THE STRANGE CASE
OF THE MAD PROFESSOR

COURTESY OF DUKE UNIVERSITY ARCHIVES

THE STRANGE CASE
OF THE MAD PROFESSOR

*A True Tale of Endangered Species, Illegal Drugs,
and Attempted Murder*

PETER KOBEL

LYONS PRESS
Guilford, Connecticut
An imprint of Globe Pequot Press

Lyons Press is an imprint of Globe Pequot Press.

Project editors: Ellen Urban and Meredith Dias
Layout: Sue Murray

Library of Congress Cataloging-in-Publication Data

Kobel, Peter.
 The strange case of the mad professor : a true tale of endangered
species, illegal drugs, and attempted murder / Peter Kobel.
    pages cm
 Includes bibliographical references and index.
 ISBN 978-0-7627-7377-0
 1. Buettner-Janusch, John, 1924- 2. Murderers—United States. 3.
Anthropologists—United States. I. Title.
 HV6248.B7717K63 2013
 364.152'30973—dc23

                                          2013010261

Printed in the United States of America

10 9 8 7 6 5 4 3 2 1

FOR THE LEMURS OF MADAGASCAR
AND THOSE WHO STUDY THEM

I must warn the reader that facts are not hard, clear, and self-evident. They are not hard little objects that yield obvious conclusions and theories when a sufficient number are gathered, counted, sorted, and listed. Facts are elusive, and they are subject to much interpretation. Indeed, facts themselves are often the products of interpretations. . . . Facts do not speak for themselves—ever.

—JOHN BUETTNER-JANUSCH, *ORIGINS OF MAN*

Who is it that can tell me who I am?

—WILLIAM SHAKESPEARE, *KING LEAR*

CONTENTS

Introduction   ix

ONE   Origins   1

TWO   Island Ecology   24

THREE   Going South   51

FOUR   Alpha Male   72

FIVE   The Tangled Web   95

SIX   Above Suspicion   140

SEVEN   Punishment and Crime   165

EIGHT   Descent of a Man   204

Epilogue   215

Acknowledgments   220

Notes   222

Further Reading   263

Index   265

INTRODUCTION

"I should say this," federal judge Joseph Lord said solemnly at the sentencing of former anthropology professor John Buettner-Janusch at the end of his 1987 trial. "I have been on the bench now since September of 1961, which brings me very close to twenty-six years. In those twenty-six years, I don't know of any sentence that has caused me more difficulty, more thought than this one. Every sentence is difficult, but this one is of transcendent difficulty."

Buettner-Janusch was about to receive forty years in federal prison for the attempted murder of another federal judge, Charles Brieant. Seven years earlier, at the peak of his career, Buettner-Janusch had been convicted of turning his New York University laboratory into a drug factory. Judge Brieant had presided over the bitterly contested jury trial. The drug conviction destroyed Buettner-Janusch's illustrious career, which had taken him from Yale to Duke to NYU. At the last of these, he served as chairman of the Anthropology Department.

Why Buettner-Janusch, a brilliant scientist, writer, and academic, committed these crimes remains an enigma. An enigmatic man—divisive, and himself divided—he made enemies as easily and as often as friends. His fall from grace, his horrific attempt to kill a judge and the man's wife, as well as several others, gave pause even to a man such as Judge Lord, who had seen many crimes over the course of a quarter-century.

This is, then, a mystery story. It details Buettner-Janusch's rise to the heights of the academic world of physical anthropology, and his precipitous decline. The story entails prestigious universities, scientific research, academic infighting, amateur sleuthing, illegal drugs, attempted murder, and, curiously but importantly, those most lovable of primates: lemurs.

Buettner-Janusch, one of the first scientists in the English-speaking world to begin studying lemurs seriously, began bringing them back to

Yale from their native Madagascar in the early 1960s, and encouraged and inspired others to study them. He later took the prosimians, as they are known, with him to Duke, where he founded a primate facility, today the Duke Lemur Center, a crucible for research, conservation, and education that holds the largest collection of lemurs outside Madagascar.

The hugely successful DreamWorks *Madagascar* trilogy has made lemurs (who like to "move it, move it") iconic in the imagination of Americans both young and young at heart, but these mostly endangered creatures have fascinated a small group of scientists, researchers, and conservationists—let's call them lemurians—for decades, often due to Buettner-Janusch's influence. Anthropologist Alison Richard, who got the lemur bug from Buettner-Janusch's Yale student Alison Jolly, said: "Madagascar has been isolated for 80 million years, and it is, as Alison Jolly memorably wrote, as if time had broken its banks and flowed to the present by a different channel. So many life forms on the island, lemurs included, are unique and uniquely different from their relatives elsewhere. Studying the rule breakers is a good way of understanding the rules."

Not only did Buettner-Janusch inspire scientists to study Madagascar and its fauna, especially lemurs, but in their wake myriad conservation organizations began working to conserve species and their habitats there.

This is also a story about academia, where Buettner-Janusch spent his career as an educator, researcher, and, as chairman at NYU, a manager. As a manager, he was a natural disaster. Buettner-Janusch was "peremptory, uncompromising, unpredictable, unreasonable, and arbitrary," said Peter Klopfer, cofounder with him of the Duke Lemur Center, who clashed with B-J, as he was known, and yet remained his friend and faithful correspondent until B-J's death in prison. As such, this book will also attempt to observe some of the rites and rituals conducted in the ivory tower. Buettner-Janusch wrote two highly regarded textbooks on physical anthropology, and nearly two hundred papers, essays, and book reviews—even while in prison. This book will also put his scientific research into perspective.

The difficult part for anyone attempting to tell Buettner-Janusch's story, however, remains that the crimes inextricably intertwine with the science. The professor claimed that the drugs found in his NYU lab— LSD and methaqualone, the latter more commonly known as Quaalude— belonged to his research on modifying lemur behavior. Lemurs, his lasting legacy, and illegal drugs, his downfall, are linked forever. When Buettner-Janusch died in a federal prison hospital in 1992, his press obituaries inevitably led with his crimes. JOHN BUETTNER-JANUSCH, 67, DIES; N.Y.U. PROFESSOR POISONED CANDY, read the *New York Times* headline, and the headline for his obituary in England's the *Guardian* summed up Buettner-Janusch succinctly: BRILLIANT BUT FLAWED.

The Strange Case
of the Mad Professor

1

Origins

THE SON OF A SUCCESSFUL ARCHITECT, JOHANNES BUETTNER-JANUSCH was born in Chicago in the Roaring Twenties, a decade that roared more loudly in that city than anywhere else. The family may have moved to a small hamlet in northern Wisconsin in time for John to attend elementary and high school, but the Windy City had a profound effect on the sensitive boy. How could it not?

John was born on December 7, 1924, to Frederick Wilhelm Janusch and Gertrude Clare Buettner. His father was born in Vienna, and Gertrude, of German descent, was herself born in Chicago. The couple had one other child, daughter Theodora, two years later.

In the wake of the stock market crash of 1929, the family moved to Eagle River, Wisconsin. But Chicago had an enormous impact on the curious, precocious boy, inspiring his lifelong passion for urban life, its culture, architecture, and politics, its opportunities and temptations. Indeed, as an anthropologist he later wrote at length about how humans were evolving into a new species, *Homo urbanus,* if you will. Many themes that marked John's later life appear like portents in his early upbringing in the 1920s: the second-city inferiority complex, John's overcompensation for his own feelings of inferiority, a deceptive normality, a hidden yet ferocious appetite for wealth and power, and a laissez-faire amorality.

Gertrude Buettner, Frederick Janusch, and B-J as a toddler.

Perhaps more than any other city in America, Chicago distilled the contradictory essence of that decade. Until World War I, its population swelled with immigrants from Europe—Czechs, Greeks, Hungarians, Italians, Lithuanians, Poles, Slovaks, Ukrainians—and during and after the war, a human tide moved there from the South, whites from Appalachia and blacks from the Deep South. In 1900, Chicago's population stood at 1,698,575 souls. By 1920, the city had swollen by over a million more. It made, as it still does today, for a rich cultural stew.

As the city's population and economy exploded, it rivaled New York architecturally, culturally, economically. The Giralda tower of Seville's cathedral gave shape downtown to the iconic Wrigley Building, completed in 1924, and just across Michigan Avenue workers capped the neo-Gothic Tribune Tower the following year.

Other arts flourished as well, enjoyed by John's parents, both well-off and cultured. Frederick loved classical music, especially opera, and imparted a lifelong love of it to his son. The world-class Chicago Symphony Orchestra had played in Orchestra Hall on South Michigan since it was built in 1904. In 1921, the Chicago Civic Opera, still a powerful cultural institution, was founded, with utilities magnate Samuel Insull serving as president. He chose the design team to build its new home, the Civic Opera House, a forty-five-story skyscraper completed on November 4, 1929, just after the stock market crashed.

Like New York, Chicago had made itself a citadel of capitalism, which, as always, has a dark side. The Chicago Board of Trade, established in 1848, first standardized futures trading in commodities, its importance to global markets impossible to overstate. As historian William Cronon, author of *Nature's Metropolis: Chicago and the Great West*, said, "Go to the Chicago Board of Trade today, and you will see one of the most extraordinary monuments to world capitalism that you can see anywhere on earth. . . . What'll be happening down on that floor are people buying and selling commodities and products from ecosystems and economies all over the world, setting prices that determine the future for people all over the world, and yet you look at it and you don't have a clue."

The dark underbelly of capitalism more readily appeared in the infamous Union Stock Yards, on the city's South Side. The site reeked, not just from the hundreds of thousands of hogs, cattle, sheep, and their excrement, but also their "processing," or mass butchering. Even decades later, Norman Mailer used the foul turn-of-the-century stockyards there—as seen in Upton Sinclair's *The Jungle*—as a metaphor for the violence at the 1968 Democratic Convention and in the Vietnam War in *Miami and the Siege of Chicago*. "Chicago was a town where no one could forget how the money was made. It was picked up from floors still slippery with blood," he writes. "In Chicago, they did it straight, they cut the animals right out of their hearts." A horrifying, if almost matter-of-fact, acceptance of carnage took place for the sake of power, money, life—capitalism red in tooth and claw.

Of course, Chicago also had a reputation for violence between people, much of it fueled and funded by Prohibition. Al Capone, Bugs Moran, and their colleagues personified the violence and lawlessness of the city. A powerful combination of political and police corruption and public indifference to justice caught the district attorneys of Chicago between a rock and a hard place. Juries absolved the blatantly guilty. The musical *Chicago* took its protagonists from two celebrated real-life Jazz Age murderesses, Belva Gaertner and Beulah Annan, who shot and killed their lovers. Despite clear evidence of their guilt, juries acquitted them in 1924.

Also that year, the murder trial of Richard Loeb and Nathan Leopold, one of the first of many "trials of the century," did result in a conviction, despite the defense of Clarence Darrow, one of the most celebrated attorneys of his day. Loeb and Leopold, wealthy and intellectual teens, planned a motiveless murder, a Nietzschean exercise to demonstrate that herd morality didn't constrain them. Their random, tragic victim was fourteen-year-old Bobby Franks. The trial both appalled and mesmerized the nation, resulting in life sentences for the two would-be supermen, who bungled their crime pathetically, leaving a trail of evidence.

Opera-loving Insull, once Thomas Edison's secretary, amassed a fortune through the electrification of the city. He diversified his holdings into railroads and radio, but he had overleveraged himself severely; his companies were valued at some $500 million, but he had only $27 million in equity. During the Depression, his firms collapsed. He was tried for fraud but acquitted. An AP story after his death in 1938 ran with the headline INSULL LEFT $1,000 CASH; AND DEBT OF $14,000,000. With the collapse of his firms went the life savings of hundreds of thousands of shareholders. John's father, heavily invested in Insull's companies, saw his family's finances devastated.

⏤ ⌁

The family left Chicago in time for John to attend first grade in a small town in northern Wisconsin, but, in those first formative years and in return trips to the Midwestern metropolis, urban life entranced him. While John was too young to understand much of his surroundings in Chicago in the 1920s, it formed part of the air he breathed. He heard stories about the city's low violence and high culture, its themes of deception, secrecy, and crime, an operatic overture to John's later life and career.

The family moved in 1931 to Eagle River, a small resort town in northern Wisconsin, popular with vacationers from Chicago and Milwaukee, about twenty miles from Michigan's Upper Peninsula. Frederick's parents already lived in the area and gave him a hundred feet of waterfront property on Cranberry Lake. Frederick designed and built a beautiful two-story, five-bedroom home with interior white-pine panel-ing and lakefront bedroom windows.

While Eagle River is just over three hundred miles from Chicago, it might as well be another planet. It is the self-styled snowmobile capital of the world. Every winter since the 1920s, around New Year's, its citizens have erected an ice palace, hauling some 3,000 twelve-inch bricks of ice from a local lake to create a twenty-foot-high edifice. Founded in 1885 by North Woods loggers and fur traders, Eagle River had a population of 1,398 in the 2010 census. The many lakes in the area provide excel-lent fishing for muskie, walleye, bass, and trout. In 1961, a local plumber, Joe Simonton, brought the town notoriety when he claimed that three aliens landed their spaceship on his chicken farm, offering him some small pancakes in exchange for water. He said they looked like they were of "Italian descent" and were bad cooks. Apparently the pancakes tasted like cardboard.

Small-town life has its charms, certainly, but John didn't fit in and left as soon as he could. John's family recognized his intellectual gifts early and treated him accordingly, although some of his relatives thought his parents spoiled him. Rather than playing with the neighborhood kids outside, he preferred to listen to opera on the radio with his father. A voracious reader, he loved classical music and theater in a small town where even few adults shared his passions.

Inevitably he began to annoy or alienate many townspeople. He went to local public schools, attending the Eagle River Grade School for eight years before the Eagle River Union Free High School, from 1939 to 1942. His teachers saw in him a scintillating intelligence but acknowledged that he made few friends because of his intellectual airs. George Richards, later an instructor at the Milwaukee School of Engineering, taught at Eagle River High. John was, Richards said, "a brilliant student, having the mental capabilities of a college soph-omore while still a junior in high school, but was unpopular with schoolmates because he considered them beneath him as to intelligence and social standing."

In later years, John boasted of having dropped out of high school at age sixteen, an account widely repeated later in the media. It made for a good story—high school dropout garners four academic degrees, then becomes famous anthropologist—but it's purely apocryphal. In 1942, he simply left Eagle River and enrolled in the University of Chicago's early admission program. He had returned to the big city.

But more than just his superior manner alienated Eagle River townsfolk. Many insisted that John was sympathetic to, even enamored of, the Nazis, and their concerns were more than just wartime paranoia. The government was tracking anyone suspected of sympathies for the Axis enemies, and many were arrested. Support for the war was widespread, and suspicions flourished in the hothouse atmosphere of small towns. Young Johannes was obviously of German-Austrian descent, and his father never lost his heavy accent.

These accusations went beyond the mere rumor and innuendo typical of Middle America, where support for the war held strong. Several Eagle River citizens went on record. Certainly, John opposed the war. He also opposed the Selective Training and Service Act of 1940, which instituted the first national conscription during peacetime. He spoke out against it in a speech at the Eagle River Women's Club in November 1941. "I wish to state that I am irrevocably and without reservations against the Selective Service Act, and that military service is abhorrent and degrading to my pacific nature. I shall not, if there is any way to avoid it, serve in any army under any flag in this world." These are bold words for a sixteen-year-old, especially in an atmosphere of growing war fever. He said unequivocally: "Militarism is an evil thing."

But many people in Eagle River saw John's antimilitarism as tainted with pro-German convictions. Joyce Larkin, editor of the local paper, the *Vilas County News-Review*, said that John told her: "The Germans are the super-race. The Germans will rule the world. No matter where you are, if you are a German, you belong to Germany."

Others supported Larkin's recollections. The postmaster, Edna Bond, said that "everyone" in the community knew that John admired Hitler. The county judge, Frank Carter, said that John "had marked Nazi leanings in the extreme and had argued personally with me and used the phrase, 'Might is right' and that 'Hitler was giving the Germans a good form of government, doing good and not harm.'"

Larkin also said, however, that she'd received a letter from John asserting that the American government was prejudiced against Jews, blacks, and the Japanese—not exactly the sentiments of a Nazi sympathizer. Later, John vociferously supported the civil rights movement, which also contradicts his early apparent pro-Nazism. Already an outsider, he may have sought merely to *épater le bourgeois,* as he might have put it. His desire for attention was enormous, and he never seemed to care much whether that notice was admiration, disdain, or loathing. His regard for Hitler may have been nothing more than youthful ignorance. Whatever his true motivation, a few years later he went to jail for failing to show up for induction. At the time, he told a prison official, William Bean, that he believed "war was illogical, unethical, completely political and irrational."

Public school in Eagle River no doubt bored John. He got good grades, but they required little effort on his part. In grade school, he easily earned As and Bs, except for penmanship. Even in adulthood, his handwriting was nearly inscrutable. He ranked first in his class his freshman year in high school, with accolades from his English and civics teachers. In his general science, English, biology, algebra, Latin, world history, civics, and business courses, he regularly scored in the 90s. He also took typing, which later proved useful in prison. He worked on the school newspaper and yearbook and took an active role in theater.

B-J, a freshman at Eagle River High School, stands (back center) among the other staff of the school's newspaper.

He grew rapidly, and pictures in the high school annual show a tall, if somewhat awkward, young man looming over his fellow students. His early sexual development followed a familiar pattern. John's first sexual experience was with another boy at age seven. According to a report by a prison doctor, Martin Ruona, he had sex with a girl, somewhat more experienced, for the first time at age sixteen. By the time a prison medical officer interviewed him after his freshman year in college, he'd had sexual relationships with a couple of other women.

In the antediluvian parlance of 1950s psychology, Ruona summarized John's mental state in his report: "Throughout the discourse patient reflects some effeminate enthusiasms. However, apart from a childhood experience, he denies other homosexual activity and reveals adequate repulsion." It's anyone's guess what those effeminate enthusiasms or adequate repulsion might have been.

With World War II raging half a world away, he left his obscure hamlet in Wisconsin and matriculated at the University of Chicago for the fall semester of 1942, which he attended for his entire freshman year, enrolling in Chicago's early admission bachelor of philosophy program.

Founded in the early 1890s, the university lies just seven miles south of downtown Chicago in the suburbs of Hyde Park and Woodlawn. Most of the core campus was built in the "collegiate gothic" style, its towers, cloisters, spires, and gargoyles imitative of Oxbridge, and resembling many other American schools, such as Princeton and Yale. The style, part of the gothic revival in American architecture, gave the colleges a physical patina of academic prestige. The University of Chicago's undergraduate core curriculum embraced the classics, while the graduate schools strongly emphasized research. For the boy from Eagle River, acceptance at the University of Chicago, with its reputation for academic excellence, proved that he was special, further validating his gifts. He began hyphenating his last name at this time because it seemed more dignified, and he began using the nickname "B-J."

But the program was rigorous and demanding, and John's performance during his freshman year at Chicago was mediocre. The transition from a remote rural school to the demands of an upper-tier university like Chicago proved formidable for him. Along with a few other elite universities, Chicago had been chosen as one of the sites of the Manhattan Project. The year before, on December 2, 1941, in the squash courts underneath the west stands of Stagg Field, Nobel Prize–winning physicist Enrico Fermi and his team of scientists had initiated the first controlled, self-sustaining nuclear chain reaction. The world would never be the same again.

B-J, however, had more mundane activities on his mind, like passing physics and German. He earned Ds in elementary and intermediate German, a D in physics, and a C in English composition. He performed much better in social science and humanities, in which he earned As, and

Gertrude Buettner and B-J as a student
at the University of Chicago. COURTESY OF
TERESA TRAUSCH

in biology, in which he received a B. Overall, his undergraduate record lacked the luster of his earlier promise—although in fairness, this was an era before grade inflation.

A larger challenge loomed beyond the classroom, however: the Draft Board.

⌁

While anti-German and even more virulent anti-Japanese sentiment festered during the war, America remained officially neutral until the Japanese attack on Pearl Harbor and Manila (the capital of America's only official colony, the Philippines) on December 7, 1941. It was B-J's seventeenth birthday. After President Franklin Roosevelt's famously rousing speech, Congress declared war on Japan the following day. Three days later, the nation officially unleashed the might of its forces on the Axis powers in Europe.

When the Selective Training and Service Act passed in 1940, it required men twenty-one years or older to register for the draft. Shortly after Pearl Harbor, however, an amendment required all men eighteen or older to register. After B-J turned eighteen, he dutifully registered. He failed, however, to report to Draft Board No. 9 in Chicago for induction on November 13, 1943. He was arrested a month later. Waiving his right to a jury trial, he was found guilty on February 4, 1944, and sentenced to three years at the federal prison in Sandstone, Minnesota. In early March, he was incarcerated briefly at the Cook County Jail before being transferred on March 31. B-J served six months at Sandstone, a low-security prison for men about a hundred miles northeast of Minneapolis/ St. Paul, before being paroled to serve his remaining sentence in community service.*

When B-J entered Sandstone, he told a prison official in an interview that he had requested a 4-E classification as a conscientious objector in January 1943, but was classified 1-A instead (meaning, he was eligible for military service), which he then appealed in June. Officials denied his appeal. He wrote the Draft Board that he would not appear for induction, and, when he failed to do so, he was arrested.

The Selective Service Act of 1940 specifically exempted only individuals who "by reason of religious training or belief, are conscientiously opposed to the participation of war in any form." Roughly half of the

---

* B-J took pride in being incarcerated as a conscientious objector, and mentioned it often later in life. Then again, he also told stories of having ridden a bicycle behind enemy lines on missions for some unnamed intelligence agency. Between school, jail, and community service, it's hard to see where he would have had the time or even the inclination, particularly given his early advocacy of Nazi *kultur*.

70,000 men who applied for CO status during the war—mainly Quakers, Mennonites, and Brethren—obtained it, but some 16,000 people went to jail for draft resistance. B-J was irreligious; indeed, he was an avowed atheist.

After being released, B-J worked at low-level jobs at a variety of institutions, mostly hospitals, usually as an orderly or clerk. He moved restlessly, and even though he sometimes took courses, he seemed unmoored, adrift, frequently receiving poor evaluations from his superiors.

From Sandstone, he moved to Ann Arbor, where he worked as an orderly at the University Hospital in the neuropsychiatric ward from September 1944 to January 1946. While working forty-eight hours a week as a male attendant in the ward, B-J also managed to take classes at the University of Michigan for three semesters. But B-J put his education above work, and surely resented having to do the menial tasks that the job required.

In late 1945, Philip Olin, the personnel chief at University Hospital, told B-J's parole clerk in Detroit, Elaine Knop, that his work was unsatisfactory and that he was planning on firing B-J soon. (B-J's last day at the hospital was January 6 of the following year.) Olin said that B-J "was ill mentally, cannot adjust mentally, and [was] interfering with ward patients and regulations."

The assistant director of the nursing hospital and an assistant professor of the nursing school, Florence Harvey, wrote in B-J's employment file: "Mr. Janusch is undoubtedly a very sick boy and one who should never have been employed in the neuropsychiatric institute. His own personal problems were such as to make it very difficult for him to work in such a situation. We have advised this boy to seek psychiatric advice and believe that he has some intentions of following advice."

Harvey's tone reveals more compassion than criticism and offers a first indication that B-J was suffering from more than overwork. After being let go, he soon moved to New York City, where he worked at Mount Sinai Hospital on the Upper East Side until August 1946, then at Sydenham Hospital in Harlem from that August to March 1947. That summer he also managed to fit in a couple of psychology courses at Columbia University in neighboring Morningside Heights.

When his probation finally ended in March 1947, B-J returned to the University of Chicago to continue his degree. B-J's grades again showed little evidence of his future academic success. He struggled with German and did average work, or just slightly better, in geometry, chemistry, biology, and a telling psychology class, Problems of Psychopathology. He truly excelled only in physiology. His philosophy degree was conferred in June 1948.

Even after transferring to biological sciences to pursue a bachelor of science degree, which he received in September 1949, his performance remained lackluster. He flunked Calculus II the first time, and managed a D in a quantitative analysis class in chemistry. He did better in organic chemistry and vertebrate zoology, but he earned his degree without a single A grade—not exactly a stellar performance from a future academic superstar.

After he finished his BS, the situation changed dramatically, however. He turned his education and his life around completely. He found an intellectual passion in anthropology and a mentor in Sherwood Washburn, widely regarded as one of the foremost physical anthropologists of the century. His grades improved strikingly, and he finally began to excel again.

Washburn, scion of a Boston Brahmin family that traced branches back to the *Mayflower,* joined the anthropology faculty at Chicago in 1947, after an eight-year stint teaching anatomy at Columbia's College of Physicians and Surgeons. He remained at Chicago until 1958, serving for a time as chair of the department, before moving west to Berkeley, where he remained until his retirement.

Sherry, as he was known, had an immense impact on the field. He synthesized the "new physical anthropology"—which embraced myriad disciplines, such as paleoanthropology and primatology—and moved physical anthropology into the realm of biology. Washburn emphasized experimental research and field studies on primates and the evolutionary links of body structure and adaptation, new directions in the discipline so profound that today his influence is almost taken for granted.

Washburn held strong convictions, some of which remain controversial even today. For instance, he supported the hunting hypothesis, which stresses the importance of hunting in human evolution. (The hypothesis has been widely disputed in recent years.) But Washburn, indisputably influential, turned Chicago into an academic hub of physical anthropology. While a grad student there, B-J basked in Washburn's sun. Washburn served as B-J's academic adviser and appointed him one of his lab assistants. At the time, B-J developed an early interest in baboons, a primate of great interest to Washburn.

Also in the Anthropology Department at Chicago was Constance Sutton, who later joined the anthro faculty at New York University. A fellow bachelor of philosophy (PhB) student, she quickly grew to dislike B-J. She remembered meeting him for the first time in the anthropology grad student lounge, where she was editing a manuscript. "He strutted in and sat down next to me," she said. "He reached over and turned my chin to look at me. 'Who are you?' he asked. And I said to myself, 'Who are *you*, you arrogant man?'"

B-J later challenged her to a game of chess. Sutton agreed, but, since she didn't know how to play, B-J had to teach her. After only a few games, she beat him, and they never played again. B-J never did learn to play well with others. Later, when they both worked at NYU, Sutton came to despise him. While at Chicago, B-J met and also alienated another student, Charles Leslie, whom he encountered again during his chairmanship at NYU. Indeed, Sutton and Leslie became two of B-J's main antagonists there. None of them fully knew it at the time, but battle lines had appeared early.

Vina Mallowitz, yet another PhB candidate, was brilliant if unattractive. Born and raised in New Orleans, the daughter of a prominent physician, she had attended the public all-girls Eleanor McMain High School and spoke with a distinctive New Orleans accent, more like Brooklynese than a Southern drawl. She had entered the PhB program in fall 1945, just a few weeks short of her sixteenth birthday, and B-J and Vina both received their PhBs at the same time, in June 1948. They began dating soon after they met. Vina acted as B-J's intellectual match and foil, and many who knew them well insisted that she reined in his excesses. They married on September 22, 1950, at the First Unitarian Church in Chicago, near the university.

Vina became B-J's closest collaborator over the course of their twenty-seven-year marriage. They worked together in the field, visiting Kenya and Madagascar; in his labs, which she ran at Yale and Duke; and on the page. She earned her BS in physical sciences in June 1949, with generally better marks than B-J's, and became an accomplished biochemist, authoring numerous papers on genetics and blood chemistry, many with B-J, but with other colleagues as well.

While pursuing his graduate studies, B-J's relationship with Washburn cooled. It's unclear exactly what happened. One story has it that he was caught siphoning cash from a graduate student fund with which he threw lavish parties. Some of that money may have come from the anthropology department, which could have angered Washburn. Whatever happened, it remained a mystery, and B-J didn't talk about it. He would pursue his PhD in anthropology at the University of Michigan. But as he neared completion of his MS, his future once again seemed uncertain. In 1952, he applied for a civilian job with the US Army in the Quartermaster Corps, a logistical branch that provides general supplies as well as field and mortuary services.

B-J and Vina on their wedding day in Chicago. COURTESY OF TERESA TRAUSCH

This was, of course, during the Korean "police action," a period of high tension in the Cold War. The FBI, then headed by J. Edgar Hoover, intensely scrutinized his application and life history, running "loyalty" investigations on him out of several field offices—Chicago, Milwaukee, Detroit, Kansas City, Denver, New York, and even Los Angeles. According to recently declassified FBI documents, special agents interviewed high school teachers, college professors, landlords, employers, fellow students, and certain unidentified "informants." They scoured bank and bookstore accounts. While many circulated reports refer to B-J's prison sentence during World War II, the thoroughness of the investigation reflects the general paranoia of the time. During the height of McCarthyism, even the suspicion of Communist sympathies could derail a career.

Some who remembered B-J from Eagle River declined to affirm his loyalty, based on their belief that he'd been a Nazi sympathizer. Joyce Larkin, editor of his hometown paper, told a special agent that "if he were not so universally disliked around the city and could get his [pro-German] ideas across to people, he could have been a very good propagandist." Others declared him somewhat odd, intellectually snobbish, or "liberal," but many thought him a loyal citizen, including some who knew about his jail term. Even Washburn endorsed his loyalty, and in the end B-J passed the investigation.

During the Korean War, the army established, through the Quartermasters Corps's American Graves Registration Service, an innovative way of handling the identification of dead soldiers. For the first time in US military history, the army began regularly repatriating the bodies of American soldiers killed during wartime. In the past, they ordinarily were buried on foreign soil, then unearthed and sent home after the war's end. During the Korean conflict, the army shipped the remains of soldiers—sometimes commingled after airplane crashes or bombing raids—to Japan to be identified with the aid of American physical or forensic anthropologists. The army that year began building a quartermaster facility in Natick, Massachusetts, west of Boston, and it was hiring anthropologists for forensic work. Ultimately B-J didn't take a position with the Quartermasters Corps, though.

Instead, in his peripatetic, mysterious way, he took a position at the University of Utah in Salt Lake City. But before leaving for the Wasatch Mountains, he made his media debut in a UPI story that ran in the *New York Times* on August 16, 1953. Datelined Prairie du Rocher, Illinois, its headline reads ANCIENT VILLAGE FOUND: DIGGINGS REVEAL INDIAN SITE OF POSSIBLY 8,000 B.C. Excavating down eighteen and a half feet, B-J had co-led, along with fellow research assistant, Howard Winters, a thirteen-member crew that unearthed the remains of a village that they estimated to be 7,000 to 10,000 years old. The findings included "the remains of four Indians, arrow heads and spearheads and a copper awl." Winters was one Chicago student with whom B-J had hit it off, and would later prove to be one of B-J's few reliable friends at NYU. It was a considerable accomplishment for both budding scientists.

B-J's life featured a series of strange segues and surprises, but his sojourn to Salt Lake City was surely one of the oddest. In Salt Lake, B-J was a stranger in a strange land, an atheist in the midst of Mormon Zion. The Salt Lake metropolitan area has grown considerably since then, and its hosting of the 2002 Winter Olympics raised its profile. Its demographics have broadened, with an influx of nonwhites and non-Mormons, but the Mormon Church remains a dominant force (it was an even stronger force then), and a deep divide still runs between Mormons and non-Mormons.

Beginning in September 1953, B-J worked as a research assistant in the University of Utah's Department of Preventive Medicine. He hired on as a part-time anthropology instructor the following school year, and

B-J (top left) on an archaeological dig in southern Illinois in the 1950s; in front row, left, Vina, and second from right, Howard Winters.
COURTESY OF ILLINOIS STATE MUSEUM

taught the autumn, winter, and spring quarters. The dean, E. Adamson Hoebel, in a May 1954 letter to the University of Utah's vice president, G. Homer Durham, endorsed hiring B-J as a part-time instructor. He noted somewhat ruefully that B-J's annual salary was $2,500, a pittance even then. Taking on the anthropology courses would add $1,000 to his yearly income. "I am afraid we have exploited Buettner-Janusch unmercifully this year," Hoebel admitted. "The salary of $3,500 for next year is low for a man of Buettner-Janusch's qualifications, but he is willing to accept it."

The anthropology chair, Jesse Jennings, was laboring under the impression that B-J was close to receiving his doctorate. "Note that Mr. Buettner-Janusch does not have the PhD degree," Jennings wrote. "His thesis subject, outline, and the first chapter all have been accepted, as has his PhD candidacy at the University of Chicago. He anticipates thesis completion by August 30. There will then remain only the formality of the oral defense of the thesis and the conferring of the degree, presumably at the Christmas 1954 convocation."

The story is a complete fabrication. According to his transcripts, B-J wasn't officially enrolled in Chicago's PhD program, and he would never return there. He obtained his doctorate at the University of Michigan instead. But the lie sealed the teaching appointment—and proved to be the first of many. He fudged his CV from then on, asserting that he'd taught anthro at the University of Utah for two years rather than one.

To be fair, Jennings saw some urgency in giving B-J the appointment. Vina had been working as a technician in the university's Laboratory for the Study of Hereditary and Metabolic Disorders, and purportedly was offered a $6,000 a year job in San Francisco, which, as Hoebel pointed out, she was unlikely to make in Salt Lake.

While there, B-J also befriended Robert Anderson—ten years his senior, and a longtime member of the anthropology faculty—and his wife, Alma. Passionately interested in the traditional Northern Plains Native cultures, Anderson authored important scholarly work on the subject. They remained friends and corresponded for the rest of Anderson's life. Utah surely felt like unholy exile to a sardonic urbane atheist among the earnest Latter-day Saints, but B-J fell in love with the sun-eaten Southwestern landscape. He even began collecting Navajo rugs and Native American pottery.

～

The Buettner-Janusches moved to Ann Arbor, Michigan, over the summer of 1955, in time for B-J to begin his PhD program with the fall semester. The University of Michigan must have come as an enormous relief for them, a more intellectually and culturally congenial environment for such sophisticates. The public research university offered a bastion of liberalism and tolerance in the otherwise tightly conservative Midwest. B-J took a full slate of classes his first year, and, having found his calling, continued to prosper. He finished his dissertation, *The A-B-O Blood Groups and Natural Selection: A Review,* his second year, and even took time to teach an introductory anthro course at Wayne University in Detroit.

Frederick Thieme, who had studied under Washburn at Columbia, supervised B-J's dissertation and had a huge impact on the young scholar. Like Washburn, Thieme also propounded the "new physical anthropology," emphasizing the importance of population genetics. A popular professor, Thieme spread his enthusiasm for the study of *Homo sapiens* well beyond the anthropology department, his classes brimming with non-anthro majors. His style of discourse and passion for teaching influenced B-J as well.

On B-J's dissertation committee sat James Spuhler, a scholar instrumental in bringing the study of human and primate genetics into the mainstream of physical anthropology. He was a man of wide erudition. In a seminal address, "Genes, Molecules, Organisms, and Behavior," presented in the late 1970s, he began with a quote from the Chinese Zen master, Lin-chi I-hsüan. B-J studied at the feet of a generation of scholars, whose areas of expertise never constrained their intellectual curiosity.

At the University of Michigan, B-J and Vina befriended another couple, Milton and Sondra Schlesinger, who both became biochemists. Lifelong friends, the couples corresponded frequently and traveled together to Santa Fe or to Glyndebourne, in southern England, for the opera. Social friends rather than work colleagues, Vina and Sondra nevertheless did collaborate on a paper. All remained fiercely loyal to one another until the end. Indeed, Milton testified at B-J's drug trial decades later as a defense witness, and loaned B-J money to pay his massive legal fees.

But that storm lay well over the horizon. For now, the future teemed with promise. B-J finished his PhD in June 1957. Then he and Vina moved to New Haven, where B-J took a position at Yale as an assistant professor in anthropology.

2

Island Ecology

BREAKING THE STILLNESS OF MORNING, FROM A TOWER ON YALE'S Science Hill, came eerie cries. These were not the lamentations of a student who had flunked an exam or the heated disputations of professors. They were the cries—songs even, you might say—of lemurs, the strange and wonderful descendants of the earliest primates, native to Madagascar, part of a menagerie that B-J had collected over several years. His unique collection of creatures, outgrowing the space available on campus, eventually became B-J's greatest scientific legacy, and an inspiration to generations of anthropology and zoology students and scientists.

When B-J and Vina arrived in New Haven, though, the lemurs and other primates were still living in Africa. Over the summer of 1958, in time for the fall semester, the couple concerned themselves with more immediate matters, like finding and settling into a new apartment. Benjamin Rouse, who chaired the anthropology department from 1957 to 1963, had recruited B-J. Called the founding father of modern Caribbean archaeology, Rouse had earned his PhD at Yale and spent his entire career there, both as a professor and as a curator at the Peabody Museum of Natural History. Until Rouse became chair, the department had split deeply between feuding factions led by George Murdock and Cornelius Osgood, each having served as chair for many years.

Murdock spearheaded a team to create an unprecedented data set of world cultures, and in 1957 authored the *World Ethnographic Sample*, which compared 565 cultures using some 30 variables. Murdock also collected information on his colleagues and informed on them to FBI director J. Edgar Hoover, according to David Price in his disturbing book, *Threatening Anthropology: McCarthyism and the FBI's Surveillance of Activist Anthropologists.* Murdoch ironically later chaired the American Anthropological Association's Committee on Scientific Freedom. Osgood, a scholar of Arctic and East Asian cultures, served at Yale for more than half a century, also both as professor and a curator at the Peabody, the collections of which he built up and organized.

Turf battles in university departments are so frequent and so contentious that they figure prominently in a significant subgenre of literature: the academic satire, which includes notable works by David Lodge and Kingsley Amis. As the old saw goes, academic politics are so vicious precisely because the stakes are so small. The maxim is variously attributed, often to Henry Kissinger. One of Rouse's roles as department chair, then, was conflict resolution.

B-J was at the time the only physical anthropologist in the department, which had until his arrival covered only three of the four major areas of the subject: social anthropology, archaeology, and linguistics. B-J began by teaching an undergraduate course in human evolution, which grew into a two-semester course, the fall term devoted to human evolution, and the spring term, to human genetics.

Getting an appointment at Yale was a coup for B-J, especially in the wake of his peripatetic life. He had started college early, true, but he didn't receive his PhD until the age of thirty-two—hardly ancient either by today's standards or his, since World War II and the Korean conflict interrupted many academic careers. In a letter to the Andersons on September 16, 1958, he wrote rather glibly: "Yale is very Yale." But he was cheery and optimistic. "I think I am going to enjoy it very much here. The department is very pleasant, some lovely people here." Happy with his lab space and his office, he found the library "absolutely, unbelievably good." B-J's office and lab took space in 51 Hillhouse Avenue, an Italianate-Victorian mansion, built in 1862, which housed most of the Anthropology Department.

Obviously, Yale doesn't stand alone as the only affluent college amid a poor urban area, but the contrast proved stark. B-J offered an assessment of the town in his letter to the Andersons: "The city of New Haven is nice, rather grimy and rotten at the core, but rotten in a nice way." He didn't elaborate on the oxymoron.

Like so many other factory towns in New England, New Haven had fallen on hard times, its middle class migrating to the suburbs. Following a familiar downward spiral, poverty and its ugly twin, crime, had become more widespread. In the mid-1950s, city planners initiated a major urban renewal, which drew much attention and praise as a model for a brighter urban landscape. Robert Dahl's 1961 case study, *Who Governs?*, became a classic text on the promise of such projects.

B-J looking dapper in his Yale University faculty photo.
COURTESY OF THE OFFICE OF PUBLIC AFFAIRS, YALE UNIVERSITY, PHOTOGRAPHS OF INDIVIDUALS (RU 686), MANUSCRIPTS AND ARCHIVES

But G. William Domhoff, a sociologist at the University of California, Santa Cruz, sharply and bluntly criticized Dahl's work in 2005: "The argument about New Haven in the 1950s, a city seen at the time as evidence for the great future made possible by urban renewal, is especially poignant in terms of how things turned out there. It is now one of the poorest cities in the United States. Yale and its faculty members are islands of increasing privilege and isolation in a sea of misery."

It is a beautiful island. Charles Dickens declared Hillhouse Avenue, home to the anthro department, "the most beautiful street in America." Another Briton, zoology professor Richard Andrew, who soon joined B-J in his research at Yale, said, "If you squinted, you might imagine you were at Cambridge." The Buettner-Janusches found a good (if expensive) apartment west of campus. "It has a genuine working fireplace, there are two large bedrooms (one is now a nice study), a huge dining room, a large entry hall and a nice kitchen," B-J wrote.

Happily ensconced in their new digs, B-J almost immediately started planning to travel to Africa to collect primate blood samples and live monkeys for research. He began with a brief sortie to Kenya over the Christmas break of 1958–59. He anticipated a much longer trip, to Kenya and Madagascar, over the summer, and expected to bring back a number of animals. The prospect produced some consternation at Yale.

B-J was working in the subbasement at 51 Hillhouse, but that space seemed too small to accommodate his animals. He appealed to Rouse, the department chair, and to S. Dillon Ripley, the patrician professor of zoology, famed ornithologist, and director of the Peabody Museum (later the secretary of the Smithsonian for twenty years), for temporary space in the subbasement next door, at 55 Hillhouse, then an annex of the museum.

Ripley wrote to Rouse, agreeing to the arrangement rather reluctantly: "In talking to Professor Buettner-Janusch, I was disturbed about the storage of baboons in the sub-basement of 55 Hillhouse where they will be in darkness away from natural light and under conditions which seem to me rather inhumane. Also, I have been under some pressure from our Zoology preparation department who object to the idea of odors or noise eminating [sic] from the proposed occupants of the sub-basement.

"I believe that we should compromise," he continued in the spirit of cross-species conciliation, "and allow him to use it . . . with the sole stipulation that should conditions appear to become intolerable, either for the occupants of the sub-basement [nonhuman primates] or for the occupants of the basement [humans], that you and I should enter into further negotiations about this problem."

Yale never really had the space to house B-J's growing menagerie properly, so the animals resided in several locations. Many who visited the monkeys and lemurs that B-J collected don't recall their being "in darkness." Certainly those in the tower of the Osborn Zoological Laboratory had plenty of natural light, and some even enjoyed an excellent view of the campus.

In Kenya, B-J made certain to meet Louis Leakey, the legendary British paleoanthropologist. Secure in the scientific pantheon, Leakey had become a much sought-after lecturer, and B-J made arrangements for the grand old man to speak at Yale and, later, Duke.

On another trip, in January 1962, B-J visited the Leakeys' home in Nairobi, which he reached "over one of the most perfectly awful roads I have ever seen." After dinner, Leakey showed him some ape jaw and tooth fossils, estimated to be 14 million years old. Then, he revealed something that B-J found quite remarkable: photos of chimpanzees from Jane Goodall. The young primatologist had been studying chimps at Gombe in western Tanzania, though at the time she was working on her PhD at Cambridge. She became one of "Leakey's Angels," three women sent by him to observe apes in their natural habitat—the other two being Dian Fossey and Birutė Galdikas, who studied gorillas and orangutans respectively.

The sense of wonder is palpable in B-J's description: "Leakey showed me some of the most astounding photographs I have ever seen in my entire life. [Goodall] has found that the chimpanzee makes tools. It is simply fantastic. It is tool-making, I swear it is." The photographs of chimpanzees using sticks to fish for termites were exhibited at a conference on primates in April, sponsored by the Zoological Society of London, where they caused an enormous buzz. Goodall's observations of tool use by wild-living chimpanzees didn't appear in print, however, until a 1964 paper in *Nature*. Leakey showed B-J some other remarkable photos from Goodall as well. "This is supposed to be a deep, dark secret," B-J declared. "The chimpanzees do what he says, if you were really anthropomorphic: a rain dance before bad storms."

He also made arrangements with Leakey's son Richard to collect animals for him. Richard Leakey would later become a paleoanthropologist, conservationist, and even politician. But while still in his teens, he'd started an animal-trapping and safari tour business.

Initially, B-J was interested in studying baboon genetics, but he was also collecting blood samples from indigenous human populations during his travels. B-J's attention soon turned to the prosimians (literally "pre-monkeys"), the most ancient of living primates, which included lemurs, pottos, and galagos (better known as bush babies). While lemurs are endemic only to Madagascar and the nearby Comoros Islands, in Kenya, B-J encountered galagos and pottos, both more widely dispersed in Africa. Richard Leakey would capture and ship a number of them to B-J at Yale in the early 1960s.

It was a different time, when trapping animals for zoos and research was quite a bit more laissez-faire. "I made use of the bush baby's widely known taste for alcohol," wrote the younger Leakey. "By placing a banana saturated in alcohol at the base of a favorite tree, one could sometimes find several animals which would be found next morning sleeping soundly on the ground. Unfortunately, many bush babies seemed to recognize their capacity for alcohol and would go off to safety before passing out."

The close relatives of the bush babies and pottos, Madagascar's weird and wonderful lemurs, were beginning to attract attention in the Western media. A 1957 issue of *Life* magazine featured a stunning portfolio of color photographs of the prosimians, including the ring-tailed lemur, running sifakas, and a red-ruffed lemur, as well as a black-and-white photo of the elusive, nocturnal aye-aye.

B-J's unique scientific contribution was to travel to Madagascar and acquire a host of different lemur species, and his "zoo" soon became an important source of research and study at Yale. During the summer of 1959, he returned to Kenya, and then made his way south to Madagascar for the first time. On his return, he reported to Washburn on September 18, himself in Nairobi at the time: "We made it back safely with our 75 animals and our 19 pieces of luggage." He probably was exaggerating— about the number of animals at least.

In December, he wrote Washburn: "Our galagos are doing beautifully.... [But] I am getting a little tired of permitting them the run of my office so that they feel free to copulate and behave as galagos are supposed to behave." Housing and even feeding the creatures at Yale that B-J kept collecting continued to prove challenging.

—✦—

It takes at least a full day to fly from New York City to Antananarivo, the capital of Madagascar, a nation so remote and exotic that it's sometimes called "the Island at the End of the Earth."

"To most Americans, Madagascar seems farther away than the bar in *Star Wars*. Actually, it is just as peculiar—and it's real," wrote Alison Jolly, a student of B-J's at Yale.

The fourth-largest island in the world—roughly twice the size of Arizona—Madagascar lies some 250 miles off the southeastern coast of Africa in the Indian Ocean. Separated from mainland Africa more than 160 million years ago, Madagascar has developed its own distinct ecosystems and unique wildlife. The island is rich in biodiversity; 70 percent of its plants and animals live naturally nowhere else.

Lemurs have become the island's most famous residents, their name deriving from the Latin *lemures*, which means ghosts or spirits, perhaps from the spooky wailing cries of some species, and the fact that many are nocturnal. Many species of lemur teeter on the brink of extinction, but

B-J on one of his research and specimen-collection trips to Madagascar.

scientists have identified a great number of them only recently, so there is too little data yet even to determine their level of risk.

Lemurs were once widely distributed: Their fossils have been found in the Americas, Asia, and Europe. That they are now native only to Madagascar and the Comoros presents a scientific mystery. Geologists have shown that Madagascar broke off from the African continent during the Age of Reptiles, long before the primate lineage, to which lemurs belong, had evolved. Scientists have theorized that lemurs—or, rather, their ancestors—arrived on Madagascar on rafts of floating vegetation. Though it seems like an extraordinary voyage, a recent study shows that ocean currents would have favored their trip.

Even more impressive than the diversity of habitats in Madagascar is the diversity of the lemurs themselves. They range in size from the one-ounce Madame Berthe's mouse lemur to the indri lemur, which can weigh as much as twenty pounds. Their behavior ranges widely as well: diurnal or nocturnal, solitary or communal.

Humans arrived on the island only around two thousand years ago, but in that relatively short time, from an evolutionary perspective, only about 16 percent of Madagascar's forest habitat remains intact, and at least 17 species of lemur have gone extinct. According to Duke University professor and lemur expert Anne Yoder, some 50 to 100 species of lemur have been identified, depending on one's definition of species, and there are many, depending, in part, on the context. Among biologists, there are splitters (who tend to see more species) and lumpers (who see fewer).

A number of naturalists had preceded B-J to the island during the great age of exploration in the eighteenth and nineteenth centuries. French botanist Philibert de Commerson wrote in 1771: "May I announce to you that Madagascar is the naturalist's promised land? Nature seems to have retreated there into a private sanctuary, where she could work on different models from any she has used elsewhere. There you meet bizarre and wondrous forms at every step."

Alfred Grandidier, the French explorer and naturalist, first visited Madagascar in 1865. He spent the better part of the next five years exploring the island, returning to France, where he devoted himself, with help from others, to writing and illustrating his magnum opus, the forty-volume *Histoire physique, naturelle et politique de Madagascar.* B-J owned an edition of the entire work, with its exquisite color illustrations of lemurs and other fauna and flora.

In more recent times, the scientific study of wild lemurs was taken up by French zoologists Jean-Jacques Petter and his wife, Arlette Petter-Rousseaux, in the 1950s. They observed various species' behavior across wide swaths of the island and returned to Paris with specimens, including a lemur they kept as a pet. They wrote numerous articles in French that appeared in scholarly journals, but little effort was made to translate their work into English—although the 1957 *Life* article did feature them.

B-J made another trip to Madagascar in 1960, returning with yet more specimens. On November 23, 1960, the *New York Times* ran a brief piece announcing that B-J had brought back twenty-five lemurs. A photo shows him wearing a white lab coat and black horn-rimmed glasses, try-ing to constrain two lemurs long enough for the picture. One is holding his hand over B-J's mouth and appears to be whispering in his ear, as if to say, *Stop talking, and let's get this over with.*

In 1961, British nature documentarian David Attenborough's *Zoo Quest to Madagascar,* part of his long-running BBC series, aired. Recalling his first trip, he said, "*Zoo Quest* started as collaboration with the London Zoo. So I found myself as an animal catcher as well as everything else." He then listed some of the animals he had acquired: one ruffed lemur, two ring-tailed lemurs, ten mouse lemurs, and so on. "A funny way to make television programs, I can tell you." The program necessarily included a shot with a ring-tailed lemur clambering on his shoulders, with Atten-borough complaining in jest, "It's difficult to talk about serious natural history with this on your shoulder."

For scientists and researchers, the allure of Madagascar would continue to grow rapidly.

—〜

As a physical anthropologist, B-J took more of an interest in studying the prosimians' blood chemistry and genetic makeup than in observing or documenting their behavior in captivity or in the wild. In fact, B-J acquired most of his animals from zoos, such as the one owned by the Institut de Recherche Scientifique de Madagascar in Antananarivo. He was not a field researcher or animal collector himself.

In his lab, with Vina's critical assistance, he frequently used gel electrophoresis, a technique for separating proteins by applying an electrical charge. B-J was especially concerned with studying hemoglobin in blood samples, which provided data on the population genetics of primates. (He is credited with being one of the first scientists to use the technique for this purpose.) He cogently described his work in layman's terms to a reporter from the *St. Louis Post-Dispatch*, who referred to him as "the affable professor."

What I am doing is taking hemoglobin (the pigment in the red corpuscles of the blood) from many primate species and finding the chemical structure. Each mammal species has a unique pigment. The protein part of hemoglobin consists of a lot of amino acids. The sequence of these essential amino acids is what makes hemoglobin different in one species from another. And the position of each one of the amino acids in this sequence is determined by one message unit of the genetic code.

Over long periods of evolutionary time, these structures change. The number of differences reflects the amount of evolutionary time for primate species to become different. And the number of differences has some relationship to the number of evolutionary years that the species has been separated.

Complicated stuff for a newspaper article, but it reveals how clearly and plainly B-J could explain complex scientific topics.

Other researchers focused on prosimian behavior, which B-J encouraged, generously sharing his collection of beasts. Richard Andrew, the British zoologist who squinted at Yale and saw Cambridge, had been studying birds, but was, as he put it, "keen to get into primates." He and B-J soon became friends and colleagues, and Andrew took some of the prosimians to his own lab, where he studied their calls and displays. Cuddly and adorable as lemurs appear, they can still be dangerous, however. "The lemurs were little bastards," Andrew said. "I once had to go to the hospital, after being bitten three times in one week. They bite into you and pull their heads sideways to make the cut deeper and longer." (To be fair—to the lemurs, at least—many researchers find them congenial to work with.)

A third scientist extremely interested in B-J's prosimians, Elwyn Simons, joined the Yale faculty in 1960, becoming head of the Division of Vertebrate Paleontology at the Peabody, and a professor in the Geology Department. While Simons was focused on the evolution of humans and higher primates, he also became intrigued by B-J's lemurs. Explaining his prosimian fascination, Simons said, "They're early chapters in our own ancestry and help us to understand ourselves. We're studying the book of life leading up to humans."

So B-J quickly had developed an interdepartmental group: Andrew in zoology, Simons in geology, and himself in anthropology. Along with his small zoo, he attempted to leverage this think tank into a permanent primate research center at Yale.

Also in 1960, Michael Coe joined the anthropology faculty, and he and B-J became fast friends. Coe, an archaeologist and social anthropologist, was an expert on pre-Columbian Mesoamerican cultures, and would become one of the world's foremost authorities on the Maya. That the two men pursued distinctly different fields of anthropology no doubt helped them to avoid any intellectual conflicts.

Coe's dazzling intelligence made him a cynosure at Yale, but a large part of his success derived from a shrewdness about academic politics. Although he had little more experience than B-J, Coe angled for and landed a tenured position not long after arriving at Yale, which shielded him from the bitter fights that divided the department. Carelessly outspoken and vulnerable, B-J, on the other hand, was no political animal. As Andrew said with a sigh, B-J could be "ebullient and charming," but he also possessed a genius for "saying exactly the wrong thing at the wrong time," a tendency that alienated many of his colleagues.

Richard Andrew acted as thesis adviser to Alison Bishop (later Alison Jolly, author of the compelling book, *Lords and Lemurs: Mad Scientists, Kings with Spears, and the Survival of Diversity in Madagascar*), and Bishop found her life's calling after seeing B-J's menagerie. As a doctoral candidate, Bishop at first wanted to write her dissertation on sponges. After her first year, 1958–59, she decided to take the fall term off to travel in Europe, "to think," as she put it. "When I got back, there were the lemurs."

"Basically, I took one look at these animals and said, 'Right, I switch theses,'" Jolly explained recently. "It wasn't even that lemurs are cute. It was really that they were this incredible array of species—diurnal or nocturnal, fast or slow, insect- or fruit-eating. It was the range of the collection that blew me away."

Bishop's committee consisted of Andrew as chief adviser and B-J, Hutchinson, and Ripley. Her thesis, *Use of the Hand in Lower Primates*, synthesized months of work studying and practically living with B-J's animals. They resided all around campus: in B-J's laboratory, in Andrew's lab in the newish Gibbs building, and in Bishop's lab on the top floor of a tower at Osborn, home to the Biology Department. There she kept several bush babies, pottos, slow lorises (another kind of prosimian), and lemurs. It was all rather makeshift—some animals in cages, some free to roam partitioned sections of the room. Jolly admits that, although a young man was hired to clean the cages, the place was pretty filthy, with feces on the windowsills and the strong natural stench of pottos and slow lorises. (She said that B-J approached a perfume company for a grant—apparently without success—to find out what gave their scents such an intense *sillage*, the perfumer's term for a smell's endurance.)

One night, while Bishop was up late studying, one of the bigger galagos was stretching elaborately in the window, backlit by her desk lamp. She heard the front door creak open and then the sound of heavy footsteps. It couldn't be the night watchman, as he'd already made his rounds. She suddenly got the kind of chill that comes over you in the early morning hours, "when you realize you are all alone in a huge building with nothing else but the skeletons on the third floor and the lab rats on the second." As footsteps reached the fifth and top floor, she leapt up and flung open her door.

"*Who is it?*" she shouted.

Two big campus cops stood before her.

"Miss, whatcha got up there?" one asked. They had spotted the creature in the window. "I says to Joe, 'That there's a raccoon,' and Joe here says, 'That ain't no raccoon. That there's a cat.' So, whatcha got there, miss?"

Bishop breathed a sigh of relief and invited the policemen in for coffee as she began lecturing them on prosimians.

B-J's critters caused further consternation. During a photo shoot, a pregnant female potto escaped and did what came naturally: climbing as high as possible—to the fourth-floor ledge of a building on Hillhouse Avenue via a drainpipe. Part of the group's mission was to breed the creatures in captivity, which made B-J particularly anxious about this female's welfare. After nothing seemed to work as a lure for the appropriately named Nudnik (Yiddish for "pain in the neck"), they called the fire department. One of B-J's assistants, Joseph Twichell, climbed the truck's ladder and retrieved the three-year-old animal, much to everyone's relief. The *New Haven Register* covered the strange twist on the cat-up-a-tree story under the headline MONKEYSHINES AT YALE PROVIDE WORRY OVER VALUABLE SPECIMEN, in its August 28, 1961, edition.

The *Register* also took an interest in another prosimian story, this one concerning a couple of picky eaters. In February 1962, two so-called "gentle lemurs," recently arrived from Madagascar in a shipment of twenty-seven other specimens, didn't like the fare at Yale, eschewing the enticements of celery, peas, apples, and even ice cream, which the other lemurs enjoyed. Instead, they ate only bamboo shoots, scarce in New Haven at the time. Bishop had to travel down to the Bronx Zoo, where she cut some bamboo leaves herself as an emergency supply.

Her doctoral thesis and bamboo runs complete, Bishop earned her PhD at the end of the spring semester of 1962. She then received a post-doctoral grant from the National Science Foundation to study the ring-tailed lemur and Verreaux's sifaka, a medium-size lemur, at Berenty, in the spiny forest in southeastern Madagascar. B-J managed to get her a Land Rover, for which she hadn't even dared to ask.

❦

That year, B-J was promoted to associate professor and soon took a year's leave of absence. He and Vina traveled to Durham, North Carolina, and to the Wellcome Trust Laboratory in Nairobi to do biochemical research, finally spending several months in Madagascar, primarily at the L'Institut Pasteur de Madagascar in Antananarivo. B-J was no ethologist—a scientist who studies animal behavior in the wild—but on this trip he spent a great deal of time traversing the country.

In the spring of 1963, B-J and Vina packed up their Land Rover and headed south from Tana (common shorthand for the capital) to meet up with Bishop in the island's southeast. Along the way, they stopped at Antsirabe, which like Tana lies in the island's central highlands, its thermal springs giving it a reputation as a spa destination in the 1920s. They passed terraced rice paddies, small brick houses

Vina and B-J (right) collect specimens in Madagascar.
COURTESY OF PRESTON BOGGESS

covered with red-orange or white plaster, or larger homes roofed with ceramic or wooden tiles. Patches of the forest consisted of European pine and hardwoods, imported from abroad, which reminded B-J of Wisconsin. They stayed, B-J wrote, in a large, rambling, down-at-the-heels hotel, "an aged and somewhat shabby remnant of the exuberant elegance that had been imported by high-caste Merina [native Malagasy] and French colonials."

They continued south through the town of Ihosy, after which the road became much rougher. As they descended from the central massif, they passed citrus and lychee plantations and great groves of palms. The scent of vanilla, an important export, wafted over them. Oxcarts were common if unusually constructed. B-J noted carts made from the bodies of a Ford biplane, a Model T, and even one from the remnants of a VW Beetle.

They collected butterflies and some of Madagascar's bizarre hissing cockroaches. Most insects that make noises do so by rubbing body parts together or by vibrating various membranes, but the Madagascar roaches hiss by breathing through air holes. B-J collected samples, taking them back to the Peabody, where several escaped from the entomology lab and frightened the cleaning staff. "Most of the building maids at Yale were Irish immigrant ladies and girls," he wrote, "and they were constantly invoking the saints and the Virgin when they would come across these large whistling insects."

At last they arrived at Bishop's home in the village of Amboasary. Bishop, then just twenty-five, was a bit nonplussed. She didn't yet regard B-J as a colleague, or even as a friend. He was an authority figure, her *professor*, and he was coming to see her in her humble Lutheran mission house.

Staying with her at the time was Preston Boggess, who had just earned his bachelor's in zoology from Yale. He had received some of B-J's grant money to explore Madagascar and scout lemur habitats. Boggess also had helped Jolly find the site for her field study at the Berenty Private Reserve.

The reserve was on property owned by the aristocratic de Heaulme family, who when they started a sisal plantation in the 1930s had preserved a section of natural habitat.* They gave Bishop full access to work and study there, but as there was no place for her to stay, she found the mission house nearby.

The reserve includes two distinct ecosystems—the gallery forest and more-arid spiny thickets—and has become one of the most popular reserves in Madagascar among ecotourists for lemur viewing, the animals having grown quite accustomed to humans over the years. They even cavort in the parking lot.

Humble though the mission house was, Bishop almost lost it shortly after arriving. She and Boggess returned to the house one day to find a

---

* The sisal plant is not endemic to Madagascar. It was introduced from Mexico, and its fibers, used to make twine and rope, remain a major Malagasy export.

Lutheran pastor there, who had arrived from upcountry, having no idea who they were. They'd left the beds unmade, empty beer cans in the sink, Boggess's cigarette butts in an empty tin, and a five-foot boa constrictor that Boggess had captured earlier. The pastor was shocked—to say the least.

"In the end," Jolly wrote in *Lords and Lemurs*, "the whole American Lutheran assembly held a meeting and prayed for me. They decided that if they rented me their house, I might be saved."

Jolly recalled: "It was a funny little house in a scrabbly little town," where sisal plantation workers "came every couple of weeks to get drunk and spend their money." Still, B-J, accustomed to traveling first-class on Air France and staying in the best hotel in Tana, acted very much at ease when he arrived, like a well-seasoned explorer who had seen it all—despite having spent little time outside the capital. "The house had no electric lights," B-J remembered years later in an undated, unpublished travelogue of the trip, "and no inside plumbing, although there was a sort of bathroom. Sponge baths were the rule . . . The only real problem was with the heat and humidity. Alison had acclimated reasonably well to it, but we had not yet."

B-J then, of course, met the de Heaulme family, finding them "most gracious." They were "aristocrats who had never actually noticed the French Revolution," Jolly wrote later. "They thought it normal to have a naturalist in their game park, as they might have a librarian in their library or an archaeologist in their museum. All I had to do was drive my Land Rover straight into the eighteenth century." B-J felt right at home in their sitting room, sipping tea, no doubt feeling an affinity with them, given his self-image as a member of some natural intellectual aristocracy.

He also noted, importantly, that the lemurs "came close to the house, and it was clear that the fact that they had been habituated to humans and protected from all poaching, etc., meant they were extremely easy to study and, unlike many wild primates, one could get very close to them."

Bishop took B-J and Vina out to a festive dinner in Fort Dauphin, a trading outpost founded by the French East India Company in 1643 that still retains an aura of colonial decay. B-J described visiting a "fancy" restaurant there and enjoying "an elegant and delightful affair," which included "a number of wealthy local colonials—Swiss who ran the garages [and] oil company and had a monopoly on gasoline for that province, various members of the D'Heaulme [*sic*] family, and one or two others."

The three of them loaded up the Land Rover and set off west across the southern part of the island to Tulear, on the Mozambique Channel. Given the horrendous state of the roads—at times simply wheel tracks through tall grass—they expected the trek to take days. As it turned out, they made it in a single day. The "boring" town and the hotel accommodations failed to impress the professor. "We went to stay in a Chinese hotely (in Malagasy *hotely* is the word for *hotel*), but a Chinese hotely is something especially awful." His description includes the casual racism that he sometimes used in letters, surprising to anyone who knew his generally liberal sympathies as an adult: "Apparently, the Chinese in Madagascar are no more tidy than the downtrodden coolies are anywhere. The hotel was not clean, the bed was not bad, the shower was crude, and the toilet was a hole in the ground with two footprints, but it flushed. All very unpleasant for us soft and luxury besotted Americans."

Next, the lemurians headed northeast to Tana. But first they stopped in the small town of Sakaraha, near which Boggess and another of B-J's students, Geoff Smith, had encamped. Boggess had come to Madagascar on several missions. In addition to scouting out lemurs, he was also searching for specimens of the Madagascar swallowtail butterfly for Yale entomologist Charles Remington, the father of modern lepidoptery. Ornithologist Ripley had asked him to look for a Malagasy duck or two for his own small preserve. Boggess explored large swaths of the island over the year, camping out of his Land Rover and living on a shoestring.

Boggess's own private passion centered on snakes. He routinely hung boa constrictors from the roof of his Land Rover, knowing well that the Malagasy believed that snakes had a special connection to *kokolampo*, forest spirits, and the locals would leave him alone. But mainly he was working for B-J, which, he admitted, could be an arduous task: "B-J could be very delightful if you did exactly what he wanted you to do. But he was very changeable and could become very angry quickly. He wasn't someone you'd want as a next-door neighbor."

Earlier, he and Smith had taken B-J, Vina, and a *Life* photographer shooting a portfolio on primates to the eastern rain forest near the village of Andasibe (also known as Périnet, the name of the train station). Today the region is called the Analamazaotra Special Reserve and the Mantadia National Park. Because it's so close to the capital, only a few hours' drive by car, it has become a great lemur-viewing spot for ecotourists. Indeed, Conservation International's field manual, *Lemurs of Madagascar*, calls it "one of the best primate-watching sites in the world."

B-J, who had never been to Andasibe, assumed the mantle of a tour guide with broad knowledge of the site, which deeply annoyed Boggess, who'd trekked the island for nearly a year. "He was a phony," he said. "He tried to create this false image of himself as a seasoned field zoologist. He didn't know how to start a fire. He'd never slept in a tent. He had no idea what he was talking about, but he always tried to grab the limelight." Still, for a young man it was the adventure of a lifetime, and B-J had made it possible.

When they all arrived back in Antananarivo, love filled the air. Bishop's diplomat boyfriend, Richard Jolly, had come on leave from his post in Uganda. They'd already decided to get married, although they were still denying it. Boggess was engaged to a woman who worked at the US embassy, and Smith was dating a diplomat's daughter. B-J and Vina invited them all for lunch one afternoon in May at the old colonial Hotel Colbert, the best hotel in the country, where B-J always stayed. He ordered an enormous strawberry tart, and the meal became the future Jollys' engagement feast, with B-J presiding over it with an air of benevolent paternalism.

"John and Vina seemed to share a delight, that somehow they had facilitated all of this love," Jolly said. In her family's lore, it became known as the Lunch of the Loving Couples and the Strawberry Tart. B-J knew that Richard and Alison would soon marry, so he bought them a painting of a Madagascar scene as a sort of engagement gift.

As the 1963 sojourn came to an end, B-J had visited several of the main geographical regions of Madagascar: the eastern rain forest, watered by the trade winds of the Indian Ocean; the temperate central highlands around the capital; the relatively drier deciduous forest on the western side of the island; and the semi-arid spiny thicket in the southwest, where the Berenty reserve lies.

—◆—

B-J returned to Yale from his sabbatical early in the summer of 1963, expecting a comfortable routine. In the fall he took up his classes again, and he continued working on the manuscript of a book, *Origins of Man: Physical Anthropology*. But the routine proved illusory. He wrote Bob Anderson ominously: "Do not write to me about what I am going to tell you in this letter unless you write to me privately at the office. Vina does not know the full extent of the disaster which has overtaken us at Yale and I cannot hold it back any longer." In November the new department chairman, Sidney Mintz, had told him to look for another job.

Mintz had replaced Rouse that academic year, and the situation might have played out differently if Rouse had remained chairman. Getting tenure isn't ever easy—particularly so at Yale—and Mintz and B-J absolutely detested each other. Mintz, a "perfect, complete fool" and "just about the most repulsive person I know in anthropology," B-J wrote, took him "to a cheap little bar and grille and over a cup of coffee told me that no one could understand what I was doing, I was too specialized for the department and they would like me to go to another university." With barely contained fury, he admitted: "I was so outraged I almost flung my coffee in his face."

B-J's rage, like a sawed-off shotgun, sprayed widely. "I shall never forgive this place. . . . It is a horrid thing to say, but I don't think I will ever get over the way they behaved." The incident formed the beginning of a murderous grudge against Mintz that B-J harbored for more than two decades. B-J then railed against Yale and his former mentor, Washburn. "It is ironical in a way because practically everybody of any stature in the profession told me not to touch this university with a ten-foot pole. Only one person suggested it was worthwhile, Washburn, the little bastard."

It was an unfair characterization made in the blindness of his rage. After B-J got his appointment at Yale, he had written to Washburn in the spring of 1958: "I decided, after much thought and debate, to accept a position in physical at Yale. I think it is going to be a marvelous opportunity. I had a wonderful two days there, enjoyed the people, got a good look at potential laboratory facilities, and think I can do some good work there." It sounds like his decision had already been made—but B-J's relationship with Washburn was never an easy one.

Yale followed the traditional tenure paradigm, which, for those who didn't get it, became a seven-year ditch. Feminist literary critic Elaine Showalter describes the potential fallout in her book, *Faculty Towers:*

> *Being turned down for tenure is one of the most stressful and traumatic events of a professional life. This is not only so for the individual but the group, the department, or the college. For unlike the corporate world, the academy does not sever connection with its terminated faculty immediately. Assistant professors who are denied tenure don't clean out their desks and go home to stick pins in wax models of their colleagues.*
>
> *What is particularly painful about the tenure process is its duration, its* longue durée. *The terminated assistant professor must linger*

for a year, or maybe two, continuing to carry out his duties, looking for another job, among senior colleagues who may have voted against him. Because of the confidentiality of the process, the candidate doesn't know for sure how the vote went, but there will be plenty of rumors and gossip. Meanwhile he has to be polite, to wear an elaborate social mask until he can leave; but so will most of his colleagues, who are struggling with their own survivors' guilt, bad faith, hypocrisy, pity, or just the wish not to be confronted with human suffering.

According to a department professor who followed the decision to deny B-J tenure, Mintz didn't play by the book at all. Tenure decisions at Yale had a strict protocol, which Mintz ignored. Typically, a professor was hired for three years, and, short of deeply disturbing the quiet groves of academe—e.g., a felony conviction or complete and total lunacy—the department renewed his term for another three years. The decision to grant tenure had to take place by the sixth year, and if denied, the professor received a year's "courtesy" appointment, during which he or she could look for another position.

When a decision was in the making, the chair sent out ten or so letters to outstanding figures in the field, requesting their assessments of the candidate's work and stature. Copies of published work circulated to other members of the department for review. After a period of time, the department gathered to decide.

Mintz apparently disregarded most of the time-honored procedures, neglecting to request letters of recommendation or circulate published papers. He simply gathered the anthropologists for lunch one day that fall at Mory's, a storied Yale eating and drinking club, and asked them to vote up or down on B-J's tenure. Several professors were on leave, including Rouse, who'd hired B-J, and the department wasn't all that large to start. While not everyone found the arrangement comfortable, B-J had few backers willing to speak up for him. According to B-J, Mintz told him that the vote against him was unanimous.

So, if B-J was telling the truth, Mintz also ignored the rule of secrecy about the tenure meeting. But this chapter of B-J's story to some extent describes a lost world, as does Showalter's description of tenure trials. Most Americans over the course of their working lives experience nothing like the job security of academic tenure, which guarantees the right of a senior professor not to have his or her job terminated without just cause. But the hierarchical system of American academia has grown ever more feudal in recent decades as the tenured professor has dwindled in numbers, supplanted by overworked, underpaid adjuncts, the moral equivalent of academic serfs, or non-tenure-track professors. Frank Donoghue explains in *The Last Professors: The Corporate University and the Fate of the Humanities* that only about a third of college and university teachers have received tenure or are working on a tenure track today.

By traditional academic standards, B-J had been doing everything right. All the right journals—such as *American Anthropologist* and the *American Journal of Physical Anthropology*—had regularly been publishing his original research and reviews. He edited a special issue of the *Annals of the New York Academy of Sciences* devoted to primates (1962) and two scholarly collections of work: *Evolutionary and Genetic Biology of Primates* (1963, 1964). His book, *Origins of Man*, based on his Yale class notes, suggested that he was a brilliant teacher. So what was the problem?

The problem was B-J himself.

Simons belonged to the geology department, so he didn't vote at the tenure lunch. But he knew B-J well. "John was very outspoken," he recalled, "and he was constantly making judgmental remarks about people. He was very acute at evaluating his colleagues, but it wasn't appreciated because he usually hit the nail on the head."

Even his best friend at Yale, Michael Coe, conceded that B-J certainly was "no diplomat." Coe admitted that while B-J could be incredibly kind to people who are often "invisible"—the custodial staff, for instance—"he didn't respect authority, and that makes it difficult to get along in academia."

As his letters reveal, B-J was remarkably caustic and derogatory about his colleagues—and not just Mintz, for whom his intense dislike was understandable, given how the chair handled the tenure decision. Apparently, Washburn had made some less-than-ideal remarks about a proposal for a Yale primate center B-J had crafted. "Unfortunately, old Washburn was asked by someone here to comment on my work, and he was pretty shitty, all things considered," wrote B-J. The department chair responsible for hiring B-J at Duke, where he went after Yale, had a "central nervous system difficulty so he can't do nonrepetitive things like making new appointments," B-J snarked. Even in writing about arranging a lecture series for Leakey, of whom he speaks with some affection, he dismisses the old man in a non sequitur as "wrong-headed."

While B-J certainly had friends at Yale, he succeeded in alienating a number of people in his department. Many explanations have been floated for why B-J—both polarized and polarizing—got along swimmingly with some people and made intense enemies of others. Some argue that he liked you only if you were in some way useful to him, or that he would cultivate your friendship if you were important, ignoring you if he deemed you somehow insignificant. In fact, a deeply arbitrary nature seems to inform many of B-J's likes and dislikes, of people and ideas. Both were like fashion—clothes that he tried on and kept if they made him look good, or discarded if they didn't.

Coe averred, somewhat incongruously, that things might have turned out very differently: "B-J loved animals. He *loved* them. He would have made a great zookeeper. Then maybe he wouldn't have got into all that trouble." Perhaps. But B-J had far too much ambition for that, and he probably already realized that his unique prosimian colony was becoming his card to greater academic success. Mintz, in fact, had left him that card to play in a last bid at Yale.

At their meeting after the tenure vote at Mory's, Mintz had suggested that B-J try to find a position elsewhere at the university. B-J put together a proposal, drawn from recent grant applications, for a primate research colony, which he sent to Hutchinson in December 1963. In a cover letter, he made it clear that he was circulating the proposal to other institutions, acknowledging that if the proposal wasn't accepted, he'd have to leave Yale at the end of the 1964–65 academic year.

In his proposal, the primate colony would serve to continue B-J's genetic research and entail an expanded breeding program, but it would also offer a platform for behavioral and field studies. The colony would provide interdisciplinary teaching opportunities and permit research by scientists from other institutions. B-J also emphasized the importance of the creative collaboration with his colleagues Andrew and Simons, who would be active participants. B-J included a list of the primates in his collection by species, with a total of eighty-six animals as of December 1963. Along with many lemurs, some pottos, bush babies, tree shrews, and African blue monkeys, the menagerie also included several baboons.

Hutchinson wasn't a primatologist, but he clearly still recognized the possibilities and prestige that an expanded, well-funded facility could bring to Yale. So he set about doing what Mintz hadn't done. Hutchinson wrote to experts in the field for their opinions on the proposal, including B-J's mentors Washburn, then at Berkeley, Spuhler at Michigan, Thieme, then vice president of the University of Washington at Seattle, as well as William Straus in the anatomy department at Johns Hopkins and prima-tologist C. R. Carpenter at Penn State.

"It appears to me at the moment that although there are other prima-tological institutes, we have something unique and dynamic," Hutchinson wrote in the form letter. "There are, however, numerous difficulties, and I am not too sanguine about the possibility of keeping the project together. . . . I am personally extremely anxious to have this work continue, [but] some of my colleagues both in and out of this department are more skeptical."

Hutchinson was right not to be sanguine, for the problems were myr-iad. The anthro department had cut B-J loose; Yale had always had difficulty housing the primates; and creating an interdisciplinary group to manage the project posed challenges of its own.

But time was running out. University bureaucracies, like those in government, often make decisions at a glacial pace. Soon after his fateful meeting with Mintz, B-J contacted Duke University about an appointment in the anatomy department and the creation of a primate center. Although negotiations dragged on for months, he would finally receive a job offer, along with space for the new facility, in July 1964.

A highlight of the academic year came in April 1964, when Louis Leakey gave his series of talks, *Man and His Cousins—Fossil and Living,* as part of Yale's annual Silliman Memorial Lectures. A bequest from Augustus Ely Silliman established the prestigious annual course of lectures to "illustrate the presence and wisdom of God as manifested in the natural and moral world," and had featured such luminaries as mathematician John von Neumann and astronomer Edwin Hubble. B-J had known the Leakeys for several years, so he facilitated the event, as he would at Duke, when Leakey lectured there as well.

In a semblance of normalcy, B-J continued teaching classes, conducting genetics research in his lab with Vina, and working on his book during his last academic year at Yale. A great deal of planning needed to take place in order to move his menagerie to Duke, where, with the aid of a grant from the National Science Foundation, he set up the proper primate facility of which he had dreamed. But bitterness at his treatment by Mintz and others consumed him. "I sure am going to have a very disagreeable year next year," he confided to Anderson, "because I have the utmost dislike and contempt for most of the people in this department now."

The year passed quickly—even if B-J's dislike and contempt didn't. While he took his prosimians with him, others from Yale, similarly smitten by lemurs, continued what B-J had begun. His legacy at Yale lasted long after he left.

3

Going South

It's hard to imagine B-J in Durham, North Carolina, in the mid-1960s. Picture Oscar Wilde on his famous 1882 lecture tour of America, drinking whiskey with miners in Leadville, Colorado, as a start. Even within the more-tolerant confines of academe, B-J stood out. He cut a striking figure, sporting finely made suits with flamboyant ties from Saks Fifth Avenue or Lord and Taylor and enormous horn-rimmed glasses, his close-cropped hair dyed blond. Jaws dropped and eyes rolled on Main Street. In return, his contempt was plain to see: He often wore a large button that read I'D RATHER BE IN PARIS.

B-J and Vina's move south in 1965 came during a tumultuous time. The Vietnam War was rapidly escalating, as was opposition to it, and the civil rights movement was in full flower. Durham and surrounding cities stood on the front lines at home.

A progressive in later life, B-J outspokenly opposed the war and supported civil rights. Indeed, the civil rights movement played an important, if indirect, role in his move, and marked the beginning of a lifelong friendship with Peter Klopfer, who was in Duke's zoology department. Police arrested Klopfer at a sit-in protest, and, B-J, learning of the plight of a fellow scientist, mailed him a check from New Haven for his defense fund. They seem, at first, a strange pair. B-J was an ostentatious and provocative atheist, Klopfer a soft-spoken but strong-willed Quaker. But liberal political convictions and a passion for lemurs cemented their friendship.

Both had been at Yale, although Klopfer received his PhD in zoology there in 1957, the same year B-J arrived. Klopfer was cosmopolitan. Born in Berlin and raised in California, he had studied at UCLA and Yale and had taught high school in Massachusetts. But even for him the move in 1958 from England—where he had done postdoc work at Cambridge—to the American South made for a profound culture shift. As Klopfer recalled in his memoir, *Politics and People in Ethology*: "Our flight that August from the United Kingdom to Durham was hardly of global proportions, but it was a change of worlds." He continued:

> *Durham's airport consisted of a single grass-lined runway, along which the baggage was dumped. The modest building (with a large sign proclaiming it an international airport) did, however, boast four separate restrooms, respectively labeled 'Ladies,' 'Gentlemen,' 'Colored Women,' and 'Colored Men.' The full significance of this dawned only some days later when we were rudely taught that launderette signs identifying certain machines as for 'colored' referred to the user and not the clothes.*

Klopfer recovered from this initial shock and soon adapted to his new environment. He and his wife, Martha, bought a farm about six miles from Duke, which they called Tierreich (kingdom of animals), where they kept their dogs and horses. They also cofounded a Friends school so that their children wouldn't have to attend segregated schools.

The battle against the Jim Crow laws was only just brewing. On February 1, 1960, four black students from North Carolina Agricultural and Technical State University in neighboring Greensboro had sat down at a segregated lunch counter in Woolworths and politely asked for coffee. Refused service, they sat at the counter until closing. Exactly one week later, fifty black students from Durham's North Carolina College and four white students from Duke filled up the segregated lunch counter at Woolworths on Durham's Main Street. The manager closed the store.

A few days later, Martin Luther King Jr. arrived and embraced the students' nonviolent action, giving his famous and fiery "Fill Up the Jails" speech at Durham's White Rock Baptist Church. The sit-ins and demonstrations spread widely and rapidly. Change was coming.

Klopfer's conscience demanded that he join the students. One chilly night in early January 1964, he and four other Duke professors, along with a couple of University of North Carolina faculty members and a black student, tried to enter Watts Grill, a Chapel Hill restaurant and motel. Unbeknownst to them, the proprietor was a Klansman, and he had anticipated their visit. Bigots attacked and beat the group while the police took their time in making arrests. Klopfer spent the night in jail and posted bail the next day, charged with trespassing.

While other protestors were soon convicted, Klopfer found himself in a legal limbo. After his first trial ended with a hung jury, subsequent trials met with endless postponements. Eventually, and at considerable cost, Klopfer's case made its way to the US Supreme Court, with Chief Justice Earl Warren reading a unanimous decision in 1967 dismissing the case on the grounds of the Sixth Amendment, which guarantees the right to a speedy trial.

Klopfer first met B-J when the latter came down to interview for a position with Duke's anatomy department. Duke's anthropology department was being reorganized at the time, but a position was open in anatomy. (Physical anthropologists make for skilled anatomists, the study of fossils and evolutionary history providing a deep understanding of the relationship of form and function.) Although B-J was hired in anatomy, he also held courtesy appointments in anthropology and zoology.

The prospect of B-J moving his prosimian colony to Durham enthralled Klopfer. "When he first asked me about bringing the lemurs to Duke," Klopfer said, "it took me thirty seconds to decide." B-J's collection

of lemurs and other prosimians was profoundly unique, so the move created an extraordinary personal opportunity to study the animals as well as
a huge coup for the university. Klopfer had already acquired a sizable tract
of land—some 40 acres in the huge Duke Forest, a 7,000-acre preserve
kept by the university—where he watched goats, studying their behavior,
especially their maternal-filial relationships.

When the anatomy department hired B-J as an associate professor
in 1965, he and Klopfer agreed to use the site's field station, which B-J
nicknamed "the Crummy Old Goat Barn," as the humble headquarters
of what eventually became the Duke University Primate Center, now the
largest sanctuary for prosimian primates in the world.

Moving the roughly ninety animals from New Haven to Durham
made for a hazardous adventure. B-J rented two Cessnas and, along with
a graduate student, Peter Nute, loaded the animals on board in their traveling cages. Nute's plane made the trip without incident, but somewhere
over New Jersey, B-J's plane narrowly missed colliding with another small
craft. Soon after, the plane encountered several violent thunderstorms
that forced them to land at a small airfield in Pennsylvania, where he
and the pilot spent the night in a motel. They arrived safely in Durham
the next day. But the pilot, "somewhat stupid and an alcoholic," as B-J
recalled, left the key to the plane doors inside as they got out, and it took
about an hour to get the doors open again.

The prosimians were soon ensconced in their new home—most of
them, that is. When B-J did a census a day or two later, several mouse
lemurs (Microcebus) had mysteriously gone missing. "It turned out that
the cages in which Microcebus was put had an opening large enough for
them to get out," he discovered. "Several had, and I still believe there are
some 'wild' microcebes in Duke Forest."

The cofounders of the primate facility soon inaugurated plans for a
new building to house the prosimians, financed by a National Science
Foundation grant of slightly more than $400,000, a substantial sum then

as now. Because B-J focused primarily on biochemical genetics, studying primate blood samples, he kept his lemurs in relatively small cages. Klopfer, on the other hand, wanted larger enclosures so that the lemurs could engage in something closer to their natural behavior.

"In the months that followed, when B-J and I saw how fruitful our collaboration could be, we enlisted an imaginative architect to help design the facility," Klopfer explained. "B-J merely needed breeding facilities. I, however, wanted space in which the animals could lead more-or-less natural lives. B-J had to periodically catch the animals in order to draw blood. I wanted to be able to watch them unobserved." They compromised by building a series of hexagonal rooms. Klopfer wanted cylindrical cages—the absence of corners diminishing the animals' sense of confinement—but that created obstacles for the local architects whom they consulted. The final cages had two stories, with one-way glass for observation, and allowed the animals access to outdoor enclosures. Workers finally completed the new building, after myriad delays, in 1968. It provided an extraordinary space for scientific study.

While B-J was devoted to his prosimian colony, he also occupied himself with teaching. During the 1966–67 academic year at Duke, undergraduates voted the skilled educator one of the five best professors on campus.

At Duke, B-J authored two textbooks based on anthropology classes he'd taught at Yale, and they offer glimpses into what it might have been like to attend one of his courses: *Origins of Man: Physical Anthropology* (1966) and *Physical Anthropology: A Perspective* (1973), both published by John Wiley & Sons.

Ian Tattersall, curator emeritus of anthropology at the American Museum of Natural History in New York, considers *Origins of Man* "one of the best books in paleoanthropology." Of course, science, like species, evolves, and new research has dated parts of the book. Science is a work in progress, but Tattersall recently declared the work "a monument of its time." Tattersall was a grad student at Yale when he met B-J while in Madagascar in 1969. B-J had by then moved on to Duke, but several people who had known B-J at Yale urged Tattersall to track him down in Madagascar. Tattersall met B-J and Vina in Antananarivo, and they shepherded him around the island. It was there that Tattersall saw his first lemur in the wild, and, like Jolly, when she'd first encountered B-J's colony, he had a sort of enlightenment.

"I had the experience of falling in love the first time I saw a lemur," he said, speaking of his deeply emotional reaction. "They are very charismatic; they exude charisma. I was a paleoanthropologist when I went to Madagascar, and I came back wanting to study them further."

One might be surprised that a scientist would describe a subject of study with such obvious feeling, but scientists are human, a species laden with emotions. They are supposed to leave their subjectivity at the door, but feelings influence interests, which, in turn, influence subjects of research. "These creatures probably best represent what our ancestors were like; they are a window into the past," he said. "But field studies are an emotional thing. It was the charismatic way they projected themselves more than my intellectual interest that made me want to study them."

B-J's writing is similarly engaging and compelling. *Origins of Man* remains remarkable for its depth of research, comprehensiveness, and readability. The writing is so lucid, so effortlessly fluid, that anyone with a strong interest in primate evolution or natural science can use it as a reference guide. Its first half discusses evolutionary theory, offers detailed descriptions of the fossil record of humans' ancestors and relatives, and then describes the major groups of living primates. The second half is devoted to *Homo sapiens* exclusively, ranging from human genetics to culture.

Not surprisingly, he gives considerable attention to lemurs (Lemuriformes). "The lemurs are so various, so relatively little known, and so fascinating to us that the discussion of them will be more detailed than the discussion of the other Prosimii." He wrote the book, as a whole, in unadorned, straightforward prose. (It was, after all, a textbook. B-J's book reviews provide a greater sense of his abilities as a prose stylist and caustic wit.) But in describing lemurs, he sometimes waxed lyrical:

> *Lemurs move with great facility through the trees. They are among the most spectacular arboreal aerialists known. Anyone who has observed these animals closely in their native habitat sees that the way they leap over extraordinary distances and grasp small branches, as they swing themselves up into a tree at the end of a jump, resembles the very greatest human trapeze artists.*

He clearly loved these creatures. In the introduction to the section on living primates, he states that

> *Some anthropologists have written that lemurs . . . are rather dull witted. Nothing could be farther from the truth to one who has worked with lemurs extensively. But we must be honest and admit it is possible that the absorption and fascination we have with these particular animals may lead us to project fantasies about their intelligence, good nature, etc. Actually almost all members of the Lemuriformes, with the exception of the tiny nocturnal Microcebus, seem to be rather gentle, placid, easily tamed creatures who might make excellent pets and whose general intelligence seems to be considerably greater than dogs and cats.*

The second half of *Origins*, centered on humans—their genetics and blood groups—inevitably raised the specter of race, a touchy subject in the South, and a difficult topic even today. Interviewers often asked about the subject because it was controversial and made for good copy. Never

57

shy of controversy, B-J began using a politically inspired description of the Caucasian integument, referring to it as "swine-pink skin."

An inveterate writer of letters to the editors of publications ranging from small-town weeklies to *Time* magazine, on any number of topics, B-J deftly mixed science and politics in a letter to the *Durham Morning Herald.*

To the Editor:

I must agree with the letter William R. Coats published in your paper July 20. It is all very well to call for "law and order" in regard to the recent riots, presumably due to race. I have not seen any particularly active call for "law and order" when those who parade around in besmirched sheets and hoods disturb, distress, threaten, and harass peaceful, decent citizens in cities such as Greensboro and in many other parts of the United States.

You recently published a number of letters from persons who advocate the superiority of people with swine-pink skin. Persons who are fundamentally inferior and who feel themselves to be inferior, as psychologists and other social scientists so well know, must often attempt to assert themselves by denigrating other persons or groups. There is no scientific evidence that people with swine-pink skin have any kind of superiority whatsoever to persons who have pigmentation predominating in their integument. It is time most of us who are colored swine-pink stopped behaving like pigs and behaved more like human beings. After all, we are a small minority on this planet.

JOHN BUETTNER-JANUSCH

Physical Anthropology: A Perspective presents a revised, abbreviated version of *Origins of Man.* Intended for a one-semester course, it is less dense and includes many more photos, drawings, and tables. It is also a bit more personal, as the subtitle suggests. In the introduction to the section on living primates, he writes:

> *I usually tell my undergraduate students that the reason I am so interested in baboons and lemurs is that baboons remind me of my colleagues on university faculties—alert, intelligent, quarrelsome, untidy, fickle, disagreeable, intriguing—and lemurs remind me of undergraduates—bright-eyed, bushy-tailed, with facial expressions that reflect incredulity and disbelief that the world is what it is.*

Later he sometimes embellished his analogy by adding: "I have been asked by graduate students where they fit into this extended metaphor, and I answer that graduate students are like sloths, not like primates."

As always, B-J was partly kidding, partly serious; it was often hard to tell which. He did get along better with undergrads than graduate students. Alison Richard, a Yale anthropologist who studied lemurs and a close friend for decades, said that B-J treated undergraduates with "kid gloves," but was incredibly demanding of graduate students. Robert Sussman, an anthro professor at Washington University, had B-J as his dissertation adviser at Duke and has fond memories of him as a mentor. But Richard, who has also known Sussman for years, remembered the latter's frequent "rants" during research stints in Madagascar about how difficult it was dealing with B-J.

B-J's many book reviews reveal more of his personality. If he didn't like a book, he often hated it. His reviews often reflected an acerbic, take-no-prisoners tone that made for good reading—except sometimes for the author or editor. Take, for instance, his review of an anthology of articles called *Primate Ethology*, edited by Desmond Morris, a British zoologist and ethologist who wrote such popular science books as *The Naked Ape* and *The Human Animal*. B-J began by opining, "The publication of

nonbooks is clearly one habit that we are not going to overcome soon."
After finding the collection a mixed bag, he concluded by asserting that
"several of the articles strike the reviewer as quite superficial and quite
weak as review articles. One or two would not have passed muster as a
term paper in a beginning graduate course."

B-J made a gifted editor as well, serving as associate editor of the
American Journal of Physical Anthropology from 1970–77 and as editor
of the *Yearbook of Physical Anthropology* from 1971–77. His editing skills
were formidable, and, for those who sought his help and input, his comments could be razor-edged. But he wasn't the only one with a strong
bite. B-J had to take from Vina what he handed out to others. He often
credited her with the success of *Origins of Man*. As he finished rough
drafts of the work, he read pages aloud to her. "Whenever she burst out
laughing at something I considered a serious scientific statement, I knew
I had to change it."

B-J made no secret of his disdain for Duke and Durham generally. He
didn't hesitate to tell anyone, including his colleagues, that it was a second-rate university in a cultural backwater. B-J and Klopfer shared a deep
love of classical music, especially opera, but North Carolina at the time
offered few opportunities to enjoy live performances. B-J and Vina often
flew up to New York to attend performances at the Metropolitan Opera.
Klopfer, who had a family and couldn't afford such excursions, joined
them infrequently.

But B-J could appreciate country pleasures. After all, he grew up a
country boy. William Hylander, then a professor of anatomy at Duke
and a subsequent director of the prosimian facility, went fishing with
B-J in the Durham area for bluegills and largemouth bass, using artifi-
cial lures or live bait. An avid angler, Hylander described B-J as merely
an "average" fisherman.

Still, B-J found little charm in Southern life, and he started looking for another position after just a few years. In an early 1967 letter to Aaron Lerner at the Yale School of Medicine, he wrote: "As for our situation, we hate it here. Duke is all right in a second-rate sort of way. The Medical School is splendid, beats Yale all the way, but I hate to build something first rate in a town that is nothing but a chilly version of Endsville. . . . I just cannot imagine dying here or retiring from here, better to get out of academic life altogether." What B-J expected to accomplish by slashing at Lerner's institution is hard to say, but Lerner fired back a letter acidly correcting his correspondent's judgment of Yale's medical school.

Late the following year, B-J wrote his friend and former Yale anthro colleague Michael Coe: "I shall get out of here within two years, either via the cemetery or the madhouse if no other way. I even told one university I wouldn't mind taking a $10,000 a year cut to get out of this hole. But it didn't work. So maybe I will be forced to clip coupons and become an executive in a publishing house." Certainly there were worse fates. B-J wrote Harry Berger, an English professor at the University of California at Santa Cruz: "Life in dismal Durham is as dismal as ever."

In the years since, Duke has built a strong reputation as a research university. The whole area—including Raleigh, Durham, and Chapel Hill—has become more culturally rich largely because of the influence of Research Triangle Park, home to many high-tech companies and research-and-development enterprises, which have drawn a cosmopolitan workforce that, in turn, has demanded more cultural amenities. The region has become a magnet for many Northerners.

Not all of his letters from Duke reflect dissatisfaction. Indeed, they often show a sense of humor. Occasionally, he closed a missive with "Lemurologically yours," and his stationery included a drawing from *Origins* depicting a squatting ring-tailed lemur with its long tail rising phallically between its legs. While the graphic seems mildly pornographic, it's typical of *Lemur catta* behavior. Male ring-tails engage in "stink fights," in which they pull their long tails up between their legs to mark them with their scent, then raise their tails over their backs, wafting the odor at their antagonists. Amusing and appropriate for a person of B-J's temperament.

His correspondence reveals a lengthy and indefatigable job search. He writes that he initially received offers from the University of Illinois at Urbana as well as Hunter College and City College in the City University of New York system. He delayed a decision about Urbana, putting off the chair of the anthropology department for months even as he sweetened the offer. For someone who so detested the cultural vacuum of Durham, it seems strange that he even considered Urbana, which, although a perfectly respectable university, was, after all, located in a small city surrounded by cornfields. It was, however, number one on his list because of the possibility of taking up the named chairmanship. He told Coe, only partly in jest, that it offered "dictatorial powers over programs."

B-J and Vina visited the Illinois campus and were underwhelmed; Vina especially disliked the idea of moving to a place that seemed like another version of Durham. An urbanite at heart, B-J finally turned them down. He also wrote that, around the same time, Columbia University made overtures toward him, but several more years still stood between him and his eventual move to New York City.

Among the many responsibilities of a professor is writing recommendation letters, which B-J did with considerable enthusiasm for those he liked or respected. In a 1969 letter to NYU anthropology chair John Middleton, he strongly endorsed the promotion of Clifford Jolly (no relation to Alison Jolly): "It is a pleasure to recommend Clifford Jolly. He is a very pleasant young man with a direct manner, and a modern outlook I find refreshing among my physical anthropological colleagues." Jolly later sat on the department committee that hired B-J as chairman there, but in time he became B-J's nemesis, the star witness against him in his drug trial a decade later.

B-J also wrote a glowing recommendation of a more personal nature for Judit Katona-Apte, wife of Mahadev Apte, a professor of social anthropology at Duke. In 1968, while a student at the University of North Carolina at Chapel Hill, Katona-Apte applied for a fellowship at the US Department of Health, Education, and Welfare. B-J began his letter by describing her as a "first-rate person" with a "fine intelligence," but added a much more compelling personal touch, a solid recommendation for someone who devoted much of her career to humanitarian causes: "Mrs. Apte is an unusually articulate and perceptive young woman. When she was a child she walked from Budapest across the Austrian border during the abortive Hungarian Revolution. She spent a short period of time in London with relatives thereafter and then came to the United States."

The Aptes and the Buettner-Janusches had met a few years earlier, in 1965, when both couples were new to Duke and next-door neighbors in university housing. Katona-Apte remembered that during their first year at Duke, no one invited them to Thanksgiving dinner—perhaps because her husband was a member of the junior faculty, and therefore ranked low in the academic pecking order. When Vina heard about the slight, she was visibly annoyed that the other faculty had snubbed the newcomers, and insisted that the Aptes join them for a holiday feast. Katona-Apte became close to both B-J and Vina, with whom she played bridge and partied regularly. B-J loved the Aptes' children and spoiled them with expensive gifts from his frequent travels. He bought them a Japanese pachinko machine, incredibly exotic for Durham at the time, and stuffed lemur toys.

Once, while her husband was out of town and Katona-Apte was attending a party with B-J, her babysitter called to say that her three-year-old son, Sharad, had cut himself and was bleeding profusely. B-J sped Judit home, picked up Sharad, and raced them to the emergency room. "The students he taught were on call," she said, "so we got lots of attention."

Although Katona-Apte's daughter, Sunita Apte, was only around seven or eight at the time, her memories of B-J and Vina still remain vivid. "Both of them were larger than life," recalls Apte, now a book editor and writer in New York City. "Vina smoked cigarettes from a holder and had this sort of stunning jet-black short haircut and crazy, super-stylish clothes and outlandish jewelry. B-J was very debonair and smoked little brown cigarettes. They were like aliens down in Durham in the sixties and seventies. The pachinko game they gave my brother and me was the coolest gift we ever got."

Because she was somewhat androgynous, people joked that Vina was really a man, according to Katona-Apte. She dressed well and had an aristocratic manner. Matt Cartmill, an anthropologist who taught anatomy at Duke, noted that she had "an interesting upper-crust, Old New Orleans accent."

They made a strange married couple, but B-J and Vina were inseparable.

"They shadowed each other," Klopfer says. Vina skillfully deflated B-J's ego when it got out of hand, and she checked his excesses. They did bicker incessantly, however. At times it was witty banter; at other times, their arguments were like George and Martha's in Edward Albee's play *Who's Afraid of Virginia Woolf?* When they were neighbors, Katona-Apte unwillingly heard many fighting matches. On one occasion, during a visit to Durham after they had moved to New York, Elwyn Simons, B-J's

A portrait of Vina, taken in the early 1970s. COURTESY OF TERESA TRAUSCH

old Yale colleague, witnessed a vicious quarrel. It went on for so long that he threatened to leave if they didn't stop fighting. It ended when B-J told Vina to "get on her broomstick and fly away."

Still, as strong collaborators they complemented each other's strengths, both in research and writing. Vina had run his laboratory for years. Indeed, B-J was always rather hands-off in the lab. Under Vina's supervision, most work was done by students. B-J, the idea man, would drop by to chew the fat, but he rarely did any of the (often tedious) work himself.

Then, something happened. On Duke University Medical Center stationery, she submitted her resignation on November 30, 1971, her note terse and formal:

To: John B-J
From: Vina B-J

I hereby submit my resignation as a member of the Department of Anatomy. I wish this to be effective January 1, 1972. You are, I believe, aware of my reason for wanting to resign at this time, and there is no point in my detailing the reason here.

She copied the department chair, J. David Robertson. Their friends still don't know what happened. Obviously someone crossed a line that ended years of collaboration. Vina never worked in B-J's lab again, at Duke or at NYU.

◆━◆

Despite the shadow of Vina's resignation, the couple continued to throw the best parties in Durham. As Klopfer said, "B-J would invite Martha and me over for a spur-of-the-moment dinner, saying it would be 'just a simple Alsatian meal.'" That meal would feature sausages, potatoes, sauerkraut . . . and the best champagne available. His students often served at his dinner parties, and Robert Sussman remembers bartending at many of them.

The main attraction, however, was always B-J himself. Simons, then director of the primate center, recalled a typical party, held at the Aptes' home during one of B-J and Vina's visits from New York. B-J, sitting like Buddha with legs crossed on the living room floor, regaled the guests surrounding him in a circle. It was theater in the round.

B-J loved the dramatic flourish. Returning from one of his trips to Madagascar, for instance, B-J entered Klopfer's office and tossed on his desk a mongoose, probably picked up on a stopover in Cairo. "Here's a pet for you, Peter," he said. Klopfer was dumbfounded. It was impossible to get a mongoose through customs. When the USDA agent had asked B-J if he had anything to declare, he pulled the animal out of his pocket and said matter-of-factly: "Oh, I do have this little viverrid I'm bringing to a colleague." Perhaps too embarrassed to admit that he didn't know the taxonomical word, the agent waved B-J through. (Like many anthropologists and zoologists, B-J sometimes kept the creatures he studied as pets. For a time he had a macaque. Klopfer hand-reared galagos and ring-tailed lemurs at home.)

But B-J also had a combative, peremptory manner, much in evidence at Duke, and he often flew into fits of rage when he didn't get his way. Klopfer, one of his closest friends, admits that they often battled like territorial primates. "We fought as often as we drank together," he says. "But I admired his intellectual acumen."

As the primate facility's cofounders and co-directors, they worked together in a mostly collegial way, making decisions jointly, or so Klopfer assumed. But while in Tel Aviv, where he was a visiting professor in the spring of 1970, Klopfer received an out-of-the-blue letter from B-J. Actually, B-J had written it to the dean and the chairs of their respective departments; Klopfer had merely been copied on it, receiving the letter weeks after it was written.

B-J apparently had become convinced that "the confused administrative policies" at the primate facility left him no choice but to take over the directorship, "fully and solely." This left Klopfer somewhat confused; he'd been away for months, uninvolved in any recent policy decisions. "There was absolutely nothing to explain his takeover," Klopfer said. But since he hated administrative duties anyway, Klopfer didn't object. "Life went on as before." It was just another example of B-J's impulsive behavior, or perhaps his burning desire to rule the primate center as alpha male.

Even when one learned to expect the unexpected from a man who cultivated eccentricity, he sometimes said odd things. He had a theory, reported in *Chemistry* magazine in 1968 when the Cold War still evoked nightmares of apocalypse, that, in the event that a nuclear holocaust wiped out mankind, lemurs might play a hugely significant role because they lived far outside the main fallout zones.

Buettner-Janusch reasons thus: Prosimians such as lemurs or galagos of Madagascar and Southern Africa represent the modern counterpart of a common ancestor from which all primates, including man, evolved. If, through evolution, man arose once (and apparently he did), then he can again. However, because evolutionary development operates at its own pace, the appearance of a new man might take some time, perhaps 40 million years.

It's a science-fiction scenario worthy of H. G. Wells or Olaf Stapledon. Of course, even if an intelligent, self-aware primate evolved from lemurs, it's unlikely that it would in any way resemble modern-day humans.

⌒

Despite all the cultural outings to New York, trips to conferences, frequent vacations, and even his beloved lemurs, none of it was enough to keep B-J down south. He longed for the freedom of an urban lifestyle.

Evidence of his love for cityscapes glows in the conclusion to *Physical Anthropology.*

Despite the fashionable whine I hear today about the debased quality of life in the great cities of the world, mankind has made its mark in these cities. It is not now, and never has been, in the rugged and invigorating atmospheres of the woods, the seashores, or the mountains that the greatest achievements of our species have been made. Rather, they have been and are being made in Tyre, Carthage, Constantinople, Cairo, Jerusalem, Seville, Damascus, Florence, Calcutta, Peking, Tokyo, Rome, London, Paris, and New York.

The chapter presents an almost absurdly biased choice of photographs. The rural environments show a despairing man leaning against a hut in Colombia, a naked toddler near a wooden shack in Brazil, and an abandoned farmhouse in Iowa, its yard strewn with debris. The urban environments depict happy diners at a cafe in Paris and a scene in Central Park so pristine it could have come straight out of a Woody Allen movie.

B-J of course eventually chose that most urban of environments, Manhattan, landing a position at New York University as chairman of the Anthropology Department. If "dictatorial powers" didn't come with the job description, he would try to assume them.

In April 1973, in an almost uncanny lecture near the end of his tenure at Duke, he addressed a meeting of zoology students, offering a typical antiauthority gibe: "The bane of academic institutions is that failing academicians become deans and provosts." But he continued by eviscerating department chairpersons as well: "You start to lose your mind, judgment, and thought when you become a chairman." Like a Shakespearean court fool, his sharp words revealed both a profound truth and prophesy.

To the end, B-J's sense of privilege and his pride resulted in frequent outbursts. If he didn't get his way, he would march into the office of the department chair or the provost, full of bluster and threats. An apocryphal story, often repeated, recounts how B-J quit Duke in 1973. Purportedly, a fateful confrontation took place at an anatomy department meeting. After being denied some request, B-J announced that he had an offer from NYU in his pocket. The chair, Robertson, turned to him and said that he wished him well in his new position.

The incident was highly unlikely. B-J had been looking for another position off and on for years, and he would never have refused a move that offered a promotion, a significant raise, and the opportunity to live in one of the cultural capitals of the world. A chairmanship at NYU was no bargaining chip.

Aside from his dissatisfaction with Durham in general, and Duke especially, B-J believed that he had never received the respect he deserved. In a March 1973 letter to Klopfer, he said frankly: "I am leaving Duke for a lot of reasons. Not the least of which is the deliberate way in which the administration has managed to make it impossible for me to be what I am, a professional anthropologist. My entire professional life is lived outside of Duke."

The following day he wrote a letter to a writer doing a feature on him and his lemurs. It seethes with bitterness: "No one who could [have done so] asked me to reconsider the offer at NYU; nobody made any sort of counteroffer or proposition. I do not believe in waving offers; I do not expect much. I do not intend, ever, to hold up any university with an offer. But I felt that those who could have made a counteroffer might have done so."

B-J felt a great sense of injustice when Yale defenestrated him, and he echoed those sentiments here. While he *chose* to leave Duke, he believed that neither he nor his accomplishments were sufficiently recognized. In both cases, a proud man's dignity and sense of self-worth had been tarnished. For him, that was simply intolerable. Even though he craved being—and thrived as—the center of attention, he still saw himself as an outsider.

Indeed, he seemed to feel a sense of persecution. While at Duke, and after leaving, he claimed that he'd seen a burning cross in a yard near his house, and that the Klan had partially burned down the wooden section of the original primate field station, the "Crummy Old Goat Barn," because of his (and Klopfer's) politics.

While Klopfer considered it *possible* that B-J had witnessed a burning cross, he never heard anything about it. A fire had occurred at the field station, but Klopfer visited the site with the fire marshal the day after it burned, and they determined that a faulty wiring job had caused the fire. The field station made for an unlikely target anyway; caretakers lived in an adjacent cabin, and campus police regularly patrolled the area. Klopfer did say that B-J was prone to conspiracy theories.

As noted, B-J often found himself in serious conflicts with graduate students and research assistants. But sometimes situations got far out of hand, and the clashes occasionally revealed a dark side of B-J's personality. Cartmill, the anatomy professor at Duke during B-J's time there, said that on several occasions he had to intervene, making "peace negotiations" in altercations between B-J and his grad students.

Richard Wiggins, who fought furiously with B-J, was one such student, although their relationship began well. Wiggins grew up poor in east Durham; his father had an eighth-grade education. Without any financial aid, he was grateful when B-J took him on as an assistant in his laboratory in the late 1960s and early '70s. Wiggins worked very hard, often coming in on Saturdays as well. B-J was frequently there on weekends, playing the Texaco–Metropolitan Opera broadcasts through the intercom, humming arias and developing the photographs that he loved to take of his lemurs. When Wiggins got married in 1967 and had no furniture for his new household, B-J gave him a hutch that he'd bought when he married Vina.

"He thrust me into an elite academic world," Wiggins said, which included traveling to scientific conferences (his first trip on an airplane) and meeting famous scientists. "I was catapulted high above and far beyond my raising in east Durham. I loved him for a while."

But their relationship soured when Wiggins discovered that B-J was taking his work—the protein-sequence analysis of hemoglobins—and submitting the results for publication as his own, or giving them away to other students to jump-start their own degrees. Fierce arguments ensued.

"B-J and Vina wanted to control everything," Wiggins said, and he occasionally faced "withering abuse." Wiggins would explode in fury, and shouting matches flared. In one dispute, the department chairman had to intervene.

Wiggins simply couldn't take it anymore, and abandoned physical anthropology to pursue a career in neurochemistry. This infuriated B-J, who had expected Wiggins to stay and mentor other students. He even went so far as to stall Wiggins's dissertation. His dissertation committee eventually forced B-J to approve his PhD in absentia. "I hated him," he said.

Wiggins went on to a sterling career in neurochemistry, becoming director of the EPA's Neurotoxicology Division. Now retired, Wiggins's ill feelings toward B-J have abated, and he's returned to a sense of gratitude. "In many ways, B-J created me from the rough earth of east Durham," he said, "and he hardened me to stand up and create my own future. He thought of all of us in his lab as his children, and could be so kind in many ways, but cruel to the core in other ways." Wiggins's strength came from a sort of mithridatism—building immunity by taking small amounts of poison.

The Duke University Primate Center produced a considerable amount of significant research, focusing on physical studies of prosimian blood chemistry and genetics, overseen by B-J, and behavioral studies, including sexual and maternal behavior and vocal communication, overseen by Klopfer. It also supported ethological studies of lemurs in the wild in Madagascar.

As he prepared to say good-bye to dismal Durham during the summer of 1973, B-J expressed a certain melancholy at leaving his lemur colony behind. He was about to reach the pinnacle of his career: chairmanship of the anthropology department of NYU. At the same time, it was the beginning of the end.

4

Alpha Male

B-J AND VINA THRIVED IN THE RICH, HIGH-CULTURE MEDIUM OF NEW York City. They breezed uptown from NYU for performances at the Metropolitan Opera, which B-J had listened to since his youth. James Levine became principal conductor at the Met in 1973, the year B-J arrived in New York, and music director in 1976. Over the succeeding decades, Levine made the Met's operatic ensemble one of the greatest in the world. B-J and Vina secured season tickets and the best seats possible.

Along with a salary said to be among the highest of the entire faculty at NYU, the school lavished B-J with a $200,000 research laboratory and the use of an apartment on historic Washington Square in Greenwich Village. The building, 29 Washington Square West, dated from the 1880s. Eleanor Roosevelt had lived there for several years after FDR died.

B-J's apartment was on the fifteenth floor, just below the penthouse. While it didn't overlook the park, it faced north, its huge windows offering an extraordinary view of Manhattan's Midtown skyline. Inside it featured a large bedroom painted Chinese red, a formal dining room, an expansive living room, and a book-lined study with a Renaissance man's library that included the multivolume works of early naturalist author-artists such as Buffon and Grandidier. It may not have been the apartment of a Wall Street tycoon, but by academic standards it was palatial.

B-J and Vina decorated it with their beloved Navajo rugs, Native American pottery, and African masks. Modern art adorned the walls:

works by Picasso, Braque, and Ellsworth Kelly. They held lavish parties, of course. Though B-J fancied himself a gourmet cook, he had the events catered with uniformed servers. The affairs resembled grand salons in the French tradition. Not only scientists and academics attended the soirees, but also musicians, dancers, artists, and writers.

The thick membrane between their lifestyle and the decay of the great city around them made their lives even more magical. New York City reached its postwar nadir in the 1970s. "Dirty, dangerous, and destitute" is how photojournalist Allan Tannenbaum described the city in his pictorial record of the decade. Crime ran rampant, fueled by all manner of drug addicts, the number of heroin users reaching about 200,000 by mid-decade. Droves of vagrants inhabited the nightmarish, graffiti-covered subways. Pimps, prostitutes, and drug dealers owned Times Square, the once and future crossroads of the world.

The nation's economic recession hit the beating heart of the Eastern Seaboard especially hard, and in 1975 the city teetered on the verge of bankruptcy. Gotham just barely missed that bullet, the teachers' union providing a ten-minutes-to-midnight infusion of cash to cover the city's ballooning debts. In October, President Gerald Ford enraged countless New Yorkers when he made a speech flatly denying the city a federal bailout, inspiring one of the most famous headlines ever to run in the *New York Daily News:* FORD TO CITY: DROP DEAD. Only two months later, Ford changed course and asked Congress to approve federal loans to NYC.

If the middle class was hurting during the recession, the underclasses were flatlining. Large swaths of the South Bronx, still the poorest congressional district in the United States, lay abandoned and decaying. The cash-strapped city had closed numerous fire stations, especially in poor neighborhoods, and in the postapocalyptic landscape, overstretched firemen couldn't respond quickly enough to the countless blazes. During Game Two of the 1977 World Series at Yankee Stadium, ABC's aerial camera panned a few blocks away, revealing a billowing cloud of smoke.

An enduring urban legend has Howard Cosell intoning, "The Bronx is burning." Cosell never actually said those words, but the phrase perfectly captured the city's fiscal and spiritual crisis.

Serial killer David Berkowitz, better known as the Son of Sam, terrorized the city from July 1976 until his arrest in August 1977, producing more horrific tabloid headlines. The city was coming apart at the seams. To paraphrase Yeats, the center would not hold. But some remained largely untouched by the decay and despair. It was, after all, what author and journalist Tom Wolfe famously called "The Me Decade." Money, power, overwhelming self-absorption, or some combination thereof insulated many from the chaos, or at least banished it to peripheral vision.

Indeed, Washington Square Park, the iconic, symbolic center of NYU, had seen better days, and, like New York City, the university had fallen into a deep financial mire. City planners laid out the now history-laden Washington Square in 1826, and NYU held its first classes in 1832. Both the area around the park—including Greenwich Village, with its rich literary and artistic history and tradition of bohemianism—and the academic institution grew up together. Columbia University, New York's other major private research university, was much older but located far uptown in Manhattan. NYU was formed in the beating heart of the city; Columbia was in the city, but not of it.

NYU's buildings, old and new, leapfrog around the park and the Village. It owns a string of elegant Greek Revival townhouses, built in the 1830s, along Washington Square North, known as the Row. You can almost feel the presence of the ghosts of Henry James and Edith Wharton. It also purchased a number of commercial and industrial loft buildings east of the park, such as Rufus D. Smith Hall at 25 Waverly Place, a former hat factory built in 1897, and home to the anthropology department, and the 1901 Brown Building a few blocks away, the site of the infamous Triangle Shirtwaist Factory fire in 1911, during which 146 garment workers tragically died. In a hodgepodge with these refurbished

B-J in his office in the Anthropology Department at NYU in 1980.
COURTESY OF DEBORAH FEINGOLD

historic buildings were strewn newer structures, such as the twelve-story
Bobst Library, which looms over the southeast corner of the park, and
Tisch Hall, a few buildings east, both designed by Philip Johnson and
Richard Foster and built of red sandstone in 1972.

When B-J arrived in 1973, drug dealers besieged Washington Square.
Drugs, muggings, rapes, and murders were not new to the area, obviously.
From the beats of the fifties to the hippies of the sixties, the park had
offered a kind of free zone for pot seekers and sellers, but those with a
taste could just as easily purchase hard drugs at the bazaar as well. The
park's various microcultures had formed, as a result, an uneasy truce of
spheres of influence.

Journalist and author Gay Talese described the square's balkanization
in a 1964 article in the *New York Times*. Junkies, homemakers with kids,
and students each had their turf with invisible boundaries. But by the
time B-J arrived, the square had declined precipitously.

"In the early 1970s, Washington Square was a dangerous place," wrote
Emily Kies Folpe in *It Happened on Washington Square*.

> *In 1973, Oscar Newman, a professor of city planning at NYU, said the
> screams of people being mugged in the park often reached the windows
> of his bedroom at 29 Washington Square [B-J's building]. Newman,
> the author of* Defensible Space, *a book on the use of design strategies
> to limit crime, proposed that a seven-foot wrought iron fence, com-
> patible in design with the historic railings along the Row, be erected
> around the park to combat muggings, vagrancy, and vandalism.*

The fence was never built, and it wasn't until 1987 that an eight-month
siege by the NYPD finally drove the dealers from the park, after netting
nearly 1,400 arrests. Until then, the only time that the dealers left was on
NYU's commencement day, when it set up folding chairs there for graduation, beginning in 1976.

A short stroll took B-J from his apartment at the northwest corner of the park along its north side past the arch to his office and lab at Rufus D. Smith Hall. His elegant office, on the second floor, had a beautiful antique rolltop desk. His lab was located on the fourth floor.

—~—

B-J had tried to bring some of his colleagues and students with him from Duke to NYU, but mostly he was unsuccessful. William Hylander interviewed for a position. Although he worked in anatomy at Duke, Hylander later made his reputation as an anthropologist, winning the prestigious Charles R. Darwin Award from the American Association of Physical Anthropologists in 2010. But at the time, his wife, Linda Dykstra, was an assistant professor of psychology at nearby University of North Carolina at Chapel Hill, and couldn't find an equivalent position at NYU. Hylander chose to stay at Duke.

B-J asked Thomas Olivier and Lon Alterman, among his favored grad students, to come up to the Big Apple as well. In the end, only Alterman followed, helping B-J move his laboratory, where he worked as a research assistant for the next few years. Alterman had completed the coursework for his PhD but needed to finish writing his dissertation on orangutan hemoglobins in New York, returning to Durham to defend his work.

The first faculty hire under B-J was Owen Lynch, a social anthropologist from SUNY-Binghamton with expertise in several areas, including the cultures and politics of India and urban anthropology. It was the latter interest that landed him the job, the newly funded, named position of Charles F. Noyes Professor of Urban Anthropology.

Lynch, who at first found B-J intimidating, said that B-J's peremptory manner quickly divided the department and alienated him. At one early meeting, the new chairman berated the social anthropologists for not attracting enough students, and accused them of undermining the department's status. Lynch checked with administration records and found B-J's remarks both unfair and untrue. At a subsequent gathering, Lynch, uncowed, said as much. Lynch had a temper, and B-J, quick to anger, hated being contradicted publicly; they were two combustible fluids with low flash points, catching fire. It was an early skirmish in what would become an academic war.

"He just wanted to make physical anthropology the most important part of the department," Lynch said. "A chairman is someone who builds things up, brings a department together. He destroyed it."

It's likely that B-J did want to boost physical anthropology's presence, and, with a limited budget and head count, he soon found fault with other social anthropologists as well. (It was strange that a social anthropologist didn't become chairman, because the department emphasized exactly that area. But the search committee couldn't reach a consensus on the first round of candidates. Then-chairman John Middleton suggested B-J as a potential compromise.)

From the beginning, Constance Sutton, who had known and detested B-J at Chicago, had deep misgivings about working with him. Sutton had taught in the anthro department at NYU for years before B-J arrived, starting as an instructor in 1961. A decade later, she became assistant professor and took over as anthropology chair of University College, NYU's uptown campus in the Bronx. When it merged back with the Washington Square campus in September 1973, she moved downtown just as B-J arrived on the scene.

A political progressive and a feminist, social anthropologist Sutton specialized in the cultures of West Africa and the Caribbean. She immersed herself in black culture in the States as well. She counted as a close friend anthropologist and author Niara Sudarkasa, born Gloria Marshall, the first black woman to hold a professorship in anthro at NYU. Sutton knew Malcolm X and was also friends with writer Maya Angelou and actress Cicely Tyson. "I had a full life outside the university," she said.

But B-J was still the old B-J she remembered. One day, he walked into her office, pushed her hair back, and said, "Nice earrings." It was aggression delivered as a compliment, like an alpha primate asserting his dominance. She saw such gestures not as sexual harassment but still woefully inappropriate and physically intrusive.

Perhaps B-J did like her earrings, but he didn't seem to like or respect her. At one department meeting that she missed, Sutton said, B-J simply announced that she wouldn't be teaching graduate classes anymore because he didn't think she was "professionally competent." It's true that she didn't have a strong publishing record when B-J arrived, but it grew steadily over the years. Sutton said that she complained to the dean, and she continued to teach graduate courses until retiring in 2002.

But B-J's single harshest critic, a man who became his archenemy in the department, was Charles Leslie, an authority in the field of medical anthropology, especially traditional Asian medicine. They had much in common. Leslie had earned his PhD at the University of Chicago, where he'd known B-J. He had a strong social conscience and worked in the civil rights movement during the summer of 1964 in Mississippi; he also confronted what he considered racist writings in his own profession. Like Klopfer, he was a Quaker, and, although he had served as a pilot in World War II, he became an ardent pacifist. Leslie's friend Triloki Nath Madan called him "a truly cultured person, ever so upright and gentle, willing to take a stand and yet, courteous."

B-J, however, couldn't stand him. By many accounts, including Leslie's, B-J made life intolerable in ways big and small, and Leslie, a tenured full professor, left for the University of Delaware in 1976, where he taught until his retirement.

"He actually hounded me out of the department," Leslie told Linda Wolff, who wrote about B-J's subsequent drug trial for *New York* magazine. "B-J was tyrannical and vindictive in the extreme. He seemed set against me because he'd heard from someone else in the department that I had opposed his coming to NYU. And it wasn't even true. But that was the way he was. He was a man who couldn't brook not just disloyalty but even the hint or rumor of disloyalty."

B-J denigrated Leslie in front of his colleagues and students and, as he did with Sutton and Lynch, excluded him from academic committees. One day, he simply strode into Leslie's office and walked out with a table and a typewriter. "He didn't need them; that was done purely as a bullying thing," he said.

B-J drove the gentle pacifist to distraction: "I hated him. I fantasized about shooting him," Leslie admitted.

B-J, of course, found Leslie's public criticism unbearable. In one of his photocopied diatribes addressed to friends, dated January 1, 1980, he wrote, "Pay no attention to that pathetic booby. He was not driven from NYU by me. I have adhered to the gentleman's code and will not discuss why he left. I should think he would rather not discuss it also."

B-J often hinted darkly at the secrets of others, frequently promising to tell the full story at some later date, which he invariably failed to do. A master of the art of innuendo, he also frequently accused his adversaries of madness. According to Sutton, B-J went to the dean of arts and sciences and insisted that Lynch was mentally unstable, making him unfit to teach graduate classes. Referring to his persecutors, he warned in one of his widely distributed, photocopied letters written just before entering prison for drug-making: "I hope that all of you learn from this that hidden in our midst are mad, envious psychopaths who will do anything to further their peculiar grasp of reality. Many of you will have read the effusions of that pathetic madman Charles Leslie," he wrote, "but there are others."

Sutton, Lynch, and Leslie understandably formed an alliance to cover one another from the alpha's domineering behavior. Sutton and Lynch stayed in the department, but Leslie was banished from the troop—despite B-J's denials.

At Duke, Klopfer didn't see much of B-J after he left for New York, but he did follow B-J's career with interest. B-J said that he went up there to clean house as the new chairman, Klopfer recalled, "But he did it in a cruel, disrespectful way. He was totally tactless, without any sensitivity to others. And that was his undoing."

Indeed, B-J was simply a terrible manager, by turns mercurial, abrasive, arbitrary, insulting. In the corporate jungle, some bosses pride themselves on over-the-top mistreatment, even humiliation, of their subordinates. Obviously, such behavior isn't nonexistent in the hierarchical world of academia. But most colleges and universities seek to maintain a veneer of studied gentility. Much of the behavior in the department seemed all too simian during B-J's time, when the professors were, after all, supposed to be respectable academics.

B-J's management style as chairman reflected that of a typical alpha male baboon—threatening subordinates, swiping palm nuts from others. Indeed, B-J's earlier expectations of "dictatorial powers" were frustrated because they simply aren't part of a chair's authority. The position more typically resembles that of a mid-level bureaucrat than a corporate honcho. An insightful piece that ran in *The Chronicle of Higher Education* is tellingly titled "Beggar, Psychologist, Mediator, Maid: the Thankless Job of a Chairman."

As writer Robin Wilson explains, "Academic chairmen lack the power of middle managers in the corporate world. Although they are responsible to administrators for their department's bottom line, they can't force their faculty members to do anything. They can't fire them either, unless their behavior is egregious."

Chafing at the limits of his authority, then, B-J resorted to intimidation and bullying. And while department chairs have to report to the deans of their colleges, other professors also can take their concerns directly to those deans. Some complained about B-J's demoralizing, even irrational behavior to the deans at NYU, and . . . nothing happened.

R. Bayly Winder, dean of the faculty of arts and sciences until 1976, heard numerous grievances about B-J, but, he claimed, they didn't go far beyond the usual grousing. "John was a first-class scientist and a good administrator," he said. "In a university, that is supposed to count for something. You hear complaints all the time about department chairmen."

Norman Cantor, the esteemed medievalist, served as dean during the time just before B-J was arrested for manufacturing drugs and during his trial. He said that NYU carefully investigated the complaints about B-J. "In the spring of 1979 I personally interviewed every member of the department. Only a very small number thought he was abrasive and hard to get along with. If the majority had opposed him, he would not have been reappointed as chair," he said. "Under his administration the anthro department grew in status and increased its ability to recruit students. It is true that he was extremely opinionated and sometimes brusque, but so are many chairs and many college presidents."

But B-J did have confederates, allies, friends, and a share of sycophants—otherwise no one would have attended his parties. One of his pals, archaeologist Howard Winters, conducted work in Mexico, the American Midwest, and in New York City. Their friendship went back to their Chicago days in the 1950s, where they co-led the Illinois dig that made news. Sadly, he was in very poor health at the time.

Anne Marie Cantwell, a student of Winters's who became a professor of anthropology at Rutgers, quoted his definition of "civilization" at a conference many years ago, and the aphorism was widely repeated. It reveals a great deal about Winters's personality and bears remembering: "Civilization is a process in which one gradually increases the number of people included in the term 'we' or 'us' and at the same time decreases those labeled 'you' or 'them' until that category has no one left in it."

"Using this definition," Cantwell said, "I think he was one of the most civilized people I have had the privilege to know."

Thomas Beidelman, on the NYU anthro faculty when B-J arrived, had known the new chairman from Duke. But as a member of the junior faculty there, Beidelman said, B-J simply ignored him. Beidelman didn't care particularly, but at NYU they connected.

With his long, thinning white hair and goatee, bow ties and sport coats, and his curious manner in the classroom, which mixed cursing like a sailor with classical allusions, Beidelman could give B-J a run for his money, at least in terms of fashion. The author of many campus novels, David Lodge has compared the literary genre to Shakespeare's comedy *As You Like It,* and Beidelman would fit right in among the eccentric characters in the Forest of Arden.

An authority on East African cultures, the history of colonialism, religion and symbolism, witchcraft, and magic, Beidelman has the longest tenure of anyone in NYU's anthropology department. He and B-J soon bonded—after a manner. Asked if they were friends, Beidelman said, "Yes, and not really, if you know what I mean. I liked B-J because he was always pleasant to me and was often good company."

They did share a deep love of opera, and Beidelman was himself attracted to the operatic tendencies of B-J's personality. Plus, B-J always had great tickets to the Met. "We would sit so close, you could see the performers sweat," he said. One evening, after seeing Mussorgsky's *Boris Godunov,* B-J insisted on taking the subway back downtown rather than a cab, even though it was after midnight. In the seventies, the screeching, dangerous trains often stopped for no apparent reason, or went dark. Middle-class people, when they couldn't afford a cab, often walked a few extra blocks to avoid them.

B-J, however, seemed oblivious to his surroundings. He pulled up his coat sleeves to show off his cuff links, boasting about how expensive they were. Beidelman cringed, inching away from him incredulously.

Beidelman almost relished recalling the bad, old days shortly after B-J assumed the chairmanship, still regretting having missed what was perhaps the most infamous battle between B-J and Lynch. Arriving late to a department meeting, at first he thought he'd missed it altogether, as the room was dark. Switching on the lights, he observed the assembled anthropologists sitting around the conference table, their faces illuminated by the overhead fluorescent tubes. Mere moments earlier, Lynch had hurled a book at B-J in disgust, barely missing him. B-J had turned on his heel and walked out, flipping off the light switch on his way out the door.

How could B-J have inspired such behavior? "B-J could be charming and kind, and he could be very cruel," Beidelman said, shrugging. "He was a monster."

If that remark seems strange coming from one of B-J's friends, it's unusual only in its extremity. Even B-J's closest friends had conflicting feelings about him, able to accept his flaws even while others found them intolerable.

B-J had few strong friendships in the department—many kept their distance by trying to remain neutral—but he did have a wide circle of companions. David Sabatini, at NYU's School of Medicine, had known B-J since Yale in the early 1960s, where Sabatini's wife had worked in his lab with Vina. B-J and Sabatini, chair of the Department of Cell Biology, developed a joint program together. When not a single person from the anthropology department testified in B-J's defense at his drug trial, Sabatini took the stand as a character witness, calling him a "very truthful and honest person," adding, "I always admired him."

B-J kept up other friendships: with the Schlesingers, with whom he and Vina sometimes traveled, and his colleagues and students from Duke, which he still visited occasionally, such as Hylander and Sussman. Like other academics, anthropologists subsist in conference culture, which kept B-J and Vina frequently in touch with old acquaintances.

One of B-J's staunch friends, Alison Richard, remembered first meeting him at one such gathering, the American Anthropological

Association convention in New Orleans in 1973, shortly after she joined the Yale anthro faculty. (B-J's reputation preceded him, as Richard, it will be recalled, took up the study of lemurs at the urging of B-J's star Yale student, Alison Jolly.)

"He was an apparition," she said, "in rose-tinted glasses with a big sweet pea crawling up a huge white kipper tie. He was such a refreshing contrast to the usual run of the bearded, beaded anthropologists of the time."

Richard readily acknowledged his dark side. "He had this capacity for vitriol, and he treated some people unbelievably badly at times. But he was capable of this generosity of spirit that transcended everything," she said. "That's why you loved him." Some more than others.

Like so many of B-J's confederates, she saw through B-J's pomposity, and could still appreciate his wit and random acts of kindness. "We were at a dinner party at their Washington Square apartment," she recounted. "John was holding forth as usual, and Vina yelled cheerfully from the other end of the table, 'If he's telling you he's descended from a Polish count, it's bullshit. Buettner-Janusch means son of a butcher.' " Vina helped keep B-J in check.

One person in the department, never really B-J's friend, appeared at least at first to be a potential ally. Clifford Jolly was born in Essex, England, and earned his PhD in physical anthropology at the University of London in 1965, where he studied under such heavy hitters as John Napier and N. A. Barnicot. NYU hired him as an assistant professor in 1967. While still at Duke, B-J had enthusiastically recommended Jolly for a promotion to associate professor. Linda Wolfe described Jolly, some fifteen years B-J's junior, in her *New York* magazine cover story at the time of B-J's drug trial, as looking like an "early Beatle."

In 1970, Jolly made his mark with a classic and deeply original paper, "The Seed-Eaters," published in *Man*, a journal of the Royal Anthropological Institute. Richard Leakey described Jolly's paper as "a milestone in the study of human prehistory." Anthropologist and science writer Roger Lewin called Jolly's hypothesis a "paradigm shift," in that it countered the long-accepted "Darwinian model, which emphasized tools and culture as the main driving force of human evolution." Darwin's theory ran that, through evolution, apes lost their large canines with the development of tool use; tool-using required the greater use of hands, which led to bipedalism, and greater intellect, which produced a larger brain and, ultimately, culture.

Jolly's hypothesis, according to Lewin, explained the evolution of humans' bipedalism and distinctly different facial and dental structure through—as is obvious from his paper's title—the biomechanics of chewing tough, small seeds. The sideways grinding action required by seed-eating could occur only in the absence of the large canines of other apes, and the dexterity necessary to collect such small objects could have led to the development of the human opposable thumb. Finally, the ability to squat down to collect seeds could have acted as an intermediary adaptation that led to bipedalism.

Jolly's areas of expertise were wide-ranging, including physical anthropology, primatology, serology, and population genetics, and the hypothesis brought him to prominence at a young age. He co-chaired the search committee that hired B-J as chairman and advocated his hiring. In turn, under B-J's chairmanship, Jolly received tenure in 1975 and was promoted to full professor the following year. B-J respected Jolly intellectually, often praising the seed-eating hypothesis in classes, calling it one of the most important papers in the field of physical anthropology written in the past few decades. They even shared laboratory space on the fourth floor of the anthropology building, Jolly having to pass through B-J's lab to get to his own.

But their personalities represented polar opposites: B-J, the flamboyant peacock, his every action and remark designed to attract attention or provoke debate, versus quiet and serious Jolly, who played his cards close to his chest. A certain coolness existed between them, polite but formal.

"We got along all right, on a professional level and day-to-day basis," Jolly said. "We and our students used many of the same lab facilities. I think he regarded me as an ally and as an asset, especially when a potential source of funding had to be shown the workings of the lab. Oddly, though, I have no memory of ever discussing the substance of our research or anything about biology in general.

"Our personal styles were just too different for us to be close," he said. "I recall one or two dinners for visiting speakers that he hosted at Village restaurants, and these were pleasant and convivial occasions.

"But I must say that at times I found his Munchausen-like tales tedious. One of his supporters in the department [said] that B-J was incapable of distinguishing reality from fantasy, and I think that might well be correct. But others seem simply to have found this to be a quality of a charming and witty raconteur. So who knows?"

As for the faculty meetings, Jolly recalled less conflict than others, more rodomontade. "My main memory," he said, "was that they were pointless. B-J would simply present his administrative decisions and justify them with a torrent of words that sometimes seemed to make some sense at first but on reflection often didn't.

"If called on a particular point, he would claim that his information and instructions came from 'the deans'—unspecified—and were nonnegotiable. But you never knew how much of this was factual and how much he had made up on the spur of the moment. Further questioning risked precipitating a tantrum, an unpleasant event that most faculty preferred to avoid."

B-J began putting his own stamp on the department, and, in the time-honored pecking order of academia, his junior faculty hires owed him some loyalty at the very least. (It should be remembered that faculty appointments are voted on by a hiring committee; the chair makes the offer, but he or she is commonly credited with the hire.)

One such hire was Glenn Conroy, a biological anthropologist straight out of Yale, in 1974. Actually Conroy taught part-time in anthro and part-time in the Department of Cell Biology and Anatomy, chaired by B-J's friend and colleague Sabatini. Conroy's wife, Jane Phillips-Conroy, was working on her PhD in physical anthro at NYU under Jolly, and, when she earned her degree in 1978, Conroy moved to Brown.

As an assistant professor just beginning his career, Conroy avoided department politics as much as possible, and he left in time to miss the fireworks of B-J's arrest the following year. "I was just glad to have a job. B-J obviously had a very blunt style of administration," he said diplomatically. "But I got along well with him, and he was a champion for me. I didn't have any illusions about him. He was very tough, but I enjoyed his eccentricities."

The Buettner-Janusches sometimes invited him and Jane over for drinks or out for a meal. Conroy remembered the evening when both couples were eating at a little restaurant in the Village during a brutal mid-July heat wave. Suddenly, the lights dimmed and then went out completely. It was the infamous blackout of 1977, with widespread looting and arson breaking out in the evening's darkness. The following month, police arrested serial killer David Berkowitz, who had haunted the city's nights and dreams for a year. It was all a bit overwhelming for the Conroys.

The same year that he recruited Conroy, B-J also brought on a young archaeologist, Robert Bettinger, as an assistant professor, still without his PhD. Bettinger hailed from a California family going back several generations, and he had earned his bachelor's from the University of California at Riverside, where he was finishing his doctorate.

Like Conroy, Bettinger learned the skills that junior faculty members need to survive and prosper. At department meetings, he kept his head down and his mouth shut, enjoying the food from Balducci's and sipping the good sherry that B-J provided. Bettinger liked B-J and felt reasonably well treated by him, even though he could of course be cutting. In B-J's office, the chairman occasionally harrumphed, "Ordinarily, I wouldn't hire someone from Riverside," referring to the college's relative lack of prestige. Once, when Bettinger was sorting through some mail in the department office, B-J started yelling at him, telling him that's what secretaries were for. B-J's colleague Howard Winters, who had a calming influence on his friend, strolled in, shook his head, said simply, "Oh, John," and walked away, defusing B-J's rant.

When it came time for a salary review, B-J carefully reminded Bettinger that the decision was entirely his. Like a silverback gorilla, dispensing favors and threats purely as a show of power, he made clear that any pay increase came simply as an act of magnanimity on B-J's part. Bettinger was laboring under no illusions. "Did John have a bad side? Yes. Does everyone have a bad side? Yes. When he said those things to me, I just really didn't let it bother me," said Bettinger. "It was just the way he was."

While living his thoroughly lavish lifestyle—dinners and parties and visits to the Met and the New York Philharmonic—B-J continued to author papers for publication, but given the slow pace of scientific journal writing and publishing, a gap of several years often yawned between the initial drawing of blood, its analysis, the writing and editing of the article, and its printing. However, not much in the way of new research was getting done in B-J's expensive NYU laboratory. B-J's reputation depended heavily on his prolific lab research and publication record during those fecund years at Duke, but in 1976, the unthinkable—at least for B-J—happened: The National Science Foundation, which had been providing him with between $60,000 and $70,000 a year for research and operating expenses, was cutting off the grants on which his lab depended. The loss came as a huge blow.

B-J, who tended to see enemies everywhere (indeed, they *were* everywhere), thought that someone at the NSF had conspired to cut his funding as a personal vendetta. He had served as a board member of the NSF's Advisory Panel for Anthropology from 1971 to 1974, and that would have given him plenty of time to charm or alienate his fellow panelists. Scientists are still human after all.

But the NSF has always had a strong merit-review process, and B-J would have known that he could apply for funding again. Nancy Gonzalez, a program director for anthropology at the NSF at the time, called B-J's suspicions "preposterous." "NSF turns people down for one reason and one reason only—their work lacks scientific merit. And before such a decision is made, their proposals and their lab work are always meticulously scrutinized."

Lon Alterman, who was running the lab at the time, had another explanation for the loss of funding. "It was because he screwed off," he said. "He was too busy being the department chair, too busy going on trips, some of dubious academic value, too busy being a social gadfly. And it's not that this interfered with his research. He didn't really have any. Graduate students were his research. I was his research." When the funding ended, Alterman moved over to work at the NYU Medical Center, but he continued using B-J's lab to prepare for his own research trip to Borneo.

One of the perks of rising to a department chair is usually a reduced teaching load. But B-J liked being in the classroom, and continued to teach both graduate and undergrad classes. Reactions were mixed. Some found him incomprehensible and arrogant. The clarity of his textbooks and the tapes of his *Sunrise Semester* television course on CBS, however, may reveal more about the shortcomings of the complainers than any lack of lucidity on B-J's part. Others found him brilliant, and . . . arrogant.

Some mainly liked his style. John Paulius, who took an anthro course the semester before B-J's arrest for drug manufacturing, said, "I was stunned at the news. I knew he was cut from a different cloth, but mad? He wore Nehru jackets ten years after they were nowhere to be found. I thought the guy was the coolest. He was the coolest. But he was apparently too cool, thinking he wouldn't get caught."

An interesting portrait of B-J as lecturer comes from an unlikely source. In the 1980s, the *New York Times* ran a former NYU student's remembrance of him, titled AN ODD, BRILLIANT PROFESSOR, LONG FORGOTTEN, IS REMEMBERED. The author feared for her safety and that of her children, so it ran under a pseudonym, Sandra Blunt (highly unusual for the *Times*). Still, the article offered a perfectly preserved snapshot of the professor in his classroom.

On the first day of his course, Introduction to Physical Anthropology, B-J "walked into the classroom very pompously in his black tuxedo. His eyes seemed simultaneously stern, yet sly." B-J announced that he had season opera tickets and that the first performance was that evening. Hence, he would be dismissing class about forty-five minutes early, and would continue to do so throughout the opera season.

"He didn't apologize," she wrote. "He just said that it was very stupid of some administrator or other to schedule his class on an evening when he had opera tickets. He was certainly not going to miss the opera, he told us."

"Sandra Blunt" had some difficulty understanding B-J's lectures (although she says that she earned her master's in social-cultural anthropology at NYU). But she encountered B-J later when he heard that she had editing experience. He asked her to edit a compilation of his colleagues' papers on physical anthropology. It would be impossible to make them "worthwhile," he told her, but he hoped that by editing them, she could make them less embarrassing. He treated her courteously, she wrote, but he held many of the volume's contributors in contempt.

"It seemed to me that he took great pleasure in deriding the work of his colleagues," she wrote. "I detected an element of disgust as well, but the pleasure at his perceived superiority over them tended to override that disgust." A sense of superiority mixed with disgust and a dash of Strauss. The article certainly rings true, and, considering the increasing irrationalities of B-J's behavior, it's no wonder the ex-student chose to write anonymously. B-J's manner intimidated many students, but his colleagues often wondered what lay hidden behind the bluster.

Vina's father died in 1974, and her mother a year later, in March 1975. B-J often boasted that he and Vina had inherited half a million dollars from her family. When the NSF ended his grants, he began supplying funds for the lab out of his own pocket. But clearly his pride smarted from the cut-off, and perhaps shelling out his own money to keep his expensive lab facilities up and running seemed too much like a vanity project. He had, after all, been getting government research grants for years.

At the beginning of the fall semester of 1977, B-J began teaching a for-credit course on CBS's program *Sunrise Semester*, called "Man's Place in Nature." The series, a prototype for distance learning, had begun in 1957 and ran for nearly twenty-five years.

B-J's course borrowed its title from an 1863 collection of essays by Thomas H. Huxley, *Man's Place in Nature*, in which Huxley—aka, "Darwin's bulldog"—argued for the evolution of humans and apes from a common ancestor. B-J's course, while primarily addressing the evolution of humans from the earliest primates, asked students to view *Homo sapiens* as animals in the broader context of the natural world.

The course provided another glimpse of B-J as an educator. On the primitive set, B-J mostly stood at a podium, occasionally moving to a chalkboard on which he scrawled such classifications as strepsirrhines (lemurs and lorises) and cercopithecines (baboons and macaques). But beyond the necessary difficulty of the taxonomy, B-J shone as an instructor: clear, compelling, witty. He spoke in a deep, resonant voice infused with authority. He physically embodied the archetype of the professor, dressed in a three-piece suit and using his reading glasses as a prop. B-J's acting abilities (he was always on stage anyway) made him a television natural.

But his television course caused another skirmish between the chair and Lynch, which devolved into a kind of low comedy. Greatly annoyed by B-J's co-opting of the department's student lounge as a prep and rehearsal room for his TV lectures, Lynch collected all of B-J's things there and threw them on his office floor. To make sure that B-J knew who did it, the expert on Asian culture planted a small flag of India on the pile.

B-J, incensed, retaliated by going into Lynch's office, pulling books off his shelves, and stacking them in the hallway, then replanting the flag at the summit. They were like apes hurling feces at each other. But as the two middle-aged men vied for dominance using boyish pranks, a real tragedy was about to interrupt the comedy of bad manners. Vina was seriously ill.

Her friends had noticed that she'd been losing weight, and she received a diagnosis of malignant liver cancer only weeks before she died that October. Primary liver cancer—that is, cancer that originates in the liver—is rare in the United States, accounting for only 2 percent of all cancers. B-J called William Hylander with the news, and the latter flew up to New York to stay with his friend for a week. Hylander visited Vina in the NYU Medical Center soon after he arrived, and he found her in severe respiratory distress. "I don't think she was aware that I was in the room," he said. She was close to the end.

B-J invited Hylander and Conroy to join him at the CBS studio the next day as guests on a shoot for *Sunrise Semester*. As they were about to begin filming, the producer alerted B-J that the hospital was on the phone. The doctors informed him that they needed to perform emergency exploratory surgery on Vina, to which B-J assented. Then the producer asked if B-J wanted to postpone the shoot. He decided to go ahead with it.

Vina's cancer had spread; her condition was inoperable. She died on October 6, 1977, at the age of forty-six, and her remains were cremated. A brief obituary noted that funeral services were held in New York, but, strangely, her close friends, including Hylander, who was in New York at the time, didn't recall a funeral or memorial service.

People express grief in myriad ways, and it's difficult to tell how B-J felt about the death of his wife of twenty-seven years. Hylander said that he was "in the dumps, just the way anyone would be. He was unhappy, sad." But B-J didn't make a great show of his emotions. According to

Hylander, who was working on a journal paper, B-J didn't spend much time reminiscing, and continued going to work.

Richard Macris, a biology undergrad who worked as B-J's lab assistant and helped B-J with his *Sunrise Semester* lecture series at the studio, noted how matter-of-factly the professor announced that Vina had died a few days later. It was as if he were talking about one of his lemurs to which he'd been particularly attached. Macris, a great lover of classical music, gratefully accepted B-J's gift of the rest of his season subscription tickets to the New York Philharmonic.

Lynch—obviously no friend—also found it surprising to see B-J in the office early the day after Vina died. B-J was standing at the department copy machine, copying what looked to Lynch like insurance documents. "He was not a man deep in mourning," he said.

Rumors swirled in the anthropology department that B-J had somehow played a part in Vina's death, but corroborating evidence is extremely slim. The risk factors for liver cancer are various, including cirrhosis, hepatitis B or C, and hemochromatosis (too much iron in the liver). Smoking, especially when combined with alcohol abuse, increases the risk as well. Vina drank and smoked, but then, so did a lot of people.

The story apparently originated when someone in the lab claimed to have seen B-J remove a bottle of a highly carcinogenic substance and leave the lab with it in his suit pocket. Because of its toxicity, there was no apparent use for it outside the lab. Such actions could, however, have been completely benign. It was only in hindsight, after B-J was convicted of drug manufacturing, that stories like this could (or did) gain any credibility. By then, a couple of years after Vina's death and subsequent cremation, any attempt at proving a crime would have been impossible.

During Christmas break, B-J traveled to Paris, London, Munich, and Vienna. In July, August, and September of 1978, he traveled to Paris, London, Nairobi, Tananarive, and Vienna. They were places that he had visited with Vina, and he returned to them, he said, in memory of her.

5

The Tangled Web

EVERYONE WHO KNEW B-J WELL SAID THAT VINA WAS HIS RUDDER. Even the august Sherry Washburn called her "a steadying influence. She guided him." Her presence reined in B-J's excesses, deflated his delusions, and brought him in for safe landings when he seemed close to spinning out of orbit. Indeed, she kept him on a tether. Freed from her steadying influence, B-J's manner and dress grew even more unrestrained.

B-J had long extolled urban living as the next stage in human evolution. In New York City, despite or because of its challenges and temptations, its trammels and freedoms, he had found a congenial habitat—or so it seemed. Its ecosystems of predators and prey, its myriad symbiotic and parasitic relationships, its hierarchies of wealth and power, its variety of subcultures—all of it fascinated him. He reveled in the sheer drama and noise.

He began to change as soon as they arrived. In the past, B-J's eccentricities had drawn attention, with which, of course, he was delighted. Before New York, he had been tolerated. But among the denizens of Greenwich Village, he had found his home. He continued to wear expensive if conventional suits and flashy, boldly colorful ties, but his style expanded to include neo-Edwardian coats and Nehru jackets.

Many recalled B-J as an elegant if eccentric dresser. But Esteban Sarmiento, an anthropology grad student in the late 1970s and '80s, who became one of B-J's good friends during the coming storm and after his release from prison, saw just a man with a sunlamp tan and coiffed, dyed-blond hair, "flamboyant and tasteless." B-J was trying hard to look New York cool, but "he had Midwest stamped all over him," Sarmiento said.

Indeed, a faculty photo taken during his last months at Duke but used by the press department at NYU pictures B-J in a bold, rather raffish plaid sport coat and bow tie, with bottle-blond hair and split ends that verged on Warholian excess. He resembled nothing so much as a children's show host from the sixties. Still, he could look perfectly respectable in a tailored suit and tie.

B-J's legendary Duke University faculty photo.
COURTESY OF DUKE UNIVERSITY ARCHIVES

But he soon began to adopt the fashions of the Village's gay subculture. After Vina's death especially, he often ditched the professorial look and sported the telling combination of a leather jacket and boots with a Greek fishing cap. Such a macho fashion statement served as a gay signifier, although B-J's Yale friend Coe insisted that the fishing cap represented nothing more than a sad fashion faux pas that B-J had picked up in France.

Was B-J gay or bisexual? Almost certainly, although until he moved to New York, he had been deeply closeted. Even in New York his sexual orientation remained ambiguous, and many of his closest friends weren't certain about his sexuality. For many of B-J's generation, or somewhat younger—given his longtime marriage to Vina—the thought of his being gay never occurred to them. Tattersall said that he usually didn't give much thought to such things, but after some reflection he admitted that "it did seem to make sense." Beidelman, openly gay, claimed that he never could be sure. "I think he was. But I had no clear idea of his sex life," he said.

Many younger people, students or staff, were more certain that he was gay. Perhaps he felt more comfortable being frank about his sexuality with them. Alterman, who moved with him from Durham to New York, had no doubts. "He came out of the closet as soon as he moved to New York," he said. NYU grad student Esteban Sarmiento said that sometime after the professor's indictment B-J told him that he was gay.

Other signs appeared as well. Students reported seeing boxes of amyl nitrite delivered to B-J's office. While its recreational use became widespread in the 1970s club scene among all sexual orientations, poppers, as amyl nitrite is known, became popular as a means of enhancing sexual pleasure among gays because of its muscle-relaxing properties. They served no apparent scientific purpose. Alterman routinely referred to them as "Colonel B-J's Poppers."

In June 1979, Danny Cornyetz, who worked in the chairman's laboratory, recorded a conversation with B-J about possibly incriminating evidence against them during the federal investigation of alleged drug manufacturing in B-J's lab. Cornyetz asked B-J if a man with whom B-J had slept in his apartment might have been an informant. B-J considered the possibility, then rejected it. After B-J's conviction at his drug trial, Alterman helped clean out his office; he said he found index cards describing men with whom B-J had had sex. They contained, Alterman said, explicit comments about his encounters.

Whatever the case, B-J was secretive about his affairs, although signs of them grew more apparent after Vina's death. Perhaps her death made him feel freer to express that aspect of his sexuality. If he were to come out, Greenwich Village was certainly the place to do it. For years, the Village, along with the Castro district in San Francisco and West Hollywood in LA, provided a safe haven for gay culture and lifestyle. The gay liberation movement roared to life after the 1969 Stonewall Riots, which began on June 28 when regulars at the Stonewall Inn in the Village's Sheridan Square resisted yet another takedown by the NYPD, sparking days of protest and a movement.

As Dudley Clendinen and Adam Nagourney write in *Out for Good*, the event created a turning point, before which gays were "a secret legion of people, known of but discounted, ignored, laughed at or despised." After Stonewall, "the lives of millions of gay men and lesbians, and the attitude toward them of the larger culture in which they lived, began to change rapidly. People began to appear in public as homosexuals, demanding respect."

Although the freethinking, freewheeling Village had had a sizable population of gays since World War I, B-J arrived there not long after the movement toward a new openness about being gay took shape, just blocks away from where he lived. Life in Greenwich Village had a profound effect on him. Over his lifetime, B-J bent the truth, fabricating tales about himself or others, exaggerating his accomplishments, demeaning other people, distorting the truth for the sake of personal advantage or simply for a good story. His confabulations may have derived, at least in part, from an attempt to conceal his inner life.

If he were telling the story of his life, he would fall into the category of what in literature is called an "unreliable narrator," a term coined by Wayne C. Booth in *The Rhetoric of Fiction*. B-J's version of what happened in his lab between 1977 and 1979 is so mired in obfuscation, omissions, and evasions that it's extremely difficult to find the truth, which of course represents the traditional pursuit of scientists.

For a biographer, the situation resembles Michelangelo Antonioni's film *Blow-Up,* in which a photographer believes that he may have unintentionally photographed a murder. But, as he keeps enlarging his pictures, they become increasingly grainy and unclear. The film becomes an existential mystery in which the truth proves elusive, receding as we approach.

What exactly happened in B-J's lab at 25 Waverly Place between the spring of 1977 and May 1979 remains difficult to untangle. With a mix of recklessness and cunning, B-J helped to make it so. But as the federal investigation progressed, B-J's lab was searched, people were interviewed on the record, and tape recordings of B-J and his confederates were made, the fog of uncertainty began to disperse.

— ~ —

There were actually two physical anthropology labs on the fourth floor— one was B-J's, the other, Clifford Jolly's. When B-J moved to NYU, the layout of the fourth floor was reconfigured to accommodate the new chairman's laboratory. As a result, Jolly had to pass through B-J's lab to enter his own. B-J's lab for the most part lay open to any number of students who worked there. Asked later by a government attorney about who had access to B-J's lab, B-J responded: "Just about anyone in creation. The security at NYU is absolutely absurd. The lab is open all the time. We just leave it open." Although Jolly and B-J each had his own students working on projects, B-J made it generously clear that Jolly or Jolly's students could use his lab facilities.

Those working on the fourth floor included B-J's lab director, Danny Cornyetz, and B-J's research assistant, Richard Macris. They made a study in contrasts. Cornyetz, an anthro grad student, had grown up in a land-marked building on Manhattan's Upper West Side, and his father was a psychologist, but he was streetwise. He wore his hair long and liked hanging out late at downtown rock venues, like CBGB or the Mudd Club. He occasionally napped on the couch in the student lounge or stepped out on the fire escape for a few drags on a joint.

Macris was, by comparison, a choirboy. He grew up in a middle-class family in Flushing, Queens, graduating from the prestigious Bronx High

School of Science. Macris was still an undergrad, majoring in biology, but after taking B-J's Introduction to Physical Anthropology, he had become deeply interested in the subject.

He began working for Jolly as an unpaid research assistant, and in June 1977 he landed a position as a lab assistant with B-J for $5,000 a year. Although Macris's family was reasonably well-off—his father was a stockbroker and his brother, Robert, a lawyer—NYU's tuition was still expensive, and, more than the salary, he was glad that the position covered his tuition as well. If Cornyetz looked a little like rock star Tom Petty, Macris wouldn't have seemed out of place in the Partridge Family.

Other students in the lab at the time, all in one way or another caught up in *l'affaire* Buettner-Janusch, included Patricia Karatsis Berman, a graduate assistant and PhD candidate under B-J; Lisa Forman, another graduate assistant who studied under Jolly; and Bruce Greenfield, a biology grad student assisting Jolly with primate dermatoglyphs (patterns of lines on the palms, soles, fingers, and toes).

Lastly, there was B-J's administrative assistant, Richard Dorfman, in a paid staff position. He worked outside B-J's office on the second floor and became embroiled in the scandal because he was so closely involved in B-J's affairs.

A fault line in the lab divided the students: those who formed a part of B-J's "research projects"—Cornyetz, Greenfield, and, unwittingly, Macris—and those who didn't—Berman and Forman. For all of the ensuing debate about what happened and who did what in that lab—which continues to this day—all except Greenfield testified for the prosecution in B-J's drug trial. Greenfield himself was prosecuted for his part in those events, but not until several years later. To use a term popularized during the Nixon era, he was an unindicted coconspirator.

B-J set in motion the cascade that would lead to his imprisonment on May 9, 1977, when he submitted a requisition with the NYU Purchasing Department for two precursor chemicals commonly used for making LSD. A book checked out from Bobst, NYU's library, called *LSD: A Total Study*, with a recipe for synthesizing the drug, lay in plain sight for months that summer and fall on B-J's desk. On October 26 of the following year, B-J ordered through NYU two precursor chemicals often used in making methaqualone. B-J's attorneys made much of the transparency of these actions. If he were involved in some drug-making conspiracy, wouldn't he have made some effort to conceal his actions? It was a very good question.

B-J's explanation for the lab's research, which he offered to Jolly, Forman (Jolly's grad student), and others was that he was making substances *like* LSD and methaqualone—*not* those drugs exactly, but rather variations on them. Jolly said that B-J told him that he was making LSD-like chemicals for research on the lemurs at Duke. Then he said, apparently in jest: "Perhaps we should be making LSD and make a lot more money. But no one does this anymore, do they?" He also told Jolly that he'd made methaqualone, but that it was a mistake, and wasn't the substance's final form.

He told Forman a similar story. After federal agents broke into the lab in May 1979, B-J called Forman and invited her to his apartment. He asked if she knew about the "lemur project," and she said that she did. Then B-J told her that "it was possible that by accident the substances that were taken out of the laboratory could have been lysergic diethylamide and methaqualone because he was trying to make some substances that were very close to those," Forman said. "By accident, he may have made those substances."

But to others, B-J revealed a different version, which unfolded in their court testimony at B-J's drug trial. According to Dorfman, B-J's administrative assistant, the chairman told him directly in 1977 that he was going to make LSD, because "money was money, so who cares?" Cornyetz, the lab director, said that B-J told him in 1979: "You are as amoral as the rest of the U.S., and therefore I can tell you that we are going to make Quaalude in the laboratory. We need some money to keep the laboratory going."

Cornyetz's and Dorfman's testimony, however, was colored by their having turned state's evidence to avoid drug convictions themselves. Several conversations with B-J were taped and entered into evidence at his trial, but there was no smoking gun. Although he often sounded evasive, B-J never admitted to making either LSD or methaqualone. Then again, by the time the tapes were being surreptitiously recorded, the feds had interviewed B-J, and he knew he was under investigation. While B-J always maintained his innocence, he never said anything remotely like "We're doing science, so there's nothing to worry about." The conversations tended to address the latest developments in the federal investigation and how best to deal with them.

LSD was clearly the first "neurotoxin"—as B-J referred to his research substances—that he considered for manufacture. But with fog-machine genius, he chose to manufacture a drug with plausible deniability. LSD, first synthesized in 1938 by Swiss chemist Albert Hofmann at the pharmaceutical company Sandoz, originally had the name LSD-25, because it was the twenty-fifth in a series of lysergic acid derivatives. After accidentally discovering the hallucinogenic effects of LSD five years later, Hofmann produced many more chemical modifications, most of which "were weakly or not at all hallucinogenic," although some had medicinal properties that Sandoz could market. In other words, the LSD precursor chemicals that B-J had ordered could be used to make other lysergic acid derivatives.

Hofmann, who began experimenting with LSD and other psychotropic drugs, became, like British author Aldous Huxley, a psychedelic mystic. He also had great hopes for the therapeutic use of LSD (for the treatment of alcoholism and anxiety associated with terminal illnesses, for instance), which Sandoz offered under the brand name Delysid, from 1947 until the mid-1960s. Hundreds of studies took place using animals and human beings, but beginning in the 1950s and cresting with the counterculture of the '60s and early '70s, LSD became a recreational drug—much to Hofmann's dismay.

"This joy at having fathered LSD," he wrote in *LSD: My Problem Child*, "was tarnished after more than ten years of uninterrupted scientific research and medicinal use when LSD was swept up in the huge wave of an inebriant mania that began to spread over the Western world, above all the United States, at the end of the 1950s."

When the Controlled Substances Act passed in the United States in 1970, LSD became a Schedule I drug, along with heroin. The Drug Enforcement Administration's Office of Diversion Control defined these drugs thusly: "Substances in this schedule have a high potential for abuse, have no currently accepted medical use in treatment in the United States, and there is a lack of accepted safety for use of the drug or other substance under medical supervision."

The act did not preclude LSD from legitimate research. But funding for LSD studies slowed to a crawl by the end of the 1970s. (In recent years, clinical studies using LSD for psychotherapy have resumed.)

Among the charges brought by the grand jury against B-J was that he and his coconspirators had formed an organization called Simian Expansions, "one of its purposes being to provide a mechanism through which the proceeds of illicit drug sales could be channeled and the source of such funds concealed."

Not surprisingly, an apparently legitimate purpose explained the non-profit's creation. In November, the month after Vina died, B-J cosigned the New York incorporation papers for Simian Expansions. Its mission statement read: "The purposes for which the corporation is to be formed are to privately and publicly receive, solicit, and maintain funds to foster, promote, coordinate and implement research on primates and apply the income and principal thereto to said research. Public solicitations shall be made by contact with charitable institutions, universities, solicitation of private and public grants for research, and any and all other public avenues available for solicitation within the purview of the law."

Signing the incorporation papers with B-J were Martin Marion, a mid-level employee at the Staten Island Zoo, and Greenfield, the NYU grad student. While it's perfectly plausible that a scientist of B-J's stature would start a nonprofit to raise funds for research—especially after losing the NSF grants on which he'd depended—it is curious that one of the nation's best-known anthropologists would found a nonprofit with people who were, by comparison, a couple of kids associated with a tiny zoo.

The Staten Island Zoo, which opened in 1936, spans about 8 acres. It has something more than 400 animals representing over 200 species. If the Staten Island Zoo isn't a major research institution, it never pretended to be. If the zoo's tenuous connection to B-J's research projects seems ludicrous, it's not the zoo's pretensions. It is that B-J, with his laddish cofounders, made it seem so. Simian Expansions was either a legitimate nonprofit fund-raising vehicle for primate research or a front for a criminal enterprise—as the government prosecutor at B-J's trial bluntly put it, supplying a means "to launder money earned by making and selling drugs." In the end, it may have been neither. Simian Expansions never raised any money, legally or illegally.

According to Marion, he and Greenfield began discussing the idea of starting a nonprofit in late 1976 and early 1977. Marion's initial idea was to try to breed a colony of lion-tailed macaques—striking, silvery-maned Old World monkeys known as wanderoos, an extremely endangered species native to the Western Ghats of India, with a population today of fewer than 2,500 mature individuals in the wild. The Staten Island Zoo had several of them, Marion said, which could be cross-bred with some wanderoos at the Central Park Zoo.

They first approached Jolly with their idea, who passed. They then took their proposal to B-J, who supported it. They filed the incorporation papers at the end of 1977, though the State of New York didn't officially approve the application until fall 1978. According to Marion, the non-profit never succeeded in raising any funds, nor did it even have a corporate bank account. It did, however, create stationery and four T-shirts.

Marion, who had originated the idea of a charity, had had some fairly trivial run-ins with the law. As a student at the State University of New York at Stony Brook, he had been arrested with a group for possession of pot and had pleaded guilty to loitering. He enrolled at NYU in 1974, the same year that he became director of education at the Staten Island Zoo. But in early 1978, Marion lost his job at the zoo, due, he said, to "irresolvable personality differences with the director." His usefulness to B-J was now greatly diminished. Without his connection to the zoo as a source of primates, or a place to breed or keep them, Marion lacked any professional connections to bring to Simian Expansions, and he felt a growing coldness from the professor.

In the spring of 1979, as suspicions about illegal drug-making in B-J's lab were growing, and federal agents were about to break in, a freelance fund-raiser in Chicago, Patricia Pronger, was completing a prospectus for Simian Expansions that included a proposal for "brain research" using lemurs. Pronger even had several prospective donors. (During an interview that summer with Assistant District Attorney Denise Cote, B-J rather heedlessly and cynically referred to the donors as "rich old ladies," sounding more predatory than grateful.) Needless to say, the "rich old ladies" lost interest in the research after his indictment.

Greenfield, the third cofounder of Simian Expansions, ostensibly was working for Jolly on dermatoglyphs. Jolly said that Greenfield didn't do a particularly good job, and he began to distance himself from his student, suspicious at first and later convinced that he was up to something. Greenfield kept odd hours and often seemed to be working on other projects.

Greenfield, like Cornyetz, wore his hair long, but he dressed preppily, often in a button-down Oxford shirt, tweed sport coat, and khakis or jeans. He smoked heavily, dragging on cigarettes down to the filter, then stabbing them out violently. He left ashtrays full of butts after working at night, and Forman emptied them in the morning. While Forman admitted that he "presented himself well," she didn't like him or his friends much.

B-J's denials that LSD was being made on the premises only aroused more suspicion. An unstable substance, LSD is sensitive to temperature, light, and air. Some of Greenfield's lab activities wouldn't have seemed all that unusual . . . except that they were necessary steps in manufacturing the drug. Greenfield sometimes worked under safety lights, like those used in a darkroom, and covered flasks with foil to protect them from light.

As Hofmann wrote in *LSD: My Problem Child,* "Claims that LSD may easily be prepared, or that every chemistry student in a half-decent laboratory is capable of producing it, are untrue." Greenfield apparently was finding the process very challenging. He wasn't a trained chemist, and the anthro lab wasn't equipped for synthesizing acid. Macris, recruited by B-J to work on the methaqualone project, but not on LSD, said, "The laboratory was not a synthetic organic chemistry lab, but a general-purpose science lab. It's not in the realm of reality that the staff of the anthropology lab would be technically capable of synthesizing [these kinds of] substances to a higher degree of purity than was available from commercial sources."

Hofmann put it plainly: "In order to isolate LSD in pure crystalline form from the reaction solution and in order to produce stable preparations . . . special equipment and not easily acquired specific experience are required." Neither could be found at Rufus D. Smith Hall.

It may be difficult to make LSD, but it isn't like making weapons-grade plutonium. Augustus Owsley Stanley III spent three weeks in 1964 in the UC Berkeley library, where he claimed to have schooled himself in the science and art of making LSD. The so-called "artisan of acid" allegedly produced somewhere between 1 and 5 million hits of acid, considered remarkably pure at the time. His name even became a byword for "an extremely potent, high-quality type of LSD." Owsley wasn't a scientist, but neither was Greenfield, and perhaps neither could have produced the quality of a good chemical supply house.

Dorfman later testified that Greenfield bluntly told him Simian Expansions was a way to launder drug money. "He also explained to me that I was a good secretary to have around," B-J's assistant said, "because I knew how to keep my mouth shut, and that there would be a raise in this for me." Marion denied that he had ever had any knowledge of illegal drug-making in the lab, but the three of them—B-J, Greenfield, and Marion—met frequently in B-J's office in late 1977 and early 1978.

And so we have the central question: Were the drugs being made in the chairman's lab part of a legitimate research project, a money-making scheme, or, even more strangely, somehow both? Was Simian Expansions a charity or a fraud? Was B-J manipulating his students, or were they putting one over on him?

Jolly didn't recall Marion or Greenfield asking him to start Simian Expansions, and he said that he never heard about a plan to breed lion-tailed macaques. He was, however, working on their genetic variety in zoo populations, and Marion did supply him with blood samples for study. Still, he would have had little interest in a breeding program, since lion-tailed macaques already formed a part of an inter-zoo breeding program. But if that ever really was to be part of Simian Expansions' mission, they set that aside after Marion was let go from the Staten Island Zoo.

Greenfield soldiered on with his LSD research project. In the fall of 1978, B-J submitted another requisition for chemical substances, this time for those used in the synthesis of Quaalude. The chemicals for making drugs were ordered openly, but an air of mystery surrounded the projects, and gossip and rumors swirled around Rufus D. Smith Hall.

Another warning signal—which shouldn't have been one at all—was that B-J was spending a lot more time in the lab. His graduate student Berman was miffed that the boys' club meant that her own dissertation research wasn't getting enough attention from B-J. She committed an act of deliberate sabotage, pouring what she assumed was LSD down the drain, although she didn't own up to it. Then she got into a shouting match with B-J over a chemical procedure of her own, and he banned her from the lab for a time. The situation was growing tense.

B-J traveled extensively over the summer of 1978, but with the fall semester the pace of "research" began to accelerate. He back-burnered the LSD project and green-lighted the Quaalude project. B-J later told federal prosecutors that after Vina's death, he "took about eighteen months off, more or less. I sort of ran the department with one hand. I looked at things going on in the lab, and there I did very little work. It was not until April of this year [1979] that I came back in the lab."

But that wasn't the case at all. B-J was in the lab frequently. According to Forman, who worked for both Jolly and B-J as a lab assistant every weekday from the beginning of the fall semester of 1978, B-J came up three or four times a week during the winter of 1978 and spring of 1979. Macris said that during the spring semester of 1979, he sometimes came to the lab several times a day. He even worked in the lab at night or on weekends.

Late in the fall semester of 1978, Forman observed chemicals, some in large quantities, arriving from Fisher Scientific. Toluene, for example—an organic solvent with many uses, but commonly used in making methaqualone—began arriving in large drums.

In January 1979, Cornyetz was assigned to find some recipes. But making methaqualone, while relatively easier to synthesize than LSD, proved challenging as well. It was shortly afterward that B-J made a fateful decision, a misjudgment that in time brought his career to ruin. He decided to recruit his longtime research assistant Macris to work on the

Quaalude project. A few days after he began working on the project in February, Macris met with B-J in his office and asked what he was working on.

The chairman recited his mantra: "We're making neurotoxins for lemur research to be used at Duke University."

"Isn't this neurotoxin available commercially?" Macris asked.

"Yes, it is," said B-J, "but I wouldn't trust any commercial product on my lemurs. It wouldn't be pure enough."

Suspicious, Macris felt something was wrong. There had been rumors that B-J was making LSD, but at first he had dismissed them. "I liked the guy," he said, "and I didn't believe it. Sure, he had a volatile personality. When something went wrong, he would start screaming. He could have used an anger-management program.

"I liked him until he did what he did. He destroyed my calling. I wanted to be an anthropologist, but after what happened, I felt that I became untenable. I was like tainted merchandise."

The day after he talked to B-J about the purpose of the research, Macris visited Jolly in his office and shared his suspicions that B-J might be asking him to make illegal drugs. Jolly suggested that he keep a record, a sort of diary, about his work with B-J.

"He was convinced there was something wrong in the state of Denmark," Macris said. "But he also didn't want to lead me on so that it looked like he was directing me."

The next day, Valentine's Day, he decided to ask Cornyetz what was going on. Different as they were, they had an easygoing work relationship. Although their taste in music was deeply dissimilar—Macris loved classical, Cornyetz, new wave—they shared a love of high-end audio equipment, devouring the latest issues of *Absolute Sound* and *Stereophile* magazines. For Forman, who as a grad student felt a maternal affection for Macris, it seemed very guyish. The two of them, she said, often tried to best each other with their esoteric knowledge of audio equipment.

Cornyetz, playing the street-smart insider to Macris's naive query, asked him to guess what they were making in the lab. Macris began by asking if they were making drugs, and Cornyetz said yes. Macris first hazarded that it was LSD, and Cornyetz said that was another project. Macris then named several other drugs, before giving up. Methaqualone, Cornyetz said finally. But Cornyetz asked Macris not to let B-J know of their conversation, because, he said, the professor had insisted that he not tell him.

Curiously, B-J only gave his assistant the formula piecemeal, with handwritten notes and sometimes more detailed, typed instructions for each stage, rather than entire copied sections of books or articles. B-J was being cautious but came off seeming just plain weird. According to Cornyetz, B-J later admitted that Macris was "too straight." But B-J needed his help.

Macris continued working on the project, keeping notes in his diary. He began photographing the lab when B-J wasn't around. He checked the *Merck Index*, an encyclopedia of chemicals, drugs, and biologicals, with monographs containing molecular formulas, melting points, and other data, as well as citations for chemical synthesis. Under the entry for methaqualone, Macris found two citations, which he hunted down in Manhattan: one in German, which he found at the library of the New York Academy of Sciences, the other in English, from the *Journal of the Indian Chemical Society*, which he found at the Chemists' Club library in Manhattan. He confirmed for himself that the fragments of the formula were for methaqualone.

"I was indignant that he was doing this at a university," Macris explained, "and I was scared and worried that I might be blamed."

Macris had reason to worry. About a month after B-J put him on the new project, Macris produced about 200 grams of the "neurotoxin." B-J said he was disappointed with the quantity and asked if he couldn't cut some corners to produce a greater yield. But that meant a less pure product. "What about your lemurs?" Macris asked pointedly. B-J turned and walked away, saying nothing.

Ironically, at the time, methaqualone was still widely available as a prescription drug, so methaqualone of considerable pharmaceutical purity would have been easily available to researchers.

Indra Kishore Kacker and Syed Hussain Zaheer first synthesized methaqualone in India in 1951. Its sedative and soporific properties made it a good prescription alternative to addictive barbiturates as a treatment for insomnia. William H. Rorer first marketed the drug in America in 1965 under the trade name Quaalude. By the early 1970s, it had become the sixth most prescribed sedative-hypnotic drug in the country, and other pharmaceutical companies began producing it under the trade names Sopor, Parest, Optimil, and Somnafac. Its popularity as a recreational drug exploded, with media stories—warning, in traditional fashion, of its dangers while simultaneously sensationalizing it—calling it "the love drug," "heroin for lovers," and "the Dr. Jekyll and Mr. Hyde drug." Young people began "luding out," a form of entertainment accomplished by taking methaqualone with alcohol, resulting in a loss of consciousness. Such effects made its reputation as a love drug seem exaggerated.

Methaqualone's allure crossed subculture boundaries: It was popular on disco dance floors, in rock clubs, and in dorm rooms. According to one survey cited by the DEA, methaqualone abuse in 1979 increased by nearly 40 percent. By 1980, it ranked as the second most popular illicitly used drug in America, after marijuana. The street supply of the drug partly came from pharmaceutical companies, but mostly it was manufactured illegally in the United States and other countries. With growing evidence that methaqualone was also addictive, in addition to its widespread abuse, Congress made methaqualone a Schedule I drug in 1984, ending its medical use. In 1979, however, it was still a Schedule II drug, legal with a prescription.

Macris and Jolly continued to meet, and Jolly began his own investigation. He regularly took photographs of B-J's lab, which Macris, an amateur photographer, developed. He took samples of drugs from flasks and bottles, storing them in a bookcase at home. He even searched through B-J's trash nearly every day, seeking evidence of illegal drugmaking. Aside from Macris, Jolly didn't discuss his detective work with anyone else.

A private investigation into the possible criminal doings of a fellow professor seems like something out of a novel, perhaps one by Amanda Cross, whose academic sleuth Kate Fansler pursues bad guys in books such as *Death in a Tenured Position*. But Jolly told reporter Selwyn Raab, who covered B-J's trial for the *New York Times*, that there was nothing out of the ordinary about his actions. "I wouldn't call what I did detective work. Scientists do investigations all the time," he said. "You don't take anyone's word. You find out for yourself." Of course, doing science rarely entails going through a colleague's trash.

In April, Macris told his brother, Robert, a lawyer and an adjunct assistant law professor at NYU, that he suspected that B-J was using him to manufacture methaqualone. At first, Robert was incredulous, certain that Richard was mistaken. They called their cousin-in-law, Edward Boyle, also an attorney, and Boyle asked Richard for a sample of the substance he'd made for B-J. Macris, convinced the lab had indeed become a drug factory, decided he couldn't keep working there. He officially stopped working on April 13, calling in sick, at first feigning the flu, then later claiming to have mononucleosis.

At the end of April, Boyle got hold of a sample, procured by Jolly, and turned it over to Bernard Fried, chief assistant US attorney for the Eastern District of New York, in charge of the narcotics unit. Boyle said that he'd sourced it from a relative concerned that he had been duped into helping make a controlled substance, "possibly Quaaludes, possibly at a university."

Two weeks later, Fried called Boyle. As Boyle later testified at a pretrial hearing, Fried told him: " 'I have good news and bad news. The good news is that your relative who is working in the laboratory is one hell of a chemist. That is the purest, strongest sample of the particular controlled substance that [my] agents have ever tested.' The bad news was implicit."

Macris and Jolly had passed the event horizon. There was no turning back. Because of B-J's connections with the dean and other top brass at the university, they decided they had to go directly to the president of NYU, John Sawhill.

Sawhill, an economist by training and a consummate bureaucrat and crisis manager, had served in a variety of government positions under Nixon and Ford. When Sawhill took over as university president in July 1975, NYU, like its namesake city, was in deep financial straits. The university's 1974–75 budget was running $4.4 million in the red. (Shortly after it was announced that the previous president, James Hester, was leaving, New York magazine asked in a headline, ANYBODY HERE WANT TO BE PRESIDENT OF NYU?—painting a formidable challenge rather than a golden opportunity.) Within a couple of years, however, Sawhill had expertly balanced the budget and built a substantial endowment.

A young, somewhat ascetic and distant administrator, Sawhill was also a devoted runner, who jogged around Washington Square Park every morning at 6:30, stopping only to pick up trash and throw it away in garbage cans that he had personally helped install and chain up. At first, Macris's brother Robert, who lived in the Village, thought he might approach Sawhill during one of his jogs in the park. (Sawhill had a standing invitation to anyone in NYU's community to join him.) But after a few days, Robert Macris gave up, and Jolly made an appointment to meet Sawhill in his office.

Early in the afternoon of May 16, Macris and Jolly were ushered into the president's office on the top floor of Bobst Library. A liveried waiter served some abstemious snacks, and Sawhill indulged in his favored beverage, a Tab. Then, the president and Andrew Schaffer, NYU's general counsel, heard Macris's and Jolly's incredible tale.

Later that afternoon, Schaffer, Jolly, and Macris drove to the US attorney's office for the Southern District of New York in downtown Manhattan, where they met with Assistant DA Dominic Amorosa and DEA Agent Jack Toal. Macris turned over his diary, and Jolly delivered chemical samples from B-J's lab and several photographs. They also told Amorosa about the anonymous test the DEA had run.

Amorosa, certain that there was sufficient evidence for probable cause, suggested they get a warrant to search the lab. Schaffer thought that was unnecessary; NYU, he insisted, could approve a warrantless search. The lab was, after all, on NYU's property. He said, however, that he needed Sawhill's approval. Sawhill, in full crisis-management mode, quickly gave his consent. All agreed that Macris and Jolly would assist the federal agents in the raid.

The search was scheduled for about ten p.m. the next evening, when B-J would be attending a formal dinner. Macris took the subway from Queens to his brother's apartment in the Village, and together they met Jolly, Toal, and five other plainclothes DEA agents, including a chemist, Jeffrey Weber, outside Rufus D. Smith Hall. Jolly went first to open the door with his key and to make sure the coast was clear; then he let everyone in to the lab.

Jolly and Macris directed the agents to collect suspicious compounds and containers. They found more than two pounds of methaqualone in various stages of purification in the fume hood and on a lab bench. The agents also seized a quantity of marijuana from the laboratory's cold room, lysergic acid hydrazide from another lab bench, and two vials of ergotamine tartrate, a precursor of LSD. (The only actual LSD from the lab—which the DEA chemist, Jeffrey Weber, described as an "immeasurable" trace—Jolly had taken earlier and turned in to the feds a while later.)

Only Jolly and the lab assistants had keys, so if the search didn't appear to be a break-in, the circle of suspects would narrow considerably. Strangely, the university didn't have a set of keys to the lab. At the last minute, they decided to make their entry look like a burglary. Conveniently, someone found a crowbar, and they bashed the doorframe.

The ruse of a "burglary" didn't last long, though. The following day, May 18, DEA Special Agent Toal arrived at B-J's apartment in the early afternoon to serve him with a subpoena to talk with federal attorneys. Sitting at the table in his study with him were Greenfield and his friend Mark Schwartz. When Toal asked who they were, B-J replied that they were "a couple of students doing some work for me." Schwartz wasn't a student, and both Greenfield and Schwartz were indicted on similar drug charges nearly five years later, as part of the goings-on in B-J's lab.

B-J, overconfident and arrogant, lied egregiously to two federal attorneys, Denise Cote and Amorosa. The charm that had so often captured hearts and minds completely failed him. He became a caricature of the privileged, brilliant man who regards the working-class servants of the law as annoyances, mere insects to be brushed away. All the while, the attorneys had in their possession two pounds of methaqualone that no amount of equivocation could explain away. Although B-J must have been alarmed that someone had informed on him, he had no idea yet how many people had marshaled against him.

B-J was called in for questioning at the federal courthouse in Manhattan on May 22. Cote, an assistant DA, tangled with B-J, who, while making a pretense of cooperation, was operating at his obfuscating, mendacious best. B-J asked to see some of her documents, perused them with his reading glasses, then tossed them back at her.

"Could you just refrain from throwing things?" she asked, her patience already tried to the limit. "If you could just hand them to me." The court stenographer dutifully noted: "Witness flipped papers onto Ms. Cote's desk."

B-J (center) and attorneys William Wachtel (in front) and Frank Amoroso (in back) leave the courthouse at pretrial hearings in December 1979.
COURTESY OF NEW YORK UNIVERSITY ARCHIVES, PHOTOGRAPH COLLECTION

Cote inquired about B-J's research, and he talked about his growing interest in primate behavior. "In the last three or four years, with a couple of grad students in college," he told her, "I have been moving into the study of lemur behavior as opposed to just their biochemistry." He cited, as proof, a paper he'd recently coauthored for the *American Journal of Physical Anthropology*, "Statistical Methods for Analyzing Data on Daily Activity Cycles of Primates."

If B-J was working on the behavior modification of lemurs, as he claimed, Cote's questioning was getting to the heart of the matter. B-J had had little work of this sort published, and had shown virtually no interest in behavior earlier in his career. On the other hand, it was certainly possible that his research interests had changed. Indeed, there are solid precedents for scientists changing the course of their work in midlife. For example, Francis Crick, the English molecular biologist and co-discoverer of the structure of the DNA molecule with James Watson, became, in later life, a neurobiologist.

But much of B-J's pretrial testimony formed a farrago of lies and half-truths, of the incredible or the incomprehensible. He'd told Cote that he wasn't in the lab much during the 1978–79 school year, when in fact he came up far more frequently than usual, even on weekends or in the evening. When asked if he had contacted anyone at Duke about his proposed lemur research, B-J said that he had "discussed this in generalities" with his old colleague, Elwyn Simons, then-director of the Duke University Primate Center, who recalled no such conversations.

He stuck with his story about trying to make substances close to LSD and methaqualone, but not those exact chemicals. Only a few weeks later, on July 14, he told Amorosa that he hadn't known until very recently that "Quaaludes were drugs sold illicitly in the streets of New York," as Amorosa put it. Quaalude was by then one of the best-selling illegal drugs in America, and countless mainstream media articles had warned of a growing methaqualone epidemic. B-J's protests of ignorance strained credulity. But then again, B-J claimed not to know what was going on in his own lab.

"To your knowledge, was methaqualone manufactured in your lab?" Amorosa asked directly.

"No," B-J said.

"Did you ever ask anybody to manufacture methaqualone in your lab?"

"No."

"Has anybody ever told you that methaqualone was manufactured in your lab?"

"Nobody has ever told me that."

"Would you be surprised if methaqualone was manufactured in your lab?" Amorosa asked finally.

The DA probably regretted pushing the question.

"I would be surprised," B-J responded, "if anything but a lot of junk was manufactured in these syntheses, because the reactions were going very poorly and the fact that a lot of phosphorus chloride was being absorbed suggested to me in the beginning of some of these reactions the chloride, or chloral, forms of substituted quinazolones were probably going to come down in the reaction mixture, but most of it was such a mess that we had no idea. I was nowhere close to even beginning to purify some of the reaction."

B-J, knowing how meaningless this language would sound to Amorosa, may have sought to convey simultaneously that his work was beyond the comprehension of the DA and that it was not going at all well—so who could say what might come of that primordial soup? Perhaps even two pounds of methaqualone. In any case, the grand jury later returned two separate counts against B-J, stemming from both conversations, for making "false, fictitious, and fraudulent statements and representations" to the federal attorneys.

The lemur research story had several flaws. It was simply too remarkable a coincidence that of all the drugs that B-J might have chosen to modify prosimian behavior, he had picked "variations" on two illegal street drugs. Also, although strictly speaking not all lemurs are threatened or endangered species, they were sufficiently rare and their habitats sufficiently at risk that using them as experimental animals should have been a nonstarter. Even those who testified that B-J had mentioned doing some kind of behavior modification with them didn't like the idea. Most significantly, *there were no lemurs.*

Jolly never bought what he sardonically called the "ludes for lemurs" project for several reasons. "As far as I know, there never was a 'lemur neurotoxin research' plan," he said. "All lemur species are to some extent endangered. Even at that time, when regulations were less strict than they are now, there would have been rules about their use in such potentially harmful experiments. Detailed plans and protocols would have to be submitted and passed, collaborations established. There would be records."

No such records or plans ever materialized as evidence in court. B-J had only talked about his project in the broadest terms, never in any detail. "I never heard B-J discuss lemur behavior, or the details of any actual behavioral project, experimental or otherwise, on lemurs," Jolly said. "He did, of course, mention the upcoming 'big study' on the Duke lemurs, as an explanation of the drugs manufactured in the lab, but nothing about its details, methods, or rationale."

Only in movies or science-fiction novels do scientists work on large experiments as lone-wolf researchers. They collaborate and make use of their colleagues' areas of expertise. It would have been, Jolly said, "very unusual to set up such an expensive and dangerous program of strongly interventional research, with no collaboration or even consultation with an established, senior neuroanatomist or neuropharmacologist. Had there been such consultation, I presume the collaborator or collaborators would have readily testified to it."

Like Cote before him, Amorosa pummeled B-J with questions about the legality of using methaqualone in academic research. "Are you aware that you can get a license to manufacture controlled substances?"

"No, frankly," B-J replied with equanimity, "I was not aware until this happened. I was for eight years a faculty member of the medical school of Duke University, and matters of that sort never came up."

"You were not aware, I take it, up until maybe two weeks ago that you can get a license to manufacture controlled substances in connection with various research in the scientific fields?"

B-J conceded, "I may have been aware because as a faculty member of the medical school at Duke I may have known that the university or the medical center had licenses for all sorts of things, but there were no restrictions on anything, including prescription drugs for our use in research and other investigations."

B-J's pretensions to ignorance in such matters looked preposterous, and the DAs, familiar with the law if not academia, knew that. B-J's colleague and friend from Duke, Peter Klopfer, who more than anyone put his reputation on the line in B-J's defense at his trial, said later, "Everyone in the field knows you need permits from the feds to use controlled substances." But, again, B-J argued that he had never intended to use controlled substances, so no permits were necessary.

Amorosa continued, "I take it, then, that it would be correct to say that you never applied for nor received a license to manufacture controlled substances?"

"No," B-J said, "because we were really not manufacturing controlled substances."

"The gang that couldn't shoot straight," as Macris later called his colleagues on the LSD and methaqualone projects, had, with B-J's supervision, somehow produced more than two pounds of methaqualone, ranging in purity from 51 percent to 98 percent, but, according to B-J, they had never intended to do so. They had worked for months and months to produce something else.

In other ways, however, during the period leading up to B-J's subpoena in May of 1979, the anthropology department had been operating under an illusion of normalcy. Professors gave lectures attended by students who took notes and read the assigned texts. Many of B-J's students were pursuing their academic goals, uninvolved in clandestine research projects and deceptions. Two anthropology grad students, Esteban Sarmiento and Jeffrey Rogers, began working on their PhDs in the fall of 1978, both of them students of B-J and Jolly. But they managed to stay out of the fray—although of course they witnessed it firsthand. They worked together as teaching assistants for B-J's Introduction to Physical Anthropology class and attended his seminars.

As different as they were, they became friends. Like B-J and Jolly, Sarmiento and Rogers were a study in contrasts. Sarmiento hailed from

New Jersey and earned his bachelor's from Rutgers. He felt thoroughly in his element at a large urban university, having traveled into Manhattan to visit friends and family from his early teens. Although Jolly was his dissertation adviser, he became one of B-J's closest friends before and after his incarceration. Sarmiento had a brusque manner—an impatience with the pretense and polite manners of academia, often concealing the grossest forms of hypocrisy—which may explain why they hit it off so well. He didn't accept B-J's blandishments and often called him on them. Perhaps B-J respected that.

Rogers graduated from Northwestern in Winnetka, Illinois, a suburb of Chicago. There he had studied under Thomas Olivier, one of B-J's top grad students at Duke. Rogers received a highly competitive three-year NSF graduate fellowship, and Olivier strongly encouraged Rogers to go to NYU. His passion centered on primate genetics, and, he said, because NYU had two of the best authorities in the field, B-J and Jolly, he quickly chose New York. The fellowship didn't require that he pick an adviser, so he could take both B-J and Jolly as mentors. But he was, he said, "a naive suburban kid from the Midwest trying to figure out if I could do this." For that very reason, his perspective was revelatory; he was, to borrow a phrase from Oliver Sacks, like an anthropologist on Mars.

Both thrilled and intimidated, Rogers admired the work of the two profoundly different men. "B-J was a really charismatic character," Rogers said. "He commanded attention in many ways. Yes, he was flamboyant, but he was intellectually astute and *very* serious about science." As for Jolly, Rogers found him "a gentle, quiet, unassuming, understated man" who was also "incredibly brilliant." He had "high integrity, high creativity, [and he was] a virtual encyclopedia of biological anthropology." Rogers and Jolly still collaborate to this day.

B-J wasn't just demanding of his students. "He was very severe with students who didn't meet his standards," Rogers said. "He could be *brutal,* and the criticism was in public. He could inspire fear, but if you met his standards, you thought, 'I can really do this.' When you were praised, you felt inspired, which, in turn, inspired great loyalty." B-J's seminars, he recalled, typically entailed reading assignments and discussions, but the professor orchestrated them in a "blunt, authoritarian" manner. Rogers made B-J sound like a staff sergeant at boot camp.

Sarmiento remembered B-J's style of teaching very differently, but it may say as much about the personalities of the two younger men as it does of B-J. "People have different sensibilities," Sarmiento said. "Jeff was a guy that spent college in books more or less. For a professor to shout at him publicly that he is doing something wrong would be mortification. I spent my college days in all kinds of activities. I played semipro soccer, cycled, and wrestled. I was used to people shouting at me, both encouragement and straight-out insults." Sarmiento insisted that B-J was often rather kind to his students. "I saw this repeatedly," he said. "What he was, was direct and loud. He was not afraid of telling you what he thought if he disagreed with you—even if he was wrong. What you had to do was ignore him or shout over him."

Sarmiento took two seminars in physical anthro from B-J over the 1978–79 school year. "The seminars were designed to let us discuss as a group whatever topics we found of interest," he said. "The idea was that B-J would be the moderator. However, he nodded off that year in almost every class. We had serious students, so we really did discuss and stick to the topics even without a moderator who was awake." B-J would talk for a while, put some cream on the bags under his eyes, and often drift off. A bit later he'd wake up, clear his throat, and then blame his nap on a drug-resistant strain of malaria he'd picked up and the drugs he took to kill it. Not exactly boot camp.

When Rogers first arrived, he *was* naive. During his first semester, in the fall of 1978, he was working alone late one Saturday night at Rufus D. Smith Hall. He was startled when B-J dropped in. He greeted him, and B-J stayed for only twenty or twenty-five minutes. "Holy cow," Rogers thought, "I've come to the right place. My professor's so dedicated he's coming in to work on weekends." He realized later that B-J was checking in on his drug research. B-J told him about his making "psychoactive drugs for lemurs," and Rogers thought it was odd. It "didn't seem to make a lot of sense." But B-J's success as an academic meant that initially Rogers accepted the explanation.

B-J could be remarkably kind as well, just as Sarmiento had said. In the spring of 1979, Rogers asked B-J about summer job possibilities. The chairman said he'd look into it. A few weeks later, B-J told Rogers that he'd received an NSF grant to create a new course next fall, a class on the intellectual history of man's place in nature, ranging from ancient Greek tragedies by Sophocles and Aeschylus through David Hume and Jean-Jacques Rousseau to Claude Lévi-Strauss. It was, Rogers recalled, a very long list. B-J said he could pay Rogers $2,000 for the summer to read the works in a preliminary syllabus so that he could help with the course in the fall. Rogers spent the summer reading only to discover that there was no grant and there was no course. B-J had just paid him out of his own pocket. "That kind of experience engenders not just gratitude, but loyalty," Rogers admitted.

As the case against B-J mounted, from the DEA break-in and the grand jury investigation through the indictment and pretrial hearings to the preparations for the drug trial, Rogers began "freaking out," as he put it. During the spring semester of 1980, he found himself caught between "two men who can't talk to each other, can't be together. I realized that B-J was really involved in something illegal."

Rogers had one year left on his fellowship, and both B-J and Jolly urged him to stay. "B-J constantly told me that he was innocent, that we'd get past it and get back to doing science. And Cliff would say about B-J, 'I know this is horrible. But I know what happened. He's going to be convicted.' But I couldn't have confidence that B-J would leave, and Cliff would stay, and I'd work with him."

Rogers decided to leave. Incredibly, both B-J and Jolly, without each other's knowledge, suggested to Rogers that he go to Yale and study under Alison Richard there. Richard and her husband, Robert Dewar, were by then good friends with B-J. Richard later helped raise funds for B-J's defense committee, and cowrote B-J's obituary with Rogers and B-J's former Duke grad student Robert Sussman for the *American Journal of Physical Anthropology*. After B-J's conviction, Richard made some very cutting remarks about Jolly's involvement in the affair in *Science* magazine.

But Jolly knew Richard professionally and had spent several weeks in 1979 in Pakistan, helping her research group trap rhesus monkeys. So Rogers went to Yale, where he finished his PhD nearly a decade later. Richard supervised his dissertation, *Genetic Structure and Microevolution in a Population of Tanzanian Yellow Baboons*, and Rogers made quite a name for himself in primate genetics at the Baylor College of Medicine.

But that summer, while Rogers was reading deeply in the classics of Western science, philosophy, and literature, cracks began to appear in the drama's set. In the wake of the lab break-in in May, Rogers was subpoenaed to testify before the grand jury. Perhaps reading Greek tragedy offered him some catharsis.

Soon after the break-in, Macris began taping conversations—first on the phone, using a conventional cassette recorder and a suction cup on the receiver, then with a more sophisticated wire provided to him by the feds. He taped B-J, Cornyetz, and Forman. Many of the tapes became evidence and were played at B-J's trial. Even though B-J never testified in his own defense, jurors heard his voice. What he said and how he said it didn't sound right.

Soon, others got into the act. Jolly taped B-J and Greenfield. Forman taped B-J, Cornyetz, and Dorfman. Cornyetz taped Macris and B-J. Interestingly, none of them ever taped each other simultaneously. If you weren't taping people in the anthropology department that summer, you weren't cool. But it created an atmosphere reminiscent of the system of informers used by the Stasi, Communist East Germany's secret police, a situation antithetical to the ideals of academic freedom.

On May 22, Macris called Cornyetz after hearing about the break-in from B-J's assistant, Dorfman, who told him that he needed to come in for a meeting the next day. Macris pretended not to know anything about it. But from the start, Cornyetz cagily watched what he said, as though he assumed the call might be recorded and he was shaping his version for an audience intentionally. Because the building, Rufus D. Smith Hall, didn't show signs of a break-in—only the lab did—it looked like an inside job. Whoever broke in knew exactly what he was looking for. That B-J was subpoenaed the very next day made it obvious that federal agents were involved.

Cornyetz talked for just a few minutes, then said he'd call Macris back. He left his apartment to call. "Umm, B-J and Bruce are operating under the assumption that no telephone lines are safe to speak on, so I'm on a pay phone."

"You want me to go to a pay phone, too?" Macris asked.

"No, no, no," Cornetz said. "Umm . . . I just, you know, thought that, ah, I just would impress upon you that, you know, we just were wanting to be careful about the kinds of statements we made about the seriousness of our research on lemurs and how, umm . . . Basically, what's happened is B-J was served with a subpoena by the government."

"Oh, no. Shit."

"Yeah," Cornyetz agreed. "Now, you know, we have no idea whether there was someone who was jealous of B-J's research and attempting to lie, you know, put an end to this research somehow, or maybe, umm, the other possibility is that Bruce's friends pulled a number."

After reiterating the "seriousness" of the lemur research, Cornyetz suggested that either an envious colleague might have tried to destroy B-J's work, or some of Greenfield's friends had stolen some street drugs. In that one sentence, Cornyetz posed the two possibilities: drugs for lemurs or drugs for people. Then, again, defensively, Cornyetz said, "B-J has nothing to worry about because, uh, he has millions of people willing to testify that, you know, this research is all on the up and up, that it was planned for Duke's lemurs."

"Well, I don't know. This worries me," Macris said, laughing nervously.

Cornyetz reassured Macris that there was really nothing to worry about. Greenfield, however, had been "worried shitless." If Macris fretted too much about it, "you'll probably end up being like Bruce. Bruce has been meeting strange people who he thinks are working for the government." Nor did that lie beyond the realm of possibility.

The next day, Macris met with B-J at his office around lunchtime, wearing a wire. B-J carefully watched his language. He was clearly concerned that his phones or his apartment and office might be bugged. B-J had spent hours with his lawyers, and they'd left him rattled. He wasn't sure whom to trust.

Over the course of a long talk, B-J told Macris several times that he would "protect" him. He had described him as "sort of an errand boy" to the assistant DA. B-J, preoccupied, mentioned the lemur project only in passing, and focused more on legal details and who might have been behind the break-in. He prepped Macris for a possible subpoena. "Just remember: I've been terribly absentminded and vague. I give instructions that you often have to interpret," he said, adding: "Never volunteer any information." Knowing that Macris's brother was a lawyer, he implored him to talk to his lawyers first before telling his parents or his brother about the case so that they could explain some of the legal technicalities.

In describing his interview with the feds, B-J said, "I answered truthfully, but not necessarily fully. But the point is, you know what we are doing, you know what the story is and so on. I speak in metaphors. I hope you understand what the metaphor means, and you simply stick to it." After the break-in, the professor often used the language of metaphor, which for B-J offered a means of turning the straight truth into a Möbius strip of dissimulation.

In wondering out loud about who had broken into the lab, B-J the wordsmith chose language that might have come from a dystopian novel, reflecting the depth of his paranoia and his knowledge of the story behind the metaphor. "We do know from something that she let slip—it's a female district attorney—that . . . I have been denounced by someone," he said.

B-J ran through the people who had keys to the lab. He later asked Macris a direct question, which marked the moment that B-J's assistant had to begin lying to keep his cover. "You don't think Cliff could've denounced me?"

To which Macris dissembled, "Oh, no. I don't think he knows, you know, really anything. I had lunch with him a lot of times. I'd see him a lot. He's a friend. He never said anything."

"He has never indicated that he hates my guts or anything, has he?" B-J asked nervously.

"He doesn't."

"I mean, I have the highest feeling for Cliff," B-J said, "but . . . but, you see, Richard, when something like this happens, you begin to wonder."

A minute later, Jolly walked in.

"Uh, hi, Cliff. How are you?" Macris greeted him.

A week later, Macris and B-J met again. B-J described taking a polygraph test requested by his lawyer, Philip Kalban. Nat Laurendi, who had worked as the NYPD's chief polygraphist for thirteen years, until 1975, and had consulted on the Patty Hearst bank robbery case in 1976, administered the test on May 30. He was working independently.

B-J passed the drug questions on the test. Previously he had referred to polygraphs contemptuously as "magic," but once he passed he began taking them seriously. As always, B-J believed firmly in whatever supported his position at the time. During his trial, it emerged that he'd had Cornyetz fetch him a couple of books from Bobst Library on how to pass a polygraph exam, and he'd suggested to others that it was perfectly okay to take a tranquilizer before an exam. At any rate, the judge at the drug trial shared B-J's original position on polygraphs and refused to accept the results.

But at the time, B-J was thrilled at having passed the test. Macris, pretending concern about being questioned by the feds at his home, kept bringing up illegal drugs and what he should say to avoid perjuring himself. "You know," Macris said, "the rumors I've heard that it was LSD and methaqualone, from Danny and others."

"You don't have to say that," B-J replied. "You . . . you . . . you must never testify to, to rumors or hearsay." Then, he added, "And don't use those two words."

For a moment, B-J let his defenses lapse and offered a strange story that showed just how tangled the web had become. While he never admitted guilt, his words, heard in the courtroom, revealed his character and intentions.

"May I spin a hypothetical scenario?" B-J said, coughing. "Suppose someone comes and says to a person of impeccable reputation, 'You know, we can make an awful lot of money doing such-and-such,' and the person of impeccable reputation thinks to himself, 'Well, students have fantasies and so forth; let's see what this is all about.' At the same time, the person of impeccable reputation is beginning to develop the notion of trying a certain kind of behavior modification to see if a certain kind of research with animals will work, and the two jive a bit."

He suggested this person of impeccable reputation might make a test, but that anyone who took anything from the lab would become violently ill.

Macris asked, a bit confused, "What do you mean?"

B-J, perhaps realizing that he'd gone too far, answered, "This is a hypothetical situation, a scenario for a TV drama. Please remember that."

What the scenario doesn't suggest is innocence. It suggests, rather, delusional and narcissistic thinking. But it was beginning to seem like a drama. Lisa Forman, the lab assistant, imagined the whole affair as a movie, and even saw the comic TV actress Imogene Coca playing her.

B-J told Macris that his lawyers had assured him he could "beat any charges" on his reputation alone. He reminded Macris not to pay attention to rumors. "Rumors are rumors. Someone told me the other day that he had heard we were making a sphincter-relaxing drug in the lab."

It was unclear if Macris got the joke.

Perhaps some of the most pathetic moments of the entire affair came when B-J turned to Jolly for help. B-J's suspicions focused on students who had worked in his lab, but he had to have his colleague on his list of possible informers. Still, shortly after the break-in, B-J told Jolly that he was about to get substantial funding for research—possibly even a grant from the MacArthur Foundation—and asked him if he'd be interested in participating "more actively."

Jolly replied blandly, "Sure, um-hmm, okay, great."

Then, in June, he talked to Jolly privately at work. B-J said he thought his apartment was bugged and that it was better that they talk there. First describing how bad the affair had become, and noting that "there's an enemy here somewhere," he asked Jolly to be a character reference.

"If you think it would be of some use," Jolly offered, even as he was taping the conversation.

On June 5, Macris and Cornyetz met at Washington Square Park and walked around. It was a beautiful day, and NYU was preparing for commencement. Cornyetz noted that the workers were putting up huge Altec speakers. To keep his cover, Macris had lied to Cornyetz and told him that DEA agents had come to his home and questioned him. They discussed, as they would time and again, the evidence and potential fallout for them. Macris knew then that the lemur story wasn't going to hold water, but Cornyetz wanted to believe it would work. He didn't want the professor to get indicted, and he wanted to keep his job.

Later at Rufus D. Smith Hall, Macris told B-J about the visit from the DEA agents. Macris was vague about the conversation, but claimed that he'd stuck with the "neurotoxins for lemurs" narrative.

Once again, B-J was unusually frank. "The whole point is, I hate to tell you, but whatever you may think, this really did start, the basic part of this started out three or four years ago as a, as a crazy notion for a real legitimate project," he said. "And the thing is, now it is a legitimate project, 'cause we're about to get two hundred and fifty thousand dollars from someone in Chicago who thinks it's hot stuff."

Whatever he really may have been thinking, B-J also claimed that he felt a sense of responsibility to his students, greater than to anyone but his wife. He said that he would explain the whole story to them someday. But was he sincere, or was he trying to get them to stick with him? He told his friends and colleagues that he'd explain the whole situation someday, perhaps even in a book, but he never did.

After they left B-J's office, Cornyetz said, "I believe what he says about protecting his students. He really is a good guy."

Macris and Cornyetz met again in the park on June 8, the day after graduation ceremonies. Sawhill had given the commencement address. Federal agents had paid a visit to Cornyetz, who had hired a lawyer. Matters were beginning to look serious, but he was still clinging to hope. "They may drop it," Cornyetz said, "due to the fact that, ya know, all these expert witnesses, testimony from scientists and stuff, the fact that it was done in a university, openly, nothing was sold, nothing was traded, nothing was borrowed."

Then Cornyetz tried to cheer himself up. "Didn't that sound like a good commercial? Nothing was bought, nothing was sold, nothing was traded, nothing was stolen. Yes, and you can get it here at Duke of Madness Mufflers. We're open every day."

But as the pressure on Cornyetz grew, the feds offered him a deal, and he turned state's evidence against B-J. On July 2, he recorded a conversation with the chairman, proving himself quite skilled at eliciting compromising statements. Perhaps B-J still trusted him most, but Cornyetz lied, telling B-J that his lawyer had informed him that they'd had a bug in the lab. Using that ruse, he got B-J to recall earlier conversations, including one in which B-J had said they were making Quaalude. While B-J equivocated about what he'd said, exactly—he was always careful—he responded: "Danny, we're going to deny that conversation. We are going to say we were talking about something else."

They both seemed to want to lay the blame on Greenfield, the mystery man.

"Why did we get involved in this in the first place?" Cornyetz asked.

"Danny, that's something we'll talk about some other day."

"Is it really Bruce's fault?"

"Yes," B-J replied.

"Why the fuck did he ever talk you into doing this?" Cornyetz said.

"Why the fuck am I so stupid?" B-J lamented. "The problem is, the point is, there is a legitimate research project buried in all of this, too."

It was buried six feet under. Macris and Cornyetz had speculated that if the pressure became too great on B-J, he might "dump" it all on Greenfield. Clearly, the growing gravity of the federal investigation made scapegoating Greenfield a more plausible scenario. B-J thought his "reputation" would protect him; his position, his career, his connections, his wealth—all of it made the unseemly spectacle of drug-making almost beyond belief, and Greenfield had done some very suspicious things.

In late fall of 1978, Macris later testified, he and a friend dropped by the lab late one night. Greenfield was putting powder into gelatin capsules. Greenfield said he was having something tested for radioimmunoassay, and asked Macris to show him how to use the sensitive balance. Then, according to Macris, Greenfield said something very odd. "He told me that after handling the balance that I was to wash my hands because the material may cause one to go crazy."

Cornyetz testified that on March 30, 1979, Greenfield came into the lab and asked him to help him tape three or four plastic garbage bags to his body. After struggling for a time, Greenfield simply stuffed them into an army knapsack along with four bottles filled with powder. Cornyetz said he didn't know what was in the bags or bottles, but clearly Greenfield wanted to keep their contents concealed.

But as the feds continued to grill the people in B-J's orbit, Greenfield seemed to vanish into thin air.

Cornyetz, however, had already been charged with lying to federal officers, and had agreed to cooperate with the government and to testify against B-J for a reduced sentence; hence, the leading questions in his taped conversations. Indeed, the anxiety of the investigation over the summer had become unbearable, and he'd been wearing himself ragged, staying out late at CBGB and the Mudd Club, then catnapping in the lab. Forman was concerned that Cornyetz was going to make himself ill if he kept it up.

The mid- to late 1970s made for heady times in the rock scene in New York City. NYU students could slam shut their textbooks and walk a few blocks to CBGB on the Bowery, where a rock 'n' roll renaissance was blossoming. The grungy venue booked punk and new-wave bands such as the Ramones, the Patti Smith Group, Television, Blondie, and Talking Heads—both clubs are immortalized in the Talking Heads' song "Life During Wartime": "This ain't no party, this ain't no disco / This ain't no fooling around / This ain't no Mudd Club or CBGB."

Because of its longevity (1973–2006), CBGB has more of a place in the cultural memory, but the Mudd Club, which opened in Tribeca in October 1978, was unique, and Cornyetz was a habitué. More than a rock venue, it became something like a 1920s Berlin cabaret, fusing music, art, and fashion. Talking Heads, James Chance and the Contortions, and

The B-52s played there, but the space, which shuttered in 1983, also had a rotating art gallery, curated by Keith Haring, and it gave significant exposure to other artists, such as Jean-Michel Basquiat and Kenny Scharf.

Cornyetz wasn't a fan of punk, but he was an aficionado of new wave, especially devoted to Blondie and its lead singer, Debbie Harry. When Assistant DA Amorosa first visited Cornyetz to question him about B-J's drug case, he noticed the pictures of Harry in Cornyetz's apartment. "Is she your girlfriend?" he asked.

The grand jury continued its investigation over the summer of 1979. Without the prodding or permission of federal agents, Jolly continued to collect evidence against B-J, taking more photographs of his lab and making tape recordings. After the break-in, B-J had changed the lock to his storeroom in the building's basement. Jolly memorized the serial number of the new lock and had a duplicate key made. He searched the storeroom himself, then turned the key over to the feds. On August 2, agents once again searched B-J's lab, again without a warrant, and, using the extra key supplied by Jolly, searched the storeroom as well.

Jolly's missionary zeal in his pursuit of further evidence against B-J later made him vulnerable to accusations by B-J's attorneys—that he was jealous of B-J's status as chairman, and that he may himself have planted drugs in B-J's lab and storeroom—though no proof of this was ever offered.

When the fall semester began in September, B-J ran into Beidelman. "Something is going to happen soon. I can't tell you the details yet, but it's going to be *big*," B-J told him with a strange enthusiasm, thrusting his index finger into the air. It was, Beidelman said, like hearing Cecil B. DeMille describing one of his cinematic epics.

Something big *did* happen. On October 4, B-J was indicted on six counts, with a maximum sentence of thirty years. He was charged with

In downtown Manhattan during his first trial, B-J often seemed to enjoy the lime-light while trying to avoid media scrutiny.
COURTESY OF BARTON SILVERMAN / *NEW YORK TIMES* / REDUX

conspiracy to manufacture and distribute LSD, methaqualone, and other controlled substances; manufacturing and possessing with intent to distribute 1.185 kilograms of methaqualone; distributing and possessing with intent to distribute Cylert (pemoline), a stimulant; conspiracy to obstruct a criminal investigation; and two counts of knowingly making false statements to two assistant US attorneys. The indictment also mentioned coconspirators, "known and unknown."

At his arraignment, the fifty-four-year-old chairman, dressed conservatively in a dark three-piece suit, pleaded not guilty, but made no further statement. The federal judge, Charles Tenney, set his bail at $50,000. B-J posted $5,000 in cash to secure the bond and turned over his passport before being released.

The indictment made the front page of the *New York Times*. The *Times* quoted the prosecutor, Roanne Mann, at the arraignment as saying that B-J had perpetrated "an egregious abuse of trust" and had turned the university lab into "a drug factory." The *Times* ran a typically subdued head: INDICTMENT CHARGES PROFESSOR USED N.Y.U. LABORATORY TO MAKE DRUGS. The *New York Post*'s front-page headline screamed, in typical grammar-challenged tabloidese: CHARGE FAMED PROF RAN NYU DRUG FACTORY.

The Associated Press story that ran on the wires put B-J in a much better light, noting that "his associates called [the charges] unbelievable." Nan Rothschild, then a research associate in the anthro department, said, "I doubt any of this will stand up. And one thing which is certain is the anthropology department is no drug factory."

In December, in a photocopied "Christmas" letter, B-J told his version of the story to his friends:

> *Something quite horrible happened in October. I am sure many of you are aware of this, for the press has carried the story all over the world. I was arrested in October (on the anniversary of Vina's fatal operation, a deliberate bit of malice, and malice is characteristic of this "case") and charged with making drugs and other nasty things in my laboratory. I want all of you to know that not a single one of the charges are true, there is not an iota, jot, or tittle of substance to them. I also would like you to know something else about why I know these are totally untrue, but am advised it is not proper to reveal this information now.*

*To be dragged about Manhattan in handcuffs for the benefit of
the press (I was arrested in my doctor's office) is not an experience I
widely recommend.*

In the letter, B-J also wrote that over the summer someone had poured
sulfuric acid on many of his slides of lemur and baboon blood, collected
over twenty years, destroying them. On this occasion, as on so many, he
invoked images of Nazi-like persecution: "It exactly resembles pictures
made in Germany after *Kristallnacht.*"

B-J's arrest stood poised to become one of NYU's biggest scandals
ever—not only because one of its professors was charged with making
drugs on university property, but also because, as the grand jury indictment charged, "In his role as supervisor of the laboratory, Buettner-
Janusch would assign student-employees to assist in the synthesis of
controlled substances." A corrupter of youth. It was hardly what parents
wanted to hear—that, having paid thousands of dollars in tuition, their
children might be conned into making drugs.

But at least at first, NYU tried to seem neutral. After all, if B-J was
exonerated and NYU appeared to have thrown him to the wolves, litigation
loomed. Ron Zaccaro, an NYU spokesman, told the *Times* that the university had cooperated fully in the federal investigation, "in an effort to preserve
the standards of the university's educational environment and the welfare of
its student body." B-J, he said, was "a valued member of the NYU faculty."

The very next day, on October 6, the *Times* ran a story headlined
N.Y.U. IS REVIEWING POSITION OF PROFESSOR NAMED IN DRUG CASE,
which revealed that support was slipping. NYU's assistant vice president for public affairs, Stephen Jacobs, said of B-J that "he is an eminent,
nationally respected educator. We have to presume him innocent until
proved guilty." But then he offered that "the professor's position is under
review." Tenure has its rewards. At least, for B-J's sake, the case fell from
the front page, buried on page 27.

B-J was granted a leave of absence as department chairman; archaeologist Bert Salwen took over as temporary chair. B-J, however, continued to teach two anthro courses.

Soon after B-J's arrest, Yale friend Michael Coe began an ad hoc defense fund, and Alison Richard soon joined him. Well over a hundred people contributed, including G. Evelyn Hutchinson and David Pilbeam, both also at Yale; Sherry Washburn, B-J's mentor at Chicago who had moved to Berkeley; and J. David Robertson, B-J's former boss at Duke. Together, they contributed more than $10,000, merely a drop in the ocean of B-J's legal fees. Coe believed strongly that B-J's colleagues should rally to his defense because the justice system presumed his innocence. There were broader issues, he believed, like academic freedom. He was shocked by how many people refused to make even a token donation, but B-J had succeeded in alienating a small army of scholars.

B-J suggested several possible sources of donations to Coe, some from people he admired, some from people he didn't. Among the latter fell science-fiction novelist Arthur Herzog, the author of *Orca* and *The Swarm*, who had attended some of B-J's parties. Herzog, B-J wrote Coe, "is a very good prospect. He is pretty rich. He has written a bunch of crappy books, but they bring in money. *The Killer Bees* [*sic*] was one of his choicer epics, and the screenplay got him a couple of million, I think."

B-J's close friends Milt and Sondra Schlesinger, the opera-loving couple whom he and Vina had known since their U Mich days, loaned him $20,000 for legal expenses. (B-J later sold some of his art collection and Native American crafts to repay them.)

On December 3, pretrial hearings convened. Among the major issues were the admissibility of the evidence seized in May and August, and the constitutionality of the warrantless searches. Federal Judge Charles Brieant, who presided over the trial the following summer, ruled that the searches were legal because it was understood that Macris and Jolly had full access to B-J's lab and indeed had been given keys. The evidence seized from B-J's basement storeroom wasn't admissible, however, because B-J had a legitimate expectation of privacy for that space. The hearings continued over a few days in December, interrupted by the holidays, and concluded on January 3, 1980.

In the following months, B-J continued writing incendiary letters, filled with venom spewed at his persecutors and complaints about the financial strains of the trial. (In late May, he wrote that he'd been spending an average of $5,000 a week since his indictment in early October.) It was unfathomable that his attorneys permitted him to mail the letters. B-J persisted in calling the prosecutor, Roanne Mann, "a slut," "a fascist whore," "a Nazi whore," "the bitch," and a "foul insane fiend." The judge was "a fascist pig" and "a lunatic." Macris and Jolly he called "the worm and the jackal," respectively. The letters were so crazy that Coe later burned all of them in his fireplace.

B-J's anger grew to rage and fantasies of revenge. "I shall certainly drive the cuckolded English fascist swine-jackal into the street as soon as possible, and all his filthy graduate students with him," he wrote in February, adding a profound understatement: "And that is not an atmosphere conducive to calm graduate study."

B-J wrote to Richard about attending the annual American Association of Physical Anthropologists meeting in Niagara Falls, New York, in April. "Are you going to be in Niagara Falls?" he asked. "I decided to go. The jackal [Jolly] will be there too, and maybe there will be a grand denouement there at the edge of the falls." (B-J—perhaps intentionally, perhaps unknowingly—evoked a scene from "The Final Problem," a Sherlock Holmes story, in which the famous detective and his archenemy, the evil Professor Moriarty, locked in mortal combat, plunge over the Reichenbach Falls in Switzerland.)

B-J knew he was in trouble emotionally. "I have been seeing a shrink," he wrote Richard. "My attorneys decided they would fire me if I didn't go. They did not want to defend a homicide case as well as a drug case. And after six days a week for a while with the shrink, I am sure they were right to be worried."

B-J struggled with his demons, even as he and his lawyers continued to refine the anthropologist's lemur defense, like a chess strategy, but it was doomed to failure. Although B-J often could convince friends and colleagues of the truth of many fabulous stories, "the lemur defense" failed to hold up under scrutiny. There were drugs but no lemurs.

There was, in the end, only a kilo of methaqualone. The trial was set to begin on June 30.

6

Above Suspicion

United States of America v. John Buettner-Janusch began promptly at ten a.m. on June 30, 1980, in a sultry courtroom in the federal courthouse at Foley Square. B-J stood accused of the six counts from the grand jury indictment. The first three consisted of the drug charges: conspiracy to make and distribute LSD, Quaalude, and sodium barbital; manufacture and possession of Quaalude; and possession with intent to distribute and distribution of the stimulant Cylert. The grand jury's three other charges addressed the alleged cover-up: one count of conspiring to obstruct justice, and two counts of lying to a US attorney during the government's investigation.

The courtroom drama attracted a lot of media attention. The *New York Times* and the *New York Daily News* and *New York Post* tabloids followed it closely. *New York* magazine even devoted a cover story to it.

But plenty of other news distracted readers during the two-week trial. It was a summer of discontent, the country adrift in economic doldrums. President Jimmy Carter earlier had declared that the American public was suffering from "a crisis of confidence" in his famous "malaise" speech, in which he never actually used the word. The Iranian hostage crisis, which would last a total of 444 days, hung another dark cloud over the American psyche. Although little progress was made, the news cycle constantly featured it that summer. On July 11 American diplomat Richard Queen was released after being diagnosed with multiple sclerosis.

The 1980 presidential election was in full swing, resulting in a three-way race among Democratic incumbent Jimmy Carter, Republican Ronald Reagan, and Republican John Anderson, who ran as an independent. Preparations for the Republican Convention were well under way, which took place at the trial's end, July 15–17, in Detroit. While the stage was set for the beatification of Reagan, there was considerable speculation about his running mate. It was, of course, George H. W. Bush. On the Democratic side, Ted Kennedy was hopelessly behind in the primaries, but he refused to concede until the vitriolic convention in New York in August.

Closer to home, and as the trial began, the New York City firefighter and police unions were on the brink of going on strike—after a public transit workers strike in March had paralyzed the city for eleven days—and Mayor Edward Koch was threatening to call in the National Guard. The strike was narrowly averted at the last minute, mainly due to the diplomatic skills of labor lawyer Edward Silver, who toned down Koch's infamous irascibility at the negotiating table.

Amid this political and economic mire, the trial of a famous anthropologist, accused by the government of turning his NYU lab into a "drug factory," took place. The case made for tabloid fodder, certainly, but it mesmerized those in academic and scientific circles as well. The estimable weekly journal *Science,* not known for its crime reporting, ran a four-page article on the trial.

Presiding was Federal Judge Charles L. Brieant Jr., whom the *New York Times* described as "a stern presence on the bench." Appointed by President Nixon to the federal bench in 1971, he served until 2007. He died the following year, and the federal courthouse in White Plains, New York, was named after him.

In his fund-raising appeals to friends and colleagues, full of sound and fury, or maybe just piss and vinegar, B-J continued to describe the prosecuting attorney, Roanne Mann, as a "Nazi whore," among many other epithets. It's unlikely that anyone on the jury would have viewed her that way. At twenty-nine, just a few years out of Stanford Law, Mann was soft-spoken and waiflike, favoring frilly dresses.

She stood in stark contrast to B-J's pin-striped chief counsel, fifty-five-year-old Jules Ritholz, a seasoned attorney with the high-powered New York City law firm of Kostelanetz and Ritholz. Ritholz, who died in 1993, had a national reputation as a tax lawyer who defended big corporations, celebrities, and politicians. Many of B-J's allies and friends thought the choice of a tax attorney, however prestigious, a strategic blunder.

Ritholz presented a two-pronged defense. First, he argued that the illicit drugs found in the lab formed part of a legitimate research project, to be used in behavior modification experiments on lemurs. But then, contradictorily, he also asserted that the prosecution's star witness, Clifford Jolly, jealous of B-J's success, had conspired with lab assistant Macris to plant the drugs to bring down B-J, and perhaps even usurp his job as department chair.

Ritholz also argued that B-J had no discernible, reasonable motive. One of the best-paid professors at NYU, B-J had inherited a large sum of money when his wife, Vina, died. In his opening statement, Ritholz said: "What is there in this that would leave probably the most prominent physical anthropologist in the world to risk reputation, career, prison, the loss of everything he has worked for by performing a criminal act? Why in the world?"

Why in the world, indeed. Mann tried to answer that question two weeks later in her summation. "In his opening statement to you, Mr. Ritholz asked you to find a motive for the crimes that Buettner-Janusch is charged with today. The proof in this case provides two answers.

"First, the same reason that anyone, rich or poor, makes up his mind to peddle drugs—to make easy money.... And as you know, rich and poor would violate the law where the money is good and the risk is small."

His second motive, she claimed, was that B-J thought he was "committing the perfect crime, a crime for which he would never get caught, never be convicted, because he already had his defense planned out. He expected that no one would ever believe that a man of his stature and reputation would be making drugs for sale the way that he was."

B-J, she declared, believed that he was "a citizen above suspicion."

As always, the burden of proof fell to the prosecution, and Mann had to prove B-J's guilt to the jury beyond a reasonable doubt. B-J always proclaimed his innocence, and he certainly seemed convinced of it. He described the trial in letters as something out of *Alice in Wonderland*. In its multiple portraits of a defendant so complex, enigmatic, and contradictory that he seemed to be a cipher, the analogy seems apt. The reader might think of the line in the Disney movie of Lewis Carroll's book, in which Alice exclaims: "It would be so nice if something made sense for a change." But B-J, who felt unfairly persecuted, may have been thinking of a line from the book, *Alice's Adventures in Wonderland*, in which the Queen declares: "Sentence first, verdict afterwards." Or the well-read professor might also have recalled the opening line of Kafka's *The Trial*: "Someone must have been telling tales about Josef K., for one morning, without having done anything wrong, he was arrested."

The government relied heavily on witnesses from Rufus D. Smith Hall: Cornyetz and Dorfman, who had made plea bargains for their testimony; Macris, who had cooperated with the DEA after determining that he was being asked to make Quaalude; and, of course, the trash-can-searching anthro professor, Jolly. Although B-J never took the stand, the secretly recorded tapes made him a kind of witness for the prosecution.

The prosecution first called Patricia Karatsis Berman, one of B-J's lab assistants. Her testimony focused on the alleged LSD project. The evidence of wrongdoing she provided was decidedly circumstantial, but it offered a sharply detailed picture of what it was like to work under B-J.

Berman, then twenty-six, was at the time of the trial the manager of an art gallery, but she had a solid education in science: a BS with distinction in zoology from Duke, and an MA in anthro from NYU. She had completed all of the requirements for a PhD from NYU except for her dissertation. Berman had done her dissertation research in the lab, with B-J as her chief adviser. Hired as a lab assistant in 1975, she had to work twenty hours a week, but she often put in up to forty to seventy hours. In the summer of 1977, B-J, who until then had seldom visited the lab, suddenly began appearing two or three times a day. "He appeared to be involved with others in an ongoing project," she said.

It deeply annoyed Berman that her own adviser was neglecting her work, certainly not an uncommon complaint among grad students. B-J, she complained, was spending a lot of time with another student, Greenfield. (Greenfield was never called as a witness in the trial, although he was often mentioned in testimony. The *New York Times* described him as "a mystery figure.")

In B-J's inner office, she asked the professor what they were working on. He said that they were extracting plant lectins (sugar-binding proteins) to be given to lemurs to study changes in their behavior. Of course, rumors were circling around and outside the lab. But an NYU library book on B-J's desk, a huge tome with a green cover called *LSD: A Total Study,* further aroused her suspicions. She later skimmed through it and noticed a chapter on making LSD by Albert Hofmann.

LSD: A Total Study, edited by D. V. Siva Sankar, isn't exactly the sort of book you would expect to find on a scientist's desk. Nearly a thousand pages long, there's something disturbingly obsessive about its size and scope. While it includes a number of scientific studies, from the molecular structure of LSD to its psychological effects, it also has a strong spiritual agenda, placing LSD in the context of other mind-altering drugs, such as mescaline and psilocybin, often used ceremonially by indigenous cultures.

But many peer-reviewed papers had appeared in scientific journals on the synthesis of LSD and research on its use on animal and human subjects—without all the mumbo jumbo. (Hofmann, along with his boss, Arthur Stoll, had even described the process of making LSD in a patent he had filed in the United States in 1948.)

To be fair, for years a number of scientists, writers, and intellectuals had been intrigued by LSD's potential for spiritual enlightenment, including Aldous Huxley and even Hofmann himself. But the prologue to *LSD: A Total Study* is more nuttily new age than scientific in tone. Sankar writes:

> *The use of LSD may have signified and started a new revolution. This revolution may end up as a cop-out philosophy or in a serious determination of mankind's future. Are we going to relapse back into a new era of Dark Ages, waiting for new Crusades to spark us? Or is the use of LSD the initial event that will guide us to a new morality and to new patterns of human life on this planet?*

Mann entered the book as Government Exhibit 1.

Berman revealed an impulsive streak. She testified that one day, her suspicions aroused by the book's chapter on making LSD, and the procedures she'd observed in the lab, she destroyed or dumped several flasks from the cold room into the sink. Then she changed a so-called safe light—a red light that doesn't produce a white light spectrum—to a regular red-colored lightbulb. When B-J discovered the sabotage, he started screaming in a rage "that a previous graduate student ripped him off," she testified.

Berman didn't admit what she'd done, but her relationship with B-J—who, she said, had a "detached sort of authoritarian relationship" with her—deteriorated. B-J and Berman clashed over an experiment she was conducting that required deionized water. B-J insisted that it be double deionized. Berman thought that since it was a crude experiment anyway, it didn't need double deionization. They had, she said, "a very, very bad argument."

While they weren't talking about religion or politics, this was a university, and such disagreements happen. But B-J, often arbitrary and quick to anger, Berman said, "dismissed me from graduate school."

B-J subsequently wrote her a note, she testified, "that I wasn't dismissed, and if I came back and was a good girl, I could continue about the path of my dissertation." She was paraphrasing, of course. B-J actually wrote: "If you appear on Monday, you in no way change the place you have on the path towards your dissertation, but you have to recognize the fact that I know what I want, that it is my laboratory and that I am not accountable to you." Berman did return, but they had little communication afterward, and she didn't finish her dissertation. So much for B-J telling Macris, "Just remember: I've been terribly absentminded and vague." He ruled his laboratory like a czar.

Ritholz seized on Berman's secret destruction of the experiment. Did she have permission to do it? No, she didn't. Did she call the police? Did she contact the dean of the college? Did she "conduct any laboratory analysis of the contents of these bottles to see what [she was] spilling out?"

To all of the questions, Berman admitted that she had not.

Mann then asked her why she had sabotaged the experiment.

"I did it because I believed that illegal activity was going on in the laboratory, and I did not want to see anybody, including the professor, hurt."

Several prosecution witnesses had turned state's evidence for immunity or reduced sentences. Mann was careful to make clear the agreement each had made because she knew that the deals had to be transparent. Each signed an agreement requiring that he tell the truth. Such deals are not uncommon, and it's sometimes the only way for the government to obtain a conviction—by getting someone involved in a crime to flip.

One element missing from the strongest part of the government's case—the manufacture and possession of methaqualone—was a sale, or even a plan for distribution. (The feds claimed that the quantity of methaqualone found in the lab could have produced 2,000 doses, with a street value of $12,000.) So they presented evidence for the sale of incredibly small amounts of "controlled" drugs—prescription drugs of such ubiquitous use they were categorized by the DEA as Schedule IV. In other words, just about every other dog or cat in New York City used them.

B-J's administrative assistant, Dorfman, had been charged with selling some ominous-sounding "synthetic cocaine" at B-J's behest. The "product" in this case was actually lidocaine, a common prescription painkiller, mixed with sodium barbital. Dorfman had been brought up on felony charges, but in his plea bargain he had admitted guilt to a misdemeanor charge. His sentence was still pending, however. (In exchange for testifying against his boss, Cornyetz cut a deal to have the drug-making charges dropped, pleading guilty to obstruction of justice and getting three years' probation.) A third person, Louis Liebling, who testified that he had purchased the faux coke from Dorfman, got immunity from prosecution.

Inevitably, testimony from people who cut such deals is tainted. But Judge Brieant explained to the jury that it was up to them to decide when or if the witnesses were telling the truth, or whether, as Ritholz argued, they were giving a version of events that the government wanted. "Some of the witnesses have been convicted of crimes," Judge Brieant said in his final instructions to the jury, "and the law requires me to point out that [this] is a consideration you may take into account."

Dorfman, the next government witness, had the most to lose because his sentence was still hanging over him, and of all the witnesses against

B-J, his testimony was perhaps the most damaging. If B-J's story at times resembled a pulp-fiction novel, Dorfman's descriptions of crimes—serious, petty, sometimes even absurd—came closest to that genre.

B-J's administrative assistant for several years, Dorfman said he had seen *LSD: A Total Study* in B-J's office and had asked him about it during the summer of 1977. B-J told him that they were going to make acid in the lab. Dorfman thought LSD was a sixties drug, and wondered if people were still taking it. B-J told him that it was becoming popular again. The following spring, B-J told him that they were going to make methaqualone in the lab. Dorfman said that he was unfamiliar with the term, and B-J explained that it was another name for Quaalude.

No one else, Dorfman admitted, heard these conversations. So, while B-J was apparently speaking to others in metaphors, he was baring his soul to Dorfman. Around that same time, Dorfman learned of a third drug scheme, this time not in the office but at B-J's home. A "doctor friend" of B-J dropped off "ten or twelve" bottles of liquid lidocaine. (The "doctor friend" in question disappeared, and the government didn't pursue this particular instance of apparent criminal activity.) B-J told Dorfman that he would be "synthesizing cocaine" from it.

Although it is possible to synthesize cocaine rather than extract it from coca leaves, doing so makes for an expensive and inefficient process. What B-J allegedly sought to do was pass off lidocaine—sometimes used to adulterate real cocaine—as the real thing. Dorfman said that B-J gave him several batches in powder form to test on his friends. The first batches deliquesced. Another batch that retained its powder form caused a burning sensation, so B-J added a tad of a sodium barbital. Then, apparently, it was good to go.

Dorfman sold two grams of the so-called synthetic coke to a friend, Louis Liebling, for $100. He gave B-J $80 and kept $20 for himself. In this case, there was a witness. The prosecution called Liebling to testify, with full immunity, that he had indeed purchased this substance from Dorfman.

A week or so after the lab was broken into in May, a package arrived in Dorfman's office containing bottles of Cylert, which Dorfman called a "mood elevator," and a prescription cold medicine. He delivered them to B-J, and a few days later B-J gave Dorfman a handful of Cylert pills. Dorfman took a few of them and gave some to his pal Liebling.

Dorfman described B-J's attempts to cover up his drug conspiracy in vivid language. After federal agents served B-J with a subpoena, the professor advised Dorfman to "deny, deny, deny." A few days later, he said, B-J told him to "get busy forgetting." B-J also told him that he would be taking a lie detector test and that he would "thwart" it. Dorfman gave B-J two Valiums, and the professor told him that "it was perfectly all right to take tranquilizers before a polygraph."

Dorfman gave the government a home run: B-J wasn't just making drugs; he was also conspiring to sell them. He said that he had only cooperated in B-J's schemes in the hopes of keeping his job. (NYU soon fired him for his troubles anyway.)

His testimony also sounded scripted, and his B-J didn't sound like B-J. Dorfman's story ran too much like a distillation of the government's case. On closer examination, Dorfman's testimony begins to seem suspect. The doctor who happens by and then is never heard from again or pursued by the DEA. B-J's bold admissions of nefarious doings, conveniently confessed without witnesses. There's a cognitive dissonance—or blatant absurdity—with the idea of B-J receiving drugs in his elegant apartment, working diligently on refining the ersatz coke, and receiving just eighty bucks for his labors. More than any witness, Dorfman had reason to tell a story that fit the prosecution's case like a glove. Dick Wolf would have called for a rewrite.

Ritholz sparred and parried with Dorfman in his cross-examination, searching for holes in his story. His main line of offense remained Dorfman's credibility—or rather the lack of it.

Clarifying a question, Judge Brieant asked Dorfman plainly, "Did your lawyer make a deal with the government for you to cooperate?"

"Yes," Dorfman answered.

Ritholz moved quickly: "And while you say that no one promised you anything, you are hopeful to be treated leniently, isn't that right?"

"I am hoping to be treated justly," Dorfman replied.

"Does justice mean what you deserve?"

"That it does."

"Is it correct, sir, that you violated the law by your own testimony in selling and/or delivering lidocaine?"

"I believe that is against the law."

"And you did it?"

"Correct."

"Is it a fact, sir, that you knowingly sold or delivered against the law a drug called Cylert?"

"I delivered that."

"Is it correct, sir, that you lied to agents of the United States government?"

"That is correct."

"And you want to be sentenced justly?"

"That's correct."

Ritholz then made clear what he thought justice might entail: "You are looking forward to a jail term, are you?"

"I have no comment," Dorfman replied, unrattled. "I do not know what it will be."

"I put it to you, sir, that you hope to be treated leniently in return for what you are doing, yesterday and today?"

"I would be a fool to not hope that."

Cornyetz, the next major prosecution witness, corroborated much of Dorfman's story. Cornyetz had taken part in or witnessed the lab work, whereas Dorfman, a secretary, worked on another floor and rarely visited the lab. Cornyetz was much more involved in whatever may have constituted drug manufacturing. Selling lidocaine adulterated with sodium barbital as "synthetic cocaine," on the other hand, barely seemed like drug dealing. It belonged more to the realm of lying.

Again, Mann carefully disclosed that Cornyetz had made a plea deal with the government but had promised to tell the truth. Cornyetz said that he had checked out books from the NYU library for B-J, including *LSD: A Total Study* and works on polygraph tests. He had also researched articles on the manufacture of methaqualone and had helped to make it. Much of the written material was beyond him, but he did know what he was doing, as B-J had bluntly told him.

Although his testimony significantly helped to convict B-J, he acknowledged later that his boss could be generous. When funds ran short, B-J paid Cornyetz's salary out of his own pocket. "Once, when he heard that my TV was broken, he loaned me $300 to buy a new one," Cornyetz said. "I paid him back every penny. He was a little overblown, overly taken with himself. Actually, he was full of shit. But he was a cool professor and a cool boss."

But turning state's evidence and his own lifestyle made Cornyetz vulnerable in court. In his cross-examination, Ritholz tried to portray him as a sinister character rather than just another lackadaisical grad student who liked to party.

"Are you familiar with a place called the Mudd Club?" Ritholz asked.

"Yes."

"Is that what is known as a punk club?"

"I don't think the owner would agree with that, but—"

"What do the people look like there?"

"A lot of lawyers go to the Mudd Club," Cornyetz cannily replied.

Ritholz didn't find the riposte particularly witty. "What do the people look like there?"

"I can't describe that. A lot of people wear suits now."

"Did a lot of people have colored paint on their faces?"

"No."

"Never when you were there?"

"No. They wear makeup sometimes."

"You call it makeup, all right."

Ritholz undermined the credibility of both Cornyetz and Dorfman for having cut deals with the government for lenience. But two witnesses who seemed above reproach, Macris and Jolly, confirmed the basic outline of their story.

Macris told his tale—from his early suspicions that he was making drugs through confirming that he was indeed making methaqualone, to cooperating with the government to build a case against the chairman. Ritholz struggled to undercut the testimony of the undergrad. First he tried to belittle his competence as a chemist. Speaking of the constituents used in making methaqualone, Ritholz confirmed that most of them were organic chemicals. Then he asked Macris if he'd taken Organic Chemistry I at NYU. Macris allowed that he had.

"You failed, didn't you?" Ritholz demanded.

"Yes, I did."

"And then in the academic year 1977–1978, did you take it over again?"

"Yes."

"You got a D that time?"

"D plus," Macris corrected him.

"D plus. You squeezed it. Then did you take Organic Chemistry II?"

"No, I dropped the course."

"You started it, and you dropped it?" Ritholz asked, feigning uncertainty when of course he had Macris's transcripts. He then announced histrionically, "On the basis of that I will move to strike the testimony of this witness."

Judge Brieant wasn't amused. "The Court will leave it to the jury to determine the weight to be given his testimony. You will consider all of the matters in evidence, including the experience of this witness. The motion is denied."

Macris in fact earned A's in all of his other chemistry courses but one, in which he received a B, and he graduated with a 3.4 grade point average. He wasn't nor did he ever intend to be a chemist. But he knew enough.

Macris was certain that there was an "LSD project," although he never worked on it. There were many signs: the LSD tome, the precursor chemicals, the trace of LSD found by Jolly. Dorfman claimed that B-J had told him LSD would be made in the lab.

The case for LSD, however, was still slim. Midway through the trial, with the jury out of the courtroom, Judge Brieant stated, "I can't help observing that the case on the LSD is not nearly as strong as the case on the methaqualone, but that is a matter of prosecutorial judgment at this point. And while I might urge you all to drop the LSD out of this case, that is not for me to say." He then ruled that only small parts of the LSD tome could be shown to the jury. "I am not going to have this jury meddling around with an entire book in the jury room and reading it to each other."

Ritholz jumped in: "Your Honor, I'd like the record to clearly show, one, there is not one word of evidence in this trial about making LSD."

Judge Brieant revealed a rare flash of humor. "I was so groggy yesterday after listening to all this boring stuff, which is putting the jury to sleep here, that I had forgotten that one of the government's cooperating individuals quotes this defendant as stating an intention to make LSD. In making my evidentiary rulings, I am entitled to observe or to assume total truthfulness on the part of these witnesses."

He continued sardonically: "Here you have a case where one of the alleged coconspirators quotes this defendant as saying, 'Goody, goody, we are going to make LSD for the money,' and thereafter you have a bunch of purchase tickets showing delivery into the laboratory of constituent chemicals. We have this testimony of Patricia what's-her-name who went in there and poured the stuff down the sink."

But no one could say exactly what Berman had poured down the sink.

Jolly, who detailed his own amateur gumshoe investigation, was another tough witness for Ritholz to crack. Ritholz tried to make Jolly's meticulous, persistent search for evidence look suspicious, acting surprised when Jolly didn't just check B-J's trash occasionally, but sometimes twice a day. Jolly's search for clues, which continued even after the feds had broken into the lab and seized evidence, did seem intensely fervent.

Macris later argued that there was nothing mysterious about it. "We both felt a high level of proof was required," he said. "I think to an outsider looking in, the detailed investigation may have appeared to be a personal attack on B-J. But we couldn't comprehend what was happening in front of us. We felt a strong necessity to dismiss every legitimate explanation before reaching the sad conclusion of B-J's involvement in an illegal drug-making operation."

If B-J weren't convicted, the fallout would be incendiary. Jolly offered this explanation for his actions: "I did ask what was going on and was given a story I didn't believe. Buettner-Janusch is not the sort of person to admit fault easily—he has such confidence in himself that he believes what he says is right and often convinces others. I knew I would have to have a firm case."

Ritholz sought to portray him as coveting B-J's prestige and seeking to undermine him in the hopes of getting the department chairmanship himself. He even suggested that Jolly might have planted the drugs in his scheme to overthrow B-J, despite the lack of evidence of such machinations. In the end, no personal gain could come out of trying to bring down B-J. Macris and Jolly earned for themselves only the enmity of B-J's friends and defenders.

At the end of the prosecution's testimony, with the jury out of the room, Judge Brieant called Mann and Ritholz to the bench. He expressed deep concerns that sufficient evidence was lacking to support Count 4, conspiracy to obstruct justice. He said that B-J was "obstructing justice to beat hell," and would keep Counts 5 and 6, but he dropped the conspiracy count. B-J had knocked down one charge at least.

—◆—

Myriad witnesses took the stand in B-J's defense, including many academic and scientific luminaries, although their luster perhaps was lost on the jury. Many of them served as character witnesses, attesting to his honesty, integrity, and sterling scientific reputation. Some testified that B-J had mentioned plans for a study of lemur behavior modification using drugs. Some said that the project was a legitimate subject for scientific research. But no one from B-J's lab, or even from the NYU anthropology department, spoke in his defense. None of the defense witnesses could attest to what had or hadn't happened on the fourth floor of 25 Waverly Place from the spring of 1977 to the spring of 1979.

The first witness called by the defense, Patricia Pronger, wasn't a scientist, however, or even an academic, although she was crucial to supporting the contention that the controlled substances found in the lab were part of legitimate scientific research. Pronger, a Chicago real estate agent and apartment manager with some experience in nonprofit fund-raising, began talking with B-J over the summer of 1978 about raising money through Simian Expansions for a variety of projects, among them the behavior modification of lemurs, which she called "brain research." Over the winter and spring, she met with B-J several times and began working on a prospectus for donors.

Although Pronger wasn't a fund-raiser by trade, she did have social connections with people known in the nonprofit world as "high net worth donors." She began networking and gauging the interest of prospects as well as crafting a document that included the proposed behavior modification project. B-J hated the term "brain research," but reluctantly agreed to its use in gaining the interest of nonscientists. The proposal emphasized projects in areas of research in which B-J had strong credentials, including hemoglobin studies, but it also included the lemur project. Their fund-raising goals were ambitious if not totally delusional. Pronger said that they were seeking up to $7 million dollars in grants and donations over a period of several years, although the lemur project's budgetary goals appeared more modest, in the range of $40,000 to $70,000 a year.

Hard of hearing, Pronger occasionally had to adjust her hearing aid, and often asked the lawyers to repeat their questions. She said that she worked diligently on the funding proposal, incorporating B-J's edits. She spent a week in New York City in March 1979, visiting the lab and going out to lunch with "the lads"—B-J's assistants, Dorfman, Cornyetz, and Greenfield. She even met with Jolly and discussed the fund-raising project with him.

She completed a draft of the proposal in early May and then flew to New York to deliver the more or less final draft at the end of the month. By this time, B-J had already been subpoenaed by the grand jury, of course, and she was soon subpoenaed as well. More meetings and editorial revisions took place over the summer, but the donors she assiduously had been cultivating would back off quickly when they learned of B-J's indictment in October. Through Pronger's testimony, Ritholz aimed to give the behavior modification project legitimacy—there was a nonprofit devoted to primate research, with a fund-raiser actively working on a proposal for foundations and donors.

Mann relentlessly cross-examined Pronger. The timeline was out of sync. Pronger believed that B-J's proposed behavior modification project was in its early planning stages, when, in fact, the chemical experiments had already been well under way for some time.

Then there was the problem with the lemurs—or, really, their absence. B-J had given Pronger the impression that Elwyn Simons, director of Duke's primate facility, which housed the lemurs, had agreed to permit B-J to experiment on them. (He hadn't, although Mann couldn't prove that because Simons didn't take the stand. His absence later became a serious issue.) Pronger had trouble making clear how many lemurs would be needed, at first seeming to suggest that it might be only two or three females and their "husbands," as she called them. Ritholz, in redirect questioning, made it clear that she was really talking about two groups of lemurs, one given the behavior-modifying drugs and a control group. In the end, Pronger's testimony probably raised as many questions in the jury's mind as it answered.

One of the academic stars on B-J's team, Michael Coe, testified that he had known B-J for two decades, and that they had served together for "two very fine years" on the anthropology panel of the National Science Foundation. William Wachtel, a newly minted attorney assisting the defense, asked him, "Knowing everything you know today, do you have any doubt whatsoever that Dr. Buettner-Janusch is an honest and truthful person?"

"I have no doubt whatsoever," Coe responded.

Coe remains certain of B-J's innocence to this day. "I've always been convinced that John was innocent during his first trial," he said, "and that he was railroaded by a very jealous and unpleasant colleague." He still regrets that his testimony "didn't do more good."

Duke's J. David Robertson attested to B-J's honesty and truthfulness, finding him to be "exemplary in every respect." He also spoke glowingly of B-J's scientific credentials. "I had to decide whether to promote John to full professor," Robertson said, "and I collected information from around the world, letters from people in physical anthropology, and found that he was what he seemed to be, certainly one of the most outstanding physical anthropologists in the world."

While Coe may have regretted not being able to help more, character testimony certainly has value. If someone stands accused of a crime that seems so out of character that it invites disbelief, character witnesses can dilute the prosecution's case. The only problem was that B-J's character was so complex that, like Walt Whitman, he contained multitudes. There were many B-Js. He was like Shakespeare in Jorge Luis Borges's essay on the playwright, at once everyone and no one, an artist ultimately unknowable yet capable of creating a universe of vivid and completely real characters.

More to the defense's point was the testimony of John Morgan, director of the pharmacology program at City College of New York's School of Biomedical Education. He explained that many behavioral studies had examined the effects of methaqualone on animals ranging from rats to chimpanzees. Indeed, two US Air Force researchers had authored a study titled "Effect of Methaqualone on Behavior of the Chimpanzee" in 1968. In other words, even the US government had shown a legitimate interest in testing methaqualone on primates. What he didn't say was that the test used only four chimps; three of them passed out and the fourth fell into a stupor. Not, perhaps, the best use of government funding.

Several defense witnesses vouched for the plausibility of such a research project. Anthropologist Laura Vick supported B-J's purported interest in lemur behavior research in greater detail than his other colleagues at the trial. But even her testimony didn't corroborate his intention to use drugs—related either to LSD or methaqualone or otherwise—in his research.

Vick at the time was a visiting assistant professor at the University of North Carolina at Chapel Hill, where she had earned her PhD in anthropology in 1977. Her dissertation examined lemur behavior, and she had spent several years studying the animals at the Duke University Primate Center. Her committee consisted of professors from both UNC and Duke, including, not surprisingly, Klopfer and B-J.

Vick liked B-J, although they almost didn't hit it off. At the Primate Center, she had told B-J about her master's thesis concept, also on lemurs, and asked if she could do research there. Skeptical, B-J acted extremely put out. He told her to go sit in the summer sun and take notes on the behavior of a couple of troops of the prosimians. North Carolina in the summer can get intolerably hot and humid—conditions pleasantly familiar to the prosimians—but Vick stuck with it for a couple of hours after moving into some shade.

When B-J returned, he didn't see her and muttered that he knew she didn't have the right stuff. In a sweat-drenched fury, she tapped him on the shoulder and announced: "You can take your damn lemurs and shove them you-know-where."

Taken aback, B-J recovered his aplomb quickly. "Hmm, no one talks to me like that except for my dear wife, Vina," he said. "Why don't you come inside for a glass of sherry?"

She soon returned to observe the creatures on a regular basis. B-J had left Duke by the time she submitted her dissertation, but he read it and critiqued it. The defense claimed that B-J's critique showed an interest in modifying lemur behavior going back several years.

Called to testify at the last minute, Vick came to New York alone with her toddler, Steven, whom she took to court with her. It was stifling in the witness waiting room, and the low window stood wide open. When called, Vick asked Coe and Alison Jolly—also in the room with her—to look after Steven and not let him near the window. Needless to say, she was distracted on the stand.

Ritholz mostly questioned Vick about the critique, entered into evidence, which suggested that where she asserted that certain lemur behaviors were learned they actually might be "pre-wired" or "biochemical." Mann showed a reasonably good grasp of the issues and asked if the critique ever mentioned modifying lemur behavior or using drugs to modify their behavior. Vick said it was a preliminary sort of analysis and that the idea of experimentation was "implicit."

Vick, like Coe, later said that she regretted not being able to help B-J more—but there really wasn't much more she could have done. Vick acknowledged in her testimony that B-J may have had help from students in writing the critique. In fact, Greenfield had told Clifford Jolly the summer before that he'd written it, which seems likely. She didn't receive the critique until April 1979, long after she'd received her PhD and long after the so-called lemur research had begun at NYU. Vick said later that she hadn't even had time to reread the critique before testifying. What it all meant, no one could say.

Alison Jolly, who had looked after little Steven carefully and considerately during his mother's testimony, had flown in from England. Although known as an expert on field studies of lemurs—that is, studies of lemurs in the wild—Jolly said that she would read a paper published on behavior modification of captive lemurs using drugs with "great interest." Under Mann's questioning, however, she said that she herself would never give LSD or methaqualone to lemurs.

Robert Sussman, then an anthropology professor at the Washington University in St. Louis, said that B-J had discussed the idea of using drugs to modify lemur behavior with him in Seattle in 1977. "I actually didn't think it was a good idea," he recalled. "I didn't like manipulating animals . . . especially the animals at Duke, which are very rare primates. So I really didn't like the idea of doing it very much. I think that after he knew I didn't like it, I think he sort of dropped the subject." But he also said that it was a legitimate scientific object of research.

Peter Klopfer, up from Durham, offered testimony that seemed to justify the quantity of methaqualone that B-J was making in his lab. Mann sought to portray lemurs as small, fragile creatures, implying that the amount of drugs produced far exceeded the needs of any scientific study. But Klopfer, in a measured way that even a lay jury member could understand, said that no certain relationship existed between an animal's size and the dosage required to achieve an effect.

He compared tiny shrews with much larger chimpanzees. "The smaller animal may require much less. It may also require much more if it's an animal such as the shrew. For example, with a very high metabolic rate it may turn out that for a particular drug the dose per body weight has to be very much higher than it does for a chimpanzee, another side of the coin. So when you learn to cross species, the usual dose-mass relationship, which so many introductory texts like to refer to, is very suspect, in my view."

Klopfer conceded that very little research had been done on the effects of drugs on lemurs, so dosages would be speculative. Mann followed up quickly: Did Klopfer have any "direct knowledge of what was actually going on in Professor Buettner-Janusch's laboratory between the spring of 1977 and May 18 of 1979?"

No, he had to admit, he hadn't.

Klopfer said recently that he had hoped that his testimony had "saved" B-J. But then he heard the tape recordings at the trial. He shrugged and shook his head. The tapes weren't at all exonerating. B-J sounded like a man with a great many secrets to hide.

B-J had called Klopfer personally, asking him to testify and trying to remind him of a discussion about lemur behavior modification. Klopfer said that he'd never had any such conversation with him. If he had been planning any kind of lemur project, he noted, B-J most certainly would have contacted him.

Mann and Ritholz entered the final phase of the trial with long and ferocious summations, both aiming for a knockout punch.

Mann dramatically replayed excerpts from the tapes in succession. Over the course of the two-week trial, they certainly had had an impact. But aggregating them, hearing B-J sounding deceptive, suspicious, and angry by turns, made him seem more like a sociopath than a scientist. B-J himself appeared amused by hearing them again. He leaned back in his chair and smiled while they played, as if he thought they contained witty repartee.

Ritholz heard nothing funny. "I think we are getting a little dramatic. Do we hear [this] ten times?" he complained.

After playing each recording, Mann addressed the jury with rhetorical questions: "Does an innocent man need to paint a hypothetical scenario as a way of explaining away damning conversations? Does an innocent man make the decision to deny activities that took place as long as those activities aren't documented?"

The litany proved both relentless and powerful. B-J wasn't speaking in the voice of innocence. He became his own undoing.

Mann reiterated that B-J's motive was money, pure and simple. "This was a way, ladies and gentlemen, to make easy money—money not earmarked for hemoglobin projects and the like, money that would not depend on the generosity of rich old ladies, but money that he could easily make and spend in any way that he saw fit. Dirty money."

Then she pictured a second motive even more fiendish, that of a privileged man who believed he was above the law, "a citizen above suspicion," protected by the carapace of his reputation and renown.

But then Mann went too far. She had mentioned Elwyn Simons several times, but in summing up she pointed to his conspicuous absence—and came close to causing a mistrial.

"I submit to you that there was one man who would have had firsthand knowledge of the defendant's lemur project, and that was Dr. Elwyn Simons, the director of Duke's lemur facility. Because if Buettner-Janusch was really making drugs to use on Dr. Simons's lemurs, he certainly would have talked to Dr. Simons. He would have obtained his approval. But the one scientist that Buettner-Janusch did not bring to this courtroom was Elwyn Simons."

In court, an absence of evidence can't be used as evidence of absence.

"Strike out that argument," Judge Brieant demanded. "I will instruct the jury at this time that the defendant does not have to prove his innocence. The duty of proving guilt beyond a reasonable doubt is a burden the government has. Furthermore, the doctor was equally accessible to subpoena to anyone, including the United States attorney. It is an improper argument that has no basis. Put it out of your minds."

"I make a motion for a mistrial," Ritholz announced.

"Your motion for a mistrial is denied on that ground. I gave my instruction."

Mann wouldn't give up. "Your Honor, you know from the evidence presented during this trial that Elwyn Simons was never told about this project."

"He is stricken out of your discussion."

"Your Honor—"

"You listen to me unless you want a mistrial," the judge reprimanded her. "No more about Simons."

Simons had become the elephant in the room. For anyone who knew his role in this story, his absence was palpable. He said later that B-J personally called him and asked him to testify, "reminding" him, as B-J had tried to do with Klopfer, that they had spoken about a lemur project. Simons said he had no recollection of any such conversation and, further, was reluctant to testify. He considered B-J a friend, but he always felt "ambivalent" about him.

It turned out that on the eve of the trial Simons had had an accident with a weed-whacker in his yard, which shot a one-inch piece of metal into his leg. Bedridden, he was unable to testify.

In his summation, Ritholz again derided the credibility of the state's witnesses. Two of them, Cornyetz and Dorfman, had made deals with the government to "save their skins." He could barely contain his contempt for Cornyetz, "a very difficult fellow to believe. He is a confessed user and seller of drugs. He is the only one here besides Dorfman, you will notice, who ever sold any drugs. The two government witnesses. And in return for his testimony, he got a suspended sentence and served not a day in the slammer. That wasn't a bad deal for him, and you can understand why he did it. Incidentally, it apparently wasn't easy, because he admitted to thirty rehearsals for that testimony." Cornyetz had "lied in the continuing pattern of lies. If you got a liar, treat him like one."

Ritholz pointed out that even Macris had lied. In taped conversations, Macris said, " 'Agents came and visited me, and this happened and that happened.' That was all made up. So he isn't too concerned about telling his old buddies lies either, and I take it, and should take it that he wouldn't be too concerned about telling you lies." (They were lies of necessity, of course, in order for Macris to maintain his cover, just as a narcotics agent sometimes has to appear to be a drug user himself.)

As for Jolly, Ritholz called him a "garbage pail scavenger," noting that "you can conclude that he harbored jealousy of Dr. Buettner-Janusch and desire for the chairmanship."

Speaking of the lidocaine drug deal that Dorfman made, Ritholz asked, "Do you think that a man with the credentials of Professor Buettner-Janusch would endanger a whole life, a chairmanship, his future, for $80? . . . The whole story is incredible."

Much of the defense's story had holes in it as well. A major lacuna undercut the primary defense claim that controlled substances might have comprised part of legitimate scientific research. The experimental subjects, the lemurs, were in Durham, and it was extremely unlikely that Simons ever would have agreed to the project.

"Why would you give drugs to lemurs? We don't know enough yet about their natural behavior," Simons said decades later. And why would a world-famous anthropologist cofound a research nonprofit with young men with no scientific credentials? Finally, why wouldn't B-J have hired a high-profile marketing agency in New York to solicit donations rather than a Chicago real estate saleswoman?

However the jury answered these questions in their deliberations, it didn't take them long to come to a decision. On July 16, after four and a half hours, they returned guilty verdicts on four counts: conspiracy to manufacture and distribute methaqualone, LSD, and sodium barbital; manufacturing and possessing methaqualone; and two counts of lying to federal investigators. The jury acquitted B-J of possessing and distributing Cylert.

B-J faced a maximum sentence of twenty years in prison. He had gambled everything on his reputation, but instead had succeeded only in destroying it.

7

Punishment and Crime

THE *TIMES* REPORTED THE GUILTY VERDICT THE FOLLOWING DAY ON the front page of the city section. Arnold Lubasch recapped the trial in his story, N.Y.U. PROFESSOR GUILTY OF ILLEGAL DRUG-MAKING, reporting that B-J would remain free on bail during his appeal, and noting NYU's cautious comments. "The university said yesterday that it was studying the case 'with great care' and would consult 'members of the administration and faculty' regarding the professor's continued employment. The university added, 'The university is confident that a careful and reasoned judgment will be made.'"

The "reasoned judgment" in this case was that B-J would lose his tenure in the fall and never teach at NYU again, or anywhere else for that matter.

On September 15, *New York* magazine published its cover story on the trial with the cover headline PROFESSOR QUAALUDE and an illustration of a man in lab coat with an enigmatic smile who in no way resembled B-J. *Science* magazine ran a much more detailed feature on the scandal and trial on October 17, under the headline DRUG-MAKING TOPPLES EMINENT ANTHROPOLOGIST. Both stories featured pictures of B-J by Deborah Feingold, a celebrity photographer better known for her portraits of Mick Jagger, Madonna, and Joey Ramone than of academics or scientists. B-J had his fifteen minutes of fame as a bad-boy rock star.

B-J's sentencing hearing wouldn't take place until later in the fall, on November 13, but he and his lawyers didn't have time for a break. In yet another photocopied letter to friends and colleagues, written just two days after his conviction, he asked them once again to write letters of support to the judge urging that he be allowed "to continue as a research scientist and teacher."

B-J struck a note of stiff upper lip, portraying himself as a lion brought down by dogs and expressing gratitude for past support: "So many of you have called and sympathized, and for those of you who have expressed a vicarious fear and horror of the high probability of an extended prison sentence I believe I must try to reassure you a bit. Prison is just another place. I have been in prison and one can learn to adjust. I do not recommend it as a way of life or as an experience, but it can be born [*sic*] and life can go on if one wants it to. I admit that I would rather, if necessary, go to prison for having committed a crime of conscience, as I did once before, rather than for the sleazy and stupid allegations that have led to this present situation. I cannot change what happened. I gambled on fighting the case and lost. I appreciate more than I can say everything so many of you have written and said and the love and sympathy and hope and respect I have received from so many of you."

Letters of support poured in once again, just as they had during the investigation, asking the judge for leniency in sentencing. Perhaps one of the most poignant and eloquent came from Matt Cartmill, still a professor at Duke. B-J's attorney read part of his letter at his sentencing trial: "When I visited him in 1979 after he had learned of the forthcoming indictment, he was in lamentable shape, depressed, incoherent, embittered, consumed by alternating spasms of rage and despair. That impression, in some letters I subsequently received from him, reminded me of nothing so much as King Lear on the 'blasted heath.'"

Cartmill then described a changed man. "I am frankly surprised and pleased by the calmness and civility he has displayed since the verdict was handed down," he continued. "His career is in ruins, his reputation destroyed. He has no job, and he is facing the prospect of large fines and prolonged imprisonment. Yet his attitude is one of calm resignation tinged with relief at finally knowing the outcome of this action, disastrous though it is for him."

While B-J's own letters during the period between his conviction and incarceration were more subdued, as Cartmill notes, they still teemed with a bitterness that sometimes devolved into self-pity. But B-J remained largely above the larger calamity he had precipitated at NYU, and even among his colleagues in the broader academic arena. (He was innocent, as he always insisted, so no apologies were necessary.) While full of contempt and hatred for the students who had testified against him, he remained indifferent to the havoc he had created in their lives.

Macris, who had so wanted to be an anthropologist, transferred to business school. Berman never completed her PhD. Cornyetz got probation, but he lost his job and was asked to leave NYU. Dorfman received a year's probation and one hundred hours of community service, but was fired. Greenfield was tried five years later for making illegal drugs in B-J's lab, but to what extent he was a coconspirator would remain unclear. If B-J was the czar of his lab, it's difficult to call Greenfield an instigator. B-J didn't take direction of any kind from his students.

Forman, however, survived unscathed, although she didn't become an anthropologist, switching instead to genetics and forensic science at the Department of Justice. Nevertheless, B-J's tenure as chair and the drug-making affair had demoralized the entire anthropology department.

Jolly, at least for a while, endured the animosity of B-J's friends. Richard told *Science* magazine after the trial that "B-J has some chance of winning on appeal, but Jolly loses either way. He was a good friend of all of B-J's friends, but has generated tremendously bad feelings by his actions." Half a year earlier, Jolly had sent Jeffrey Rogers up to Yale to study under her.

Many years later, after B-J's drug conviction and his conviction for attempted murder, James Spuhler, B-J's dissertation adviser from the University of Michigan, still harbored a grudge against Jolly. Spuhler, who died in 1992, said: "All I know is I think Cliff Jolly is a shit. He, or someone, destroyed a lot of things out of sheer jealousy. I mean, someone poured acid on the slides of lemur chromosome studies that B-J had done."

As for the risk involved in alienating B-J's supporters in academia, Jolly remained sanguine. "It was unavoidable," he said. "But I was naive enough to believe that when the facts of the case came out, even his admirers would judge them carefully and objectively—after all, biological anthropologists are supposed to be scientists. In the event, it was sobering to see how little regard B-J's supporters seemed to have for the actual evidence.

"Much later, after B-J confessed to multiple attempted murders, some of his supporters apparently began to have doubts." But many of them "apparently concluded that he had simply been unhinged by the unwarranted prosecution and conviction in the drug case. And so it goes . . ."

The greater risk for him would have been doing nothing, he insisted. By May 1979, Jolly had become convinced that B-J and his coconspirators were moving from "R&D" to production. "There was imminent danger of this concoction finding its way onto the street," he said. "I shared the lab. Had B-J's homemade drugs hit the streets, quite possibly causing injury or death, and then been traced to their source, I am quite sure that B-J would have claimed ignorance (and distraction by Vina's death), and tried to throw the blame on the students—and probably on me too."

How could opinions about B-J have been so divided? B-J could be charming or brutal, kind or cruel, studied or impulsive, brilliant or inept. A complicated man, he provoked strong reactions. If you encountered him, neutrality was impossible. You were either for or against him. He too was either for or against you—unless of course he decided that you didn't matter, in which case he consigned you to nonexistence.

Many people—foes and some friends—saw him as a Jekyll and Hyde figure. The analogy is tempting, for not only does it deal with the duality of human nature, but the protagonist of Stevenson's novella, Dr. Jekyll, also experimented with mind-altering drugs. But perhaps the metaphor of the bifurcated self is too simple, especially for someone as complex as B-J.

The ancient Greek myth of Proteus may make more sense. The Homeric tradition calls him "the old man of the sea." A shape shifter of remarkable wisdom who possessed the gift of prophecy, he only revealed his secrets if caught and subdued. In *The Odyssey*, when Menelaus tries to capture him, Proteus assumes the forms of a lion, snake, boar, and even water. Although the word "protean" often has a positive connotation, it can also suggest the inauthenticity of acting. B-J could, like Proteus, assume many shapes and many roles. Like a great actor, he could improvise as well. This skill prompted Mann to ask rhetorically in her summation at B-J's drug trial: "Ladies and gentlemen, has the defendant simply concocted different stories, different fabrications at different times, whatever was necessary for him to say at the time, in order to answer the evidence that he knew the government had against him?"

Just as B-J could improvise stories to fit the evidence, he could also assume various personae, adopting different selves like a player on the stage.

At B-J's sentencing hearing on November 13, 1980, Ritholz presented a man deserving not only of consideration but indeed leniency: "a dedicated professor nurturing the young student, a kindly mentor, a charitable benefactor, a selfless friend." While some of his colleagues may have nodded, others would have found this description unrecognizable.

Ritholz continued eloquently: "Oh, how he has suffered. Gone is the lifetime-built reputation. Gone is a professional status earned by dint of the hardest kind of work there is, intellectual work. Gone is his chairmanship, his professorship, his tenure, and soon his home.

"I think I have never seen a more convincing demonstration, and encouraging one, of the rehabilitation which the law sets up as the purpose of this proceeding we are going through right now."

B-J's attorneys had been preparing for a possible conviction for some time. As such, they had submitted a very detailed proposal for an alternative sentence entailing extensive community service. A Washington-based nonprofit called the National Center on Institutions and Alternatives had developed it, offering three different alternatives: working at the Delta Regional Primate Research Center at Tulane University, the Blood Research Center with the American Red Cross, and with the Fortune Society. Each would have entailed close monitoring of B-J's living situation and life outside work, but not time behind bars.

In Judge Brieant's verdict, he carefully balanced B-J's contributions as a scientist and educator with his crimes. "I am prepared to concede that this defendant has a big credit balance with society, but it is also a very serious crime, actually two crimes here, and they, in my view, create a big debit balance also," he said.

"I have observed before that I think that the narcotics conspiracy was a serious crime, and it was vicious, the fashion in which it was conducted. This is not just a case of a defendant finding an empty building or a kitchen to stir up his own drugs. . . . This defendant also violated the trusts which he owed to society and to the academic community, which looked upon him as a leader."

Judge Brieant criticized both B-J and NYU. "I would have to say that I think the proof of guilt . . . is overwhelming," he continued. "I would view the case much differently but for his conduct, which has been characterized by his arrogance." B-J's sense of superiority—in his testimony to federal attorneys and in the tape recordings played in court—played a part in his undoing, one of his many tragic flaws.

But the judge deeply criticized NYU's negligence as well. "The court wants to observe that the university officials cooperated fully with the government once it was known what was going on in the laboratory of the anthropology department. However, the proof at this trial indicates that during the period of time when this conspiracy was in existence and ongoing, right in the laboratory, that there was no peer review whatsoever of what was being undertaken or allegedly undertaken in the laboratory in the nature of research or the compounding of chemicals. Furthermore, there was no supervision whatsoever by the trustees or the lay administration of the university as to what use was being made of its property, of its assets, and its employees, to the extent that they were being used in connection with this drug manufacturing conspiracy. There should be a lesson in this for everybody."

Judge Brieant sentenced B-J to five years in prison and a parole term of two years. (The ex-professor could have received five years for each of the four counts, with a maximum sentence of twenty years.) The judge also noted that the court was "interested" in the alternative service proposal, but Judge Brieant declined to implement it at the time.

B-J remained free on bail and managed to hang on to his apartment on Washington Square Park. But he became a pariah at NYU, shunned by many of the people who had enjoyed his company, his prestige, and his splendid parties. His lawyers began working on an appeal immediately, but it wouldn't go before the Second Circuit Court until March 5 of the following year. His letters grew somewhat more sober, at his lawyers' insistence, so as not to endanger the chances of his appeal. But B-J was still B-J, and he could never let any injustice—done to him, perceived or actual, at least—go forgotten.

Another photocopied letter sent to friends and supporters in March, after his appeal but before the court's decision, drips with sadness and self-pity: "It is difficult for me, in some ways, for I live quite alone. I have no one I can talk to about the case, and it festers and sickens within me. I have lost two years of work; I am shut up like a recluse in my apartment. . . . It is hard to bear."

Inevitably he paints his situation on an enormous canvas, portraying the martyrdom of freedom: "The cry *DRUGS* masks the invasion of the academy by the monster outside. It has been used to conceal the betrayal and destruction of collegiality and friendship by the fifth column that is always in our midst. There is no difference in substance between the cry *DRUGS* or the cries *BLASPHEMY*, or *WITCHCRAFT*, or *UNGERMAN*, or *UNAMERICAN*—cries that we all remember were used to obscure what was really at stake."

In his self-absorption, he conflates imagery of the persecution of witches, foreigners during the two world wars, the Holocaust, and McCarthyism with his conviction for possession of street drugs and lying to federal investigators.

—⁓—

B-J's appeal was rejected on April 6, 1981. Circuit Judge Irving Kaufman, referring to the case as "the tragic culmination of the career of Dr. John Buettner-Janusch, one of the world's leading authorities on physical anthropology," saw no basis for the constitutional objections raised by B-J's lawyers, which centered on the warrantless search of the lab. The appeals court reaffirmed Macris's and Jolly's legal right to permit federal agents to search and seize evidence from the lab without a search warrant.

"We are faced with the difficult task of evaluating the power of third parties to permit governmental intrusion into an area which a defendant reasonably regards as private," Judge Kaufman wrote for the court. "We are of the view that the circumstances present confirm that the two men had the requisite authority."

In writing his decision, Judge Kaufman recognized the pathos inherent in the case: "This is one of those hard cases in which it is difficult to explain the motives for criminal acts ruinous of an otherwise distinguished career. We do not possess the omniscience to supply the answer. The judgment of conviction is affirmed."

Unwilling to admit defeat, B-J decided to appeal to the Supreme Court. His chances were slim, his legal costs enormous, but he never gave up easily. At the same time, he faced a prosecutor who pursued the maximum sentence against him with the single-minded persistence of Javert in *Les Misérables*. Still, for the time being, B-J remained out of jail during his final appeal.

But time was running out. The government had set May 28 as the beginning of B-J's incarceration at the minimum-security federal prison at Eglin Air Force Base in Florida's panhandle. Just a week before, however, Supreme Court Justice Thurgood Marshall turned down an emergency request to keep B-J out of prison until he could make a formal appeal before the full Supreme Court. It seemed likely, given how quickly B-J had to prepare for prison, that he had held out hope until the last moment.

Thomas Olivier, B-J's former grad student at Duke, had been working in England but returned to America shortly before B-J left for jail, and stayed with him for about a week. He recalled B-J's housekeeper and the building's custodian getting into a dispute in the apartment about who would get his aquarium. Each claimed to have been promised it. Olivier, who called B-J "perhaps the smartest person I've ever known," found the situation absurd. A scientist whom he greatly admired was going to federal prison, and the help were arguing over who would get his fish.

Although B-J wore a brave face in his final days of freedom, he was alone, and greatly welcomed Olivier's company. "I think I might not have survived if Tom had not been with me," he said shortly after arriving at Eglin. "He is a great person, and he really did wonders for me. He persuaded me that it might be worth fighting on a little longer."

Once, during Olivier's visit, B-J wanted to make a special dinner and insisted on going to Balducci's in the Village for fresh asparagus. There, while strolling through the aisles, B-J extolled the virtues of the organic peanut butter at the gourmet grocery. "He loved to hold forth on any subject," Olivier said.

Back at the apartment, B-J steamed the asparagus while Olivier followed him around with a dishrag, wiping up spilled water. At one point, B-J turned to him, annoyed. "What's happened to you? I don't remember you being this neat when you worked in my lab at Duke!"

"B-J," Olivier answered patiently, "I've been married for years to a wife who insists on neatness."

"The irony of B-J's exclamation was that at Duke he was famous for making messes in the lab, especially with water," Olivier explained. Vina, his lab director, "had the authority, which she seemed to enjoy exercising, of banning him from working in the lab for periods of up to a week at time when he made what she called 'water pie.'"

Lon Alterman remembered a couple of "raids" on B-J's wine cellar just before the professor left for what he called "summer camp." "That was the first and only time that I drank 1964 Château Margaux," Alterman recalled fondly of the famous (and famously expensive) Bordeaux wine.

Olivier helped B-J pack a few personal items to take to prison with him. On May 27, the day before his incarceration began, B-J dashed off a letter to Sondra Schlesinger, asking her to help with arranging the packing and storage of his apartment's belongings. (Nearly everything ended up in the Schlesingers' St. Louis home—in the basement, attic, and scattered throughout the house—until they moved in 1986, when B-J stored his possessions at his Eagle River home.)

B-J's hurried exit left his apartment looking lived in when NYU showed it to philosophy and law professor Thomas Nagel and his wife, the art historian Anne Hollander, a few months later. "It was like he'd just left that morning," said Hollander. "The bathrobes were still hanging up on hooks." They moved into the apartment in the spring of 1982 and have lived there ever since.

The following day Olivier drove B-J to LaGuardia Airport in Queens for his flight to Florida, where he entered the federal prison camp at Eglin.

⌐∾⌐

Eglin Air Force Base, sprawling over more than 720 square miles near Pensacola, in northwest Florida, is home to stunning white-sand beaches, old-growth longleaf pine forests, and ancient oaks. It is an incredibly bio-diverse area; over fifty species on Florida's threatened and endangered species list live on the base.

Despite B-J's intense dislike of the heat and humidity of the Gulf summers, he could at least appreciate the area's beauty and bounty. "There are many large live oaks with Spanish moss draped in great artistic swaths from the branches," he wrote Alison Richard in an early letter. "Huge magnolia trees with gorgeous blossoms, pine trees and lots of grass and flowers. There are sea trout that the inmates are allowed to fish for from time to time. The fauna around here is quite something. The airbase is full of the pygmy rattlesnake that is supposed to be deadly. There are lots of fascinating birds—shore birds, forest birds, and open-space birds. At least five kinds of woodpeckers. And plenty of fire ants and cow-killer ants. Also some marvelous birds that dive into the water after minnows. They are called kestrels here. I have always thought of them as fisher-martins."

Typical of minimum-security institutions, the prison camp, which closed in 2006 in a cost-cutting measure, housed mostly white-collar criminals with little flight risk. It had no barbed-wire fences or guard towers. It even featured soccer and softball fields. Escape would have been easy—called simply "a walk away"—but fleeing prisoners invariably were caught, resulting in extended sentences and transfers to higher-security, and far less pleasant, institutions. Other Eglin alums included Watergate coconspirator E. Howard Hunt and former Maryland governor Marvin Mandel.

Eglin was the original "Club Fed" before that nickname became a generic term for the federal prison camp system. It may sound cushy, but prison camps are not country clubs. FPC prisoners live in dormitory-style quarters, working for pennies an hour, separated from friends and family. It's small consolation that your fellow inmates may have advanced degrees or once ran big corporations.

B-J hated it, of course. He said "it was basically a slave labor camp for the convenience of the airbase, keeping the golf course and swimming pool neat, tarring the runways, and so on."

Because of his celebrity, B-J couldn't leave camp grounds to work at the base, but that kind of "slave labor" was a sort of inside joke. When B-J first arrived, he went through a fairly typical hazing. As a newbie, B-J got the worst room in the house. For his first two weeks, he slept in a dormitory full of fleas and gnats that lacked air-conditioning or even a fan. The temperatures soared over a hundred degrees and barely cooled off at night. For his first work assignment, he had to clean bathrooms and sweep porches.

But B-J's situation improved quickly. He moved to an air-conditioned dormitory that housed twenty-four men, with small cubicles ingeniously consisting of a small army bed, a desk with a lamp and chair, shelves for books, and carpeting. His doorless cubicle rose to his chin. The well-lit bathrooms had private toilet and shower stalls. B-J began working in the laundry, washing the other inmates' dirty underwear and socks, but he soon rose through the ranks to dispensing clean clothes, which gave him a certain cachet among the prisoners, many of whom liked to show off their buff biceps and pecs with V-neck T-shirts. For a fashionista such as B-J, who harbored an aesthetic disdain for V-necks, it was theater of the absurd.

B-J also landed a job with the prison newsletter, *The Doin' Times*, where he worked as a typist. For a highly regarded editor and author of books and papers, it wasn't exactly a position of prestige—and his name fell low on the masthead—but it did give him access to a typewriter, an advantage to his correspondents who no longer had to decipher his Linear B handwriting.

The Doin' Times listed the times of movie broadcasts on cable channels and described the wide range of classes offered at the prison. B-J displayed little interest in any of the educational opportunities or sports events at the camp, and while it's hard to imagine the scientist taking any of the voluntary courses, they weren't the kind of classes you might expect.

"Many of the men here are 100% crooked," he wrote in a 1983 letter. "They spend all their time figuring out ways to do crooked things better than they did them before they got sent here." The classes, in his mind, mainly facilitated this process. "The business courses are fundamentally courses in stealing, and the celestial navigation course is one that is designed to make smugglers have an easier time of it out on the Caribbean. Then there are very special courses in gems, which clearly used the lapidary shop to train individuals in ways to cut stones, etc., when fencing them."

Indeed, many of B-J's letters from Eglin brim with wit and insight into what he called the "bureau of injustice." Instead of playing tennis or bocce, B-J was writing letters prolifically, working on papers, editing the works of his colleagues, such as Richard and Sussman, and reading voraciously. He could receive paperback books with no problem, but hardcover books had to come directly from the publisher or a bookstore. Journals or other mail sometimes proved problematic.

He also had to deal with the pettifoggery of low-level prison bureaucrats. When his usual caseworker was out sick, a poor benighted substitute attempted to deal with B-J's mail. His lawyer had sent a couple of large packages of journals and letters, which had to be opened in front of a caseworker, lest the prisoner receive contraband.

"I got a call from someone who sounded like Mr. Wuffmuff," he wrote. "Mr. Wuffmuff looked at these two packages and first accused me of running a business with my attorney. I managed to convey that business was, as far as I was concerned, some sort of venereal disease. Then old Wormvomit said we must open the packages. First he found the *AJHG* [*American Journal of Human Genetics*]. My god, said Whiffenpoof, you must have the base hospital commandant's approval for that. Then came the *AJPA* [*American Journal of Physical Anthropology*]. Well, that ought to have the approval of the education officer, says old Wormvomit. Then he got to the *American Ethnologist* and knew that he had something, and old Whufflehump said that it must be subversive."

B-J suggested that he take it all to the associate warden, who he knew hated trivia. Then, veering into the realm of fantasy, he imagined Wuffmuff being flayed alive by the associate warden and attacked by horseflies. In B-J's mind it was a well-deserved punishment.

In another description that perfectly conveys B-J's fish-out-of-water condition in a Southern jail, he eviscerated a prison official in charge of parole appeals. "The head case manager for the region is a man named Skaggs, a name redolent of the Faulknerian universe of the South—alcoholism, paranoia, sadomasochism, and religious fanaticism. All of which are typical of that man."

B-J's letter writing, often amusing, sometimes threatening or insulting, harmed his chances for a reduced sentence and for alternative service. On October 5, 1981, the Supreme Court declined, without comment, to hear B-J's appeal. The Parole Commission set a presumptive release date of November 27, 1983, for a total sentence of thirty months.

The defense had learned, shortly before the parole hearing, that prosecutor Mann had submitted, just a week before B-J's incarceration, a Form 792. Ordinarily a two-page questionnaire, it assesses both aggravating and mitigating factors in sentencing. Mann's report ran thirteen pages and included some of B-J's angry and threatening letters written after his indictment—a number of which referred to her as a fascist prostitute. Needless to say, Mann found no mitigating factors in the case, and the document surely influenced the parole board's decision. The court repeatedly declined to permit an alternative sentence, despite numerous appeals.

B-J turned his cell into a tiny office. Richard asked B-J to review the manuscript for her book *Primates in Nature,* published in 1985, which remained an essential text for several years. B-J read every page and gave copious comments in his nearly indecipherable handwriting. On the first page, he had scrawled, "What a load of mellifluous shit," she said. "He was blunt. But he was an extraordinary editor. He demanded mainly that things be expressed simply, clearly, and in a logical sequence."

B-J also helpfully offered writing advice to Richard in a letter, which if he weren't such a brilliant editor, might have been taken amiss. B-J used outstanding models outside the world of anthropology to illustrate his point: "The next manuscript you do, take some time with the sentences in the first draft. That is, I think, where it counts. I am always fond of old Flaubert, who sweated and strained and worried to death over the perfect sentence. There is no reason why the perfect sentence should not be the aim of scientific writers, too. Think of old Proust. Neurasthenic? Crazy? Self-centered? Nutsy, he wrote thousands of pages, hundreds of thousands of ms. pages, and produced one of the few genuine masterpieces of the 20th century. Darwin was ill? Kept to himself at Down House. Yet look at how productive he was. Ill, my foot. He was smart. He kept out the busybody and idiot and finished one masterpiece after the other. Look at our mad poet, Robert Lowell, crazy from teen age, yet he worked and worked and worked and produced many of the best poems of the century in English."

Richard was grateful for his help, despite the chiding. Clearly B-J set a very high bar for himself as well. He also worked with Olivier on some papers while in prison. Typically scientific journals provide an academic or institutional affiliation for their articles' authors, and surely one of the strangest appeared on a paper in the *American Journal of Physical Anthropology* that B-J coauthored with Olivier and others. The editors had prepared "Models for Lineal Effects in Rhesus Group Fissions" for publication while B-J was still in Eglin, and at a meeting they discussed how to describe B-J's affiliation. Finally, the chief editor decided that it would read: Federal Prison Camp, Eglin AFB, Florida 32542.

"It is, after all, his institution," the editor said laconically.

B-J remained busy, but he was lonely and bored. He complained to Richard in a June 1983 letter that none of his colleagues and friends, with the exception of Olivier, had visited him during the past two years. Of course, his colleagues were busy teaching and doing field research over the summers, but for a social animal like B-J, such isolation made life difficult.

Olivier visited B-J a few times. Once he brought him a biography of Robert Oppenheimer, the nuclear physicist stripped of his security clearance during the McCarthy era. "I brought some fresh oysters, and we sat outside at a picnic table in a big patio eating them," Olivier recalled. "B-J was a hoot. He kept bringing up these people and saying, 'Tom, I'd like you to meet one of my colleagues.' And he'd turn out to be a drug dealer or a politician."

But if B-J managed to work and write amusing anecdotes about his stay at "summer camp," anger was still eating away at him. Robert Dewar, Richard's husband and a fellow anthropologist, knew B-J well. "He had a lot of trouble letting go of things," he said, summing up in just a few words one of B-J's most profound flaws.

Occasionally, during phone calls from Eglin, B-J boiled over with rage about having been set up. His anger and fury could reach frightening levels, and his letters often alluded to a deep desire for revenge. Shortly after arriving at Eglin, he wrote, "If I survive, and it is not at all likely that I will, I will certainly take the most awful revenge upon certain people. I have a list, and it is already working." Perhaps even more telling: "I shall come out of here with such a load of hatred and bitterness that only blood will wash it away. The Greeks are correct. Blood is a corrective for many wrongs."

B-J's evocations of pity and terror—his brooding on revenge—mixed with signs of how low he had truly sunk. The Parole Board had shaved two months off his sentence, but his "colleagues" at Eglin were under the impression that he was to be released later, on his original and presumptive release date. Traditionally, when paroled from Eglin, a prisoner gave a party providing as much ice cream as he could afford to the ice cream–obsessed inmates. Shortly before B-J's discharge, another prisoner gave a release party, at which the criminals ate 95 half-gallons of Borden's. B-J boasted coldly that he "would change the tradition. I shall merely leave. No ice cream, no nothing."

He just didn't want to waste the money. He left Eglin for New York City on September 27, 1983. He had gained forty pounds since Vina died. Ever the bon vivant, he had always struggled with his weight. Since he wasn't interested in sports or weight-lifting like other prisoners, eating prison food, especially ice cream, did tend to pack on the pounds. He was, he said, a quarter-million dollars in debt to his attorneys. The Bureau of Justice gave him $40 and a bus ticket to New York, his destination a halfway house on the seedy Bowery.

B-J was now on parole, which requires strict adherence to rules, that, if violated, could result in a swift return visit to jail. But right out of prison, the first edict proved intolerable—a two-day bus ride to New York—so B-J got on a plane. Lon Alterman picked him up at LaGuardia Airport. B-J called his sister and told her he was back in New York, then Alterman drove B-J to the Village, where he spent $30 on a bottle of cologne in a shop on Sixth Avenue. Finally, he drove him to the halfway house, which lay not far from CBGB, where Cornyetz and his friends used to hang out.

The Salvation Army ran the place and housed a number of ex-cons there. Perhaps its most notorious previous resident, criminal and author of *In the Belly of the Beast*, Jack Henry Abbott, paroled from a Utah prison with Norman Mailer's help, was living at the halfway house when he stabbed a waiter to death.

B-J spent two months there and surprisingly had good things to say about it. B-J praised the Salvation Army, "a most admirable organization," before describing its halfway house, which at first sight was "rather horrifying." "Directly across the street is the City of New York's Shelter for Homeless Men, a chamber of horrors. The street is littered with the sad victims of the policy of the benign governor and the mayor to drive everyone out of the mental hospitals in the state and put them on the street. So the poor, homeless madmen must live on the street sleeping in the shelter.

"But the Salvation Army maintains the halfway house with excellent security. It is clean, and the food is excellent. The personnel decent and humane and the experience, of all those weird and unusual I have had the past three years, was just fine."

Over the next several years, B-J moved around a lot, living, as he often pointed out, without income. For a while, he stayed at the legendary Chelsea Hotel, rather liking its bohemian allure. Its residents had included Thomas Wolfe, William Burroughs, Patti Smith, and Sid Vicious. "It now includes such luminaries as Virgil Thompson," he wrote Richard, and then couldn't resist adding, "and perhaps me. I find it a strangely cozy place, with a remarkable number of friendly people. Dogs are allowed, as are bicycles and god knows what else." Like so many once and future residents, he complained about the cockroaches.

B-J often mentioned "sleeping on the couch" at Ian Tattersall's home in the Village at this time, although Tattersall himself said he didn't remember B-J staying over that much. At any rate, they had an extra bedroom, so B-J wouldn't have had to sleep on the couch. But perhaps he liked depicting himself as some kind of intellectual hobo. B-J was a frequent dinner guest, Tattersall recalled, and usually arrived with a good bottle of wine.

Finding work became an enormous challenge, for no colleges were willing to take a risk on him. His trial had been so widely publicized that it was impossible to find a job in academia, which, at first, was the only kind of position that he wanted. He might have lighted out for the territories, but news of his prison time likely would have preceded him even at more remote, less prestigious institutions.

B-J also had a chip on his shoulder about the injustice of his incarceration. In a CV from the time, his "Professional Positions" sounded upwardly mobile: instructor, assistant professor, associate professor, professor, chairman, until they took a sharp Orwellian turn at the end: "prisoner of the state."

While B-J had become a pariah among many of his former colleagues, Tattersall remained a staunch friend. "We tried to take care of him," Tattersall said. "I tried to help him out professionally. The guy had a career, and then he had his career taken away from him. He was still a man of talent."

Tattersall helped secure B-J a position as an honorary research associate at the American Museum of Natural History on the Upper West Side, where Tattersall worked as a curator in anthropology. B-J set to work cataloging the museum's lemur collection, one of the best in the world. The remains—consisting of preserved skins and bones—were documented and published in a pamphlet cowritten by B-J and Tattersall in November 1985. B-J wasn't getting paid, but at least it made for interesting and important work.

The remains, stored in metal drawers in the museum's back rooms, look rather sad. Most of the specimens date from hunting expeditions in Madagascar in the early twentieth century. "We would never do this today," Tattersall said, explaining that researchers would use trap-and-release techniques, photographing the animals and taking blood samples for DNA.

❦

In a strange turn of events in a story with many strange turns, just eight months after B-J's release *New York Times* readers who had followed the scandal read on May 25, 1984, a brief AP article that began: "Two men were charged yesterday with making illegal drugs in a New York University laboratory under the supervision of a prominent anthropology professor who was later convicted in the scheme."

The professor obviously was B-J. The men charged were his unindicted coconspirators, Bruce Greenfield and his friend Mark Schwartz. Both of them had been in B-J's apartment when the professor was first subpoenaed to testify before government attorneys. They were indicted for their involvement in the events at NYU, for which B-J had been convicted and served his twenty-eight-month sentence, charged with three counts: conspiring to make LSD and methaqualone, making and possessing methaqualone, and a second conspiracy to come up with an alibi.

Federal District Judge Thomas P. Griesa released the pair on a $75,000 bond. They faced five years in jail for each count, and fines of $15,000 for each drug count and $10,000 for the conspiracy count.

Greenfield and Schwartz, having gone on with their lives for years, reeled. Their lawyers claimed that the hiatus between the first DEA break-in at B-J's lab, on May 17, 1979, and their indictment so much later raised constitutional issues. They argued that the delayed charges violated the statute of limitations—five years in non-capital and non-tax cases—and due process.

Schwartz's lawyer, Michael Washor, and Greenfield's attorney, Daniel Markewich, made motions to this effect, which the court rejected. The government's response was simple and direct: The grand jury had found probable cause that until May 18, 1979, Greenfield and Schwartz were involved in a drug conspiracy, and until that date had possessed illegal drugs with intent to distribute. The current grand jury charged both men on May 15, 1984, just within the five-year limit.

If it seemed unfair to the defendants, the government found it legally proper. Mann, the prosecutor from B-J's trial, offered the reasons for the delay in a deposition on July 23. (Assistant DA John Carroll prosecuted the second trial.)

Greenfield and Schwartz weren't satisfied with her explanation, but it did clear up some mysteries, as did the second trial itself. Mann said that in June 1979, Greenfield had appeared in Amorosa's office with his attorney, Henry Bayles, a family friend getting on in years. (He was seventy-two at the time.) Amorosa and Mann, who was also present, wanted Greenfield to cooperate with the government in the case against B-J. But Greenfield was sticking to the lemur story, which the government felt it had ample evidence to refute. They just weren't interested in pursuing an interview along that line.

Mann didn't want to try Greenfield or Schwartz with B-J for several reasons. She didn't think she had enough evidence to convict Schwartz, and she worried that if she indicted Greenfield, she might have to redact some taped statements made by B-J. Her hope, she said, was to convict B-J and then get the professor to flip and testify against his unindicted coconspirators. The government did in fact get immunity for B-J, who offered testimony against Schwartz and Greenfield to a grand jury in June 1982. She claimed his testimony wasn't particularly useful, however. Still, it does undercut one theory put forward by B-J's defenders—that he went down to protect his students.

Then life got busy. The case was reassigned a few times, and importantly, there was new evidence. There was, she insisted, no intentional delay.

The jury trial of *United States of America v. Bruce P. Greenfield and Mark Schwartz* began on November 5, 1984, presided over by Judge Whitman Knapp, and ran for twelve days. The prosecution witnesses made repeat performances: Jolly, Macris, Dorfman, Cornyetz, Berman, Forman. All returned and told substantially the same stories. (That Dorfman and Cornyetz, deals made and sentences erased from their records, stuck so closely to their earlier testimony was notable, certainly.) Typical of such trials, Schwartz and Greenfield didn't take the stand.

Only two new witnesses appeared. Martin Marion testified for the defense, recounting his earlier grand jury statements about the genesis of

Simian Expansions as a benign captive-breeding project. But the other new witness for the prosecution, Stephen Lichtman, offered stunning and disturbing testimony.

The government's earlier case against B-J still had two related holes: a clear motive, and a sale—more specifically, a sale of the only real drug produced in any quantity at the lab, methaqualone. The sale of a minuscule amount of faux coke for a hundred bucks legally and morally amounted to a game of Show and Tell. Mann's purported motive of money looked absurd, given B-J's income, savings, and investments.

But with Schwartz and Lichtman, the government hoped to connect the dots. Schwartz, a nonstudent, had been seen in meetings with B-J and Greenfield. Schwartz and Greenfield, longtime friends, were at B-J's apartment when DEA Agent Toal served B-J with a subpoena the day after the break-in. Lichtman was also a friend of Schwartz. The broken link in the chain—if there was one—was that Lichtman and Greenfield both said they didn't know each other.

The feds already knew Lichtman well as a drug user and seller. He had received immunity for his grand jury testimony before B-J's trial and for his testimony at the Greenfield-Schwartz trial. Lichtman's sad tale of human degradation in the grip of addiction proved as sordid and pathetic as any heard during the course of both trials.

If B-J was, in the realm of literature, an unreliable narrator, Lichtman was, in the sphere of tabloid journalism, an unreliable witness. When he testified to the grand jury in 1979, he admitted that he was taking twenty to twenty-five Quaaludes *a day*. He also had used LSD, heroin, and coke, and had served time in prison on drug charges. He said that he had been doing outpatient therapy for five or six years, trying to deal with the demons that bit and soothed him.

Under questioning by the prosecution, he testified that he acquired some methaqualone from Schwartz in powder form sometime in March or April 1979. He said he had a pill-making machine and thought they could do business. In early April, he took a gram or a gram and a half before going shopping in Brooklyn with his stepdaughter to buy her a gift. During dinner he blacked out. "I woke up in the hospital three days later, or two days later," he said. "It seems that it wasn't ready for consumption."

Lichtman said he called Schwartz and complained about the drug's side effects. But after cross-examination, it appeared that Lichtman wasn't entirely certain that the substance that had put him in the hospital was what Schwartz had given him to test, or whether it was his own concoction. With the jury out of the room, prosecution attorney Washor approached the bench and told Judge Knapp that he thought Lichtman was high during his testimony. "From the way he sat, from the way he spoke, from the way he testified," he said.

Judge Knapp wasn't overly concerned. It really was up to the jury to make judgments about the credibility of testimony. "He's not the most impressive witness I've ever seen in my life," he said blandly. Lichtman's testimony utterly lacked credibility. If the witness wasn't sure what happened, how could a jury know? That credibility gap helped get Schwartz off the hook.

It turned out, though, that Schwartz and B-J shared an enthusiasm, not provably for drugs but certainly for dogs. Schwartz had been raising and showing Rottweilers for years, and had been president of the Long Island Rottweiler Club. They had even attended the Westminster Kennel Club Dog Show in New York together. It seems highly improbable that B-J, Greenfield, and Schwartz, sequestered in B-J's office or study, were discussing AKC breed standards, but without Lichtman no connection linked the drug conspiracy to Schwartz. Schwartz was acquitted on all counts.

Curiously, it was revealed that Jolly, who had pushed Greenfield away with a stick and still distances himself from him today, was much closer than he wanted to admit. Greenfield's attorney produced a document signed by Jolly asserting that Greenfield was pursuing a dual major— biology and anthropology—and that Jolly was in fact his adviser.

In his summation, Markewich portrayed his client as B-J's stooge. "No one intelligent can argue with you that LSD and methaqualone were being manufactured in that lab during the spring of 1979.

"Greenfield didn't know that LSD and methaqualone were being made in the lab in the spring of 1979, not because he is a stupid man, but rather because he is an intelligent man, and as a graduate student, he was being used. He was being manipulated by B-J. The lemur research project was being corrupted to B-J's own ends."

It's anyone's guess who corrupted whom. But someone was certainly making illegal drugs, and from the evidence of two trials, both B-J and Greenfield knew what was going on.

During the trial, Judge Knapp dropped the third charge, the cover-up conspiracy, against both men. Greenfield was found guilty on the first two drug counts. At his sentencing hearing on January 14, 1985, Judge Knapp summed up Greenfield's situation succinctly: "Now, what to do? Now, it's perfectly obvious to me that if this case had been prosecuted at or about the time that the first case was prosecuted, Mr. Greenfield would have had to go to jail." But it wasn't prosecuted then.

Judge Knapp continued: "Of the two, the professor and Mr. Greenfield, the professor is clearly the more culpable. I mean, it is absurd to accept his hypothetical . . . the hypothesis that Mr. Greenfield came to him and persuaded him to do this. I mean, whatever happened to Professor B-J, I don't know. He wasn't before me. Something terrible caused his values to go askew. But to say that as between the student and the professor, to assign blame to the student is ridiculous. So obviously, as between the two, the professor is the more culpable."

In America, the law doesn't allow for double jeopardy; that is, you can't be tried twice for the same crime. But science encourages experiments to replicate results, and the jury in the second drug case confirmed the hypothesis that B-J manufactured illegal drugs in his NYU lab.

Judge Knapp sentenced Greenfield to three years' probation and one hundred hours of community service. The defendant's mother was in the courtroom and approached the bench after sentencing to say thankfully and gracefully: "Though this was my son on trial, I was very impressed with your evenhandedness in the courtroom. And I almost went to law school in my day. But I didn't listen to my father, and I always felt it would be a privilege to try a case before you. And I say this sincerely."

The judge replied simply: "Thank you very much."

—~—

While cataloging lemurs at the Museum of Natural History, B-J renewed his friendship with Esteban Sarmiento, who had finished his doctorate in anthropology at NYU (with Jolly as his adviser). Sarmiento also served as a research associate at the museum.

Although B-J could produce a good bottle of wine or a bag of groceries from Dean & DeLuca, living without income in New York had taken its toll. Sarmiento recalled going out to lunch with B-J and another colleague at an inexpensive restaurant near the museum. They split the bill, and Sarmiento threw down a few dollars as a tip, which B-J pocketed and replaced with some small change.

"We mustn't spoil the natives," B-J said.

B-J and Sarmiento went on several long road trips together, often traveling to conferences of the American Association of Physical Anthropology. They had driven together to the AAPA convention in Niagara Falls that had provoked B-J's fantasies about pushing Jolly over the cascade. That trip took place in April 1980, shortly before the trial. They drove together a few weeks later to Duke, where B-J tried to marshal evidence for his lemur behavior research. On all these trips, B-J brought a bottle of wine and packed lunches from Balducci's so they could stop at a roadside picnic table for a meal.

After B-J's release from prison, they drove together to the 1985 AAPA convention in Knoxville, Tennessee. They arrived late at night after the long trip and stayed with Sarmiento's parents instead of at a hotel. It must have been humbling for a man who had fallen so far from grace, but professional conferences flow through academics' blood.

Anthropology professor Susan Brin Hyatt of Indiana University wrote eloquently about the rites and rituals of conventions in *Times Higher Education*. She began by quoting from the prologue to David Lodge's academic satire *Small World:* "The modern conference resembles the pilgrimages of medieval Christendom in that it allows the participants to indulge themselves in all the pleasures and diversions of travel while appearing to be austerely bent on self-improvement." In his novel, Lodge portrayed the gatherings as opportunities for sex, gossip, and competition for jobs, a veritable anthropology of academia.

In describing the annual gathering of the American Anthropological Association (a larger organization and meeting than the AAPA's), Hyatt continued, "And so it is for anthropologists. Like natives of a village that is both particularly fractious and extraordinarily intellectual, we undertake regular pilgrimages to these events, where we gather ostensibly to debate issues such as Marxism versus poststructuralism, but as we anthropologists are, like novelists, students of social life, we secretly know that it is in the parallel conference of personal networks that the real dramas take place."

B-J probably forced himself to go to the Knoxville conference primarily for the networking opportunities, although they proved fruitless. But when B-J was released from prison, he tried to remain upbeat about his future life and career. In the spring of 1984, Alison Jolly visited the States with her family, and B-J stayed with them for a while at their apartment on Roosevelt Island on the East River. Jolly expressed surprise at how much fatter B-J had grown in prison, which B-J explained as common among prisoners. He seemed in relatively good spirits, she said.

Tattersall said that after Eglin, B-J seemed more "at peace with himself," observing that "he came out of prison much less abrasive, a much nicer man than when he went in." In early letters to Alison Richard after his release, B-J seemed optimistic about finding work and making a fresh start. Perhaps realizing that teaching again was unrealistic, he said that he was exploring editing or even becoming a lab technician or administrative assistant. But even as B-J considered positions of a much less prestige, they weren't forthcoming.

B-J became restlessly itinerant. He lived in the Village near NYU on East Eighth Street, on the Upper East Side, at the Chelsea Hotel, and near the Cloisters in Inwood at the top of Manhattan.

Glad to get out of New York, B-J frequently visited the Connecticut home of Richard and her husband, Robert Dewar. (Richard and Dewar were then both associate professors of anthropology at Yale and the University of Connecticut at Storrs, respectively.) Richard remembers many pleasant weekends when B-J came up with bags of groceries from Balducci's and cooked. Once, as he was making dinner, she walked into the kitchen and saw B-J cracking eggs and separating the whites from the yolks with his fingers. "It was sort of appalling and incredibly sensual at the same time," she said. It was the kind of dichotomy, she suggested, that made B-J so endlessly fascinating.

B-J talked grandly of authoring more books. He spoke of writing about *l'affaire* Buettner-Janusch, to explain what had really happened, and about his prison experience and the prison system generally; substantially revising his classic *Origins of Man*; and working on a major book about lemurs. Robert Sussman, who became his literary executor, said that B-J managed to collect a lot of notes and did a small amount of writing on his lemur book, but it really amounted to very little. He couldn't concentrate or focus. Indeed, he never published another book on any subject ever again.

B-J wasn't at peace for long. His brilliant career was over. Facing an intolerable situation—a future without any opportunity to work in anthropology—his wrath grew and became more palpable. He vented to Sarmiento, ranting about taking vengeance on the people who had ruined him. Sarmiento grew increasingly impatient with the crazy talk and challenged B-J boldly.

"On the road, his thoughts would wander, and then he would come out with the revenge talk," Sarmiento said. "It would start with him calling the prosecutrix a Nazi whore. He would go on about the judge. But most of it would be about Cliff Jolly, and he talked about him with the venom of a scorned lover. He also talked about the 'worm' [Richard Macris], saying that in his day, students like that would be pushed off high buildings.

"For all those he bad-mouthed, I sometimes suggested he blow them away with a shotgun," Sarmiento continued candidly. "My idea was that when confronted with reality, he would drop the hate thing and figure out it wasn't productive."

Sarmiento felt sorry for B-J. "Where he ended up—homeless and jobless—was so much the opposite of how he saw himself. His vision of the future must have made him crazy." Sarmiento truly seemed to think that calling B-J on his mad rantings might help, but the shock therapy didn't work. B-J plotted revenge, but it wouldn't involve guns. He wasn't good with weapons.

Over the summer of 1986, B-J finally collected his scattered belongings and moved everything to his family home in Eagle River, Wisconsin. In a letter to Klopfer dated September 14, he talked about unpacking "over 1,000 boxes," and said that he looked forward, after five years, to having an income with the new year, when his pension and Social Security would begin.

But then he entered a fantasy world. He described applying for a grant to go to Madagascar. After his years of lurking around as persona non grata, what organization would have given him a grant? He went on: "I have been practicing for Madagascar by going up to the Porcupine

Mountain wilderness on Lake Superior to spend a few days hunting up salmon streams and sleeping out."

The pure air and wilderness, far from New York, offered a reprieve from his troubles. That fall he planted hundreds of bulbs, pickled "quarts and quarts" of apples, baked fruit cakes, and made pâtés. In mid-December he wrote Richard a lyrical letter that extolled the beauty of his surroundings and revealed a certain serenity: "The Great North Woods are beautiful, and it is relaxing and great fun to go after trout and salmon in the quiet and peaceful streams that run through the forests in Wisconsin and the Upper Peninsula of Michigan.

"The region has been covered with hoar frost the past few days. It is incredibly lovely, especially when a few stray rays of the sun shine out around three in the afternoon. The mornings are foggy, so that there is little contrast except between jet black tree trunks and the white universe."

But the quietude and stillness couldn't silence the fury of B-J's grudges. He still referred to Clifford Jolly as "that English psychopath," the "scandalous behavior of the prosecutrix," "the bribe asked for by the judge," and "that whining little twit Charles Leslie." B-J also mentioned in a postscript that he'd soon be in New York City, dog-sitting for Tattersall and bringing his own dog, Coco, named after Coco Chanel. He said that he looked forward to seeing Richard and Dewar. They had no idea what madness that innocent, slightly importunate PS portended.

Tattersall and his girlfriend (soon-to-be wife) Andrea Dunaif lived on Gay Street, a quiet, bending block-long street in the West Village that connects Christopher Street and Waverly Place. Originally an alley for horse stables, it later housed black servants who worked for wealthy white families on Washington Square. Today, it's a block of expensive Federal townhouses and homes with vestiges of Greek Revival detail.

Although B-J had considerable freedom of movement, he was still on parole, so he had to get permission for the trip from his probation officer, Paul Billmeyer, in Eau Claire, Wisconsin. He had grown, he admitted, a bit bored by the beauty of the woods and eagerly looked forward to enjoying the pleasures of the city again.

Tattersall was lecturing on one of the Museum of Natural History's discovery tours, educational voyages to all corners of the world that also raise substantial amounts of money for the museum. Experts in anthropology, archaeology, biodiversity, conservation, and cultural history accompany the tours, now called "expeditions." Not surprisingly, Tattersall, erudite and engaging, made for a discovery tour superstar. On this occasion, Tattersall's assignment took him to Indonesia during most of February 1987. B-J was dog-sitting for Dunaif's teacup poodle, Zoe, Coco's littermate.

On Valentine's Day, Richard and Dewar came down from Connecticut for the opera and dropped off their daughters with B-J. Richard said that nothing seemed amiss. She knew B-J's dark side all too well from his prison letters and his shouts and murmurs after his release from Eglin, and she easily saw through the platitudes about B-J's being a changed and chastened man after prison. But, she said, he truly seemed "at peace" that day. What she didn't know at the time was that the serenity came from an unfolding murder plot.

B-J's seeming peace stemmed from a sinister source. He had sent poisoned Valentine's Day chocolates to Justice Charles Brieant, the judge who had sent him to prison, at his home on Shady Lane in Ossining, New York. For the second and last time, B-J was about to make the front page of the *New York Times*.

A box of Godiva chocolates arrived at the judge's home on February 13. They came with a Hallmark card decorated with hearts addressed to the judge and his wife, Virginia, signed cryptically with only a question mark. Judge Brieant didn't eat any of the candies, but Virginia ate four pieces and became critically ill. Found unconscious by the judge that evening when he returned home, she was rushed to Phelps Memorial Hospital in North Tarrytown in Westchester County. Always vulnerable to retaliation, criminal justices keep their addresses and phone numbers private, and few acts draw the attention of the FBI more swiftly than attempts on their lives. B-J soon made the list of suspects, having been sentenced by Judge Brieant in a bitterly contested and controversial trial.

Virginia Brieant was found to have ingested two substances, atropine and sparteine. An FBI laboratory also discovered that one piece of uneaten candy contained "a lethal concentration" of pilocarpine hydrochloride. Atropine is a naturally occurring poison found in deadly nightshade, or belladonna. Its scientific name, *Atropa belladonna*, is resonant. *Atropa* derives from Greek mythology: Atropos was one of the three Fates, who by cutting the thread of life with her shears determined the time of one's death. *Belladonna* comes from the Italian for "beautiful woman," which refers to its use by Renaissance courtesans, who would squeeze drops of juice from the nightshade berry into their eyes to dilate their pupils, presumably to make them more comely. Such use became even more common among fashionable ladies in Europe in the seventeenth and eighteenth centuries. Despite this curious fashion, atropine is extremely deadly, and its toxic effects have been known since ancient times. It has long been a favored method of murder in real life and in mystery novels.

Atropine poisoning has been described in the mnemonic "hot as a hare, blind as a bat, dry as a bone, red as a beet, and mad as a hatter." But this only hints at the suffering it can cause, including dry mouth, intense thirst, tachycardia, labored breathing, blurred vision, confusion, and hallucinations. If left untreated, it can result in coma or death.

Sparteine is found in both common broom and lupines. According to the *Illustrated Handbook of Toxicology*, "an overdose leads to curare-like paralysis, spasms and death by respiratory paralysis after two to three hours."

Pilocarpine is another alkaloid, obtained from the leaves of the rainforest shrub jaborandi. Symptoms of overdose include nausea and vomiting, irregular heartbeat, sweating, dizziness, headache, and diarrhea. In very high doses, it can be fatal.

All three substances were commercially available, and B-J could have gotten access to them relatively easily. But, as British chemist and science writer John Emsley noted in his book *Molecules of Murder: Criminal Molecules and Classic Cases*, poisoning is a dying art. He writes that in 1989, of the 19,000 murders committed in the United States, fewer than 30 were caused by poison.

FBI agent William Doran said that when he interviewed Judge Brieant, B-J soon became a suspect; the judge himself characterized B-J as a "sociopath." Other clues presented themselves. The chocolates had been mailed from the Patchin Post Office on 10th Street in Greenwich Village on February 12—just a fifteen-minute walk from Tattersall's home.

The case broke in less than a week. With B-J as a prime suspect, the feds contacted his parole officer in Wisconsin and learned that he was in New York, staying at Tattersall's apartment. On February 19, FBI headquarters in Washington, D.C., identified a print on the box mailed to the Brieants as belonging to B-J's right pinky finger. The federal agents moved quickly. B-J was arrested at 11:45 p.m. that night on his way home from the Met, where he'd seen Mozart's *La Clemenza di Tito*, a story of conspiracy, attempted murder, betrayal, and forgiveness set in the Roman Empire. Of forgiveness, B-J had expressed none, nor would he receive any.

B-J was officially charged with the attempted murder of Judge Brieant the following day, February 20, in the federal courthouse in White Plains. The *New York Times* depicted a broken man: "Weary-looking, apparently ill and wearing a hearing aid, the white-bearded, 62-year-old Dr. Buettner-Janusch, who once cut a flamboyant figure on the campuses of Yale and Duke universities as well as at N.Y.U., stood silent but took notes."

The federal prosecutor, James DeVita, called B-J a "danger to the community," and charged that he had proved B-J would "try to get vengeance against those who stand in his way." Magistrate Joel Tyler ordered B-J held without bail at the Metropolitan Correctional Center in Manhattan.

A public defender, John Byrnes, represented B-J after he claimed that he couldn't afford a lawyer. Byrnes noted that B-J suffered from high blood pressure and gout and wore a knee brace. The magistrate, who spoke up when he noticed the hearing aid, permitted B-J to have access to his meds and to wear his brace.

By the time of the hearing, Virginia Brieant had escaped danger and been released from the hospital. At a press conference following the hearing, however, Doran, head of the criminal division at the FBI's New York office, asserted that the poison "was sufficient to kill. I would say that, yes, Mrs. Brieant's life was in danger."

At a news conference, US District Attorney Rudolph Giuliani—who never shied away from the limelight when it came to boasting about breaking a case—said, "In less than a week the FBI solved an attempt to murder Chief Judge Charles Brieant and his wife." True, obviously, although B-J hadn't even entered a plea yet, much less been convicted.

The FBI hastened to alert everyone connected with the prosecution in B-J's drug trial, including the witnesses. It was a rational precaution to take, although the FBI wasn't dealing with a rational suspect. B-J did, in fact, send three other poisoned packages. One went to a former graduate student at Duke, J. Bolling Sullivan, who two decades earlier had done research on primate genetics in B-J's lab. Sullivan, then a postdoctoral fellow, worked with Vina, the lab's manager, but wasn't really close to the couple. When B-J sent the candies, Sullivan was working as an associate professor of biochemistry at Duke's marine laboratory in Beaufort, North Carolina.

The Sullivans had been away during Valentine's Day, but when they returned they found a Godiva box in the mail, sent anonymously. Sullivan had no reason to be suspicious, and, while he didn't partake of the candies, his wife, Ashley, and daughter Ann ate a few pieces and became ill. "It was like food poisoning," Sullivan said, noting that his wife vomited and experienced mild hallucinations. They didn't immediately suspect the candies. Sullivan tried one and decided it "didn't taste right," so he put the piece back unfinished and tossed the box out on the back porch. A few days later, when Sullivan read about the poisoning attempt on Judge Brieant and his wife, he immediately called the FBI, who determined the box had also come from B-J.

B-J had mailed two other boxes of poisoned candies—one to his outspoken critic from NYU, Charles Leslie, and one to the man whom he blamed for his failure to get tenure at Yale, Sid Mintz. The FBI intercepted both those packages. The one to Leslie had been returned because he was on sabbatical, and the one sent to Mintz, then at Johns Hopkins, never reached him because he had moved temporarily to Washington, D.C.

The FBI soon learned that B-J had mailed "gifts" to Judge Brieant, Leslie, and Mintz the year before, which were quite likely poisoned as well. But through a series of coincidences, B-J's schemes had come to nothing. Earlier, he mistakenly had sent candies to the Brieants at the address of their son, who had thrown the contents away but kept the box as a good mailer. Leslie had received a package with chocolates and a papier-mâché Easter egg; he had thrown away the chocolates because the box was damaged, but he had kept the egg. B-J had been especially generous to Mintz, having sent him a bottle of Jameson Irish whiskey, Twinings tea, and a Passover greeting card. Mintz had tried both the whiskey and the tea and told federal agents that they "tasted unusual and unpleasant." B-J proved a persistent if inept poisoner.

Although the attempts to harm Judge Brieant, Leslie, and Mintz obviously qualified as acts of vengeance, the assault on Sullivan remained a mystery. They had known each other casually at Duke, but they had been out of touch for twenty years. At first, B-J's actions completely baffled Sullivan, but over time he hypothesized an explanation that if true reflects academia through a glass darkly.

In the mid- to late 1960s at Duke, Sullivan and B-J's student Peter Nute collaborated on orangutan genetics, authoring a published paper on their research. They briefly discussed whether to give B-J—who had contributed nothing to the research—an authorship byline for the use of his lab. Nute, who had helped B-J move his prosimians from Yale to Duke and knew the professor well, decided against it. So the 1968 paper, "Structural and Functional Properties of Polymorphic Hemoglobins from Orangutans," published in *Genetics*, cited Sullivan and Nute as authors . . . sans "Buettner-Janusch." Sullivan speculated that perhaps this was why B-J, aggrieved by the slight, tried to murder him some twenty years later.

Tattersall was on the Museum of Natural History's cruise ship near New Guinea when he received the news. His downstairs neighbor on Gay Street had called via ship-to-shore radio. The FBI had raided Tattersall's apartment, the neighbor said, and left it in a complete shambles.

When the agents searched Tattersall's apartment—with a warrant signed by Magistrate Tyler—they seized candy boxes, chocolate candies, pens, ribbons, tape, but also myriad cooking utensils from the Tattersalls' kitchen. The items gathered by the FBI, which included a copper pot, metal candy molds, and wooden spoons, revealed that B-J, ever the epicure, had made the chocolates himself. The list of seized items reads like a list of holiday supplies from a Martha Stewart cookbook, but the house was a wreck even before the feds arrived. "He left a hideous mess," Tattersall said. "The dogs were shitting all over the place."

The FBI can hardly be expected to put everything back after a raid with a ticking clock, but a thoroughly upended house hits home hard. "We never got our double-boiler back," Tattersall said with only a trace of humor. Tattersall wasn't just angry that B-J had turned his apartment into a shit show and a crime scene; he also knew the Brieants, and was very close to Virginia. "She was a great old friend," Tattersall said. They also had a soon-to-be-familial connection. Dunaif's brother was seeing the Brieants' daughter, and they eventually married. Moreover, B-J knew about the relationship between Tattersall and the Brieants.

Tattersall, not given to shows of emotion, recalled the events with strong feelings even after all the intervening years. "We were gutted by it," he said. "Why? We'd been very kind to him. We did everything we could. It was a hideous betrayal. It makes me shudder in retrospect. I never spoke to him again."

Some while later, one of B-J's attorneys showed up at Tattersall's house with some ruby and gold cuff links, saying that B-J wanted him to have them. Tattersall refused to accept them and sent the man packing.

On March 5, 1987, B-J appeared at an arraignment hearing to face four charges: attempted murder of a federal judge, attempted murder of a family member of a judge, mailing injurious matter, and tampering with a consumer product. The maximum sentence was sixty-three years in prison and $1 million in fines.

B-J by then had hired the law firm of Gallop, Dawson & Clayman to represent him. Curiously he pleaded not guilty. Because the case would be tried in the Southern District of New York, where Brieant was chief judge, it was announced that Judge Joseph Lord of the Eastern District of Pennsylvania would preside.

B-J subsequently cut a deal, and on June 9 the poisoned-candy professor pleaded guilty to mailing poisoned chocolates to Judge Brieant and to Sullivan. Both counts—mailing poisonous articles with intent to injure and kill—carried maximum sentences of twenty years each, and fines of $250,000 apiece. In exchange for a guilty plea, the government agreed not to prosecute B-J for the boxes sent to his former colleagues. It was the first time that B-J's wider murder plot had been publicly revealed, but Mintz and Leslie weren't identified as targets.

B-J stood up to plead guilty, admitting that he had made the chocolates himself, inserted poisons into them, put them in Godiva boxes, and mailed them, "with intent to do great bodily harm." Judge Lord told the defendant that, by pleading guilty, he was giving up his right to a trial.

"I understand that," B-J responded.

Sentencing was set for July 14.

Shortly before B-J's sentencing, the *ABA Journal,* the magazine of the American Bar Association, published a story, "Danger in the Courts," about the threats to federal court officials. Pegged to B-J's trial for the attempted murder of a federal judge, the article covered murder plots against other justices.

In the story, Judge Brieant said bluntly that the safety of judges was threatened. "I think it is getting more dangerous than it used to be. I think that we are getting more cases involving people who are not in the mainstream, who don't respect the system of justice. All you can do is resolve to be as careful as possible and not be afraid."

He also noted that he had begun to change his daily schedule so that his travels wouldn't appear predictable to potential assassins. That obviously wouldn't have prevented the candy poisoning, but it showed how much the murder attempt had shaken the judge.

It was just that threat to federal judges and the justice system generally that loomed large at B-J's sentencing hearing. Judge Lord told the court that he felt "there are hundreds of other federal judges looking over my shoulder at this minute. I feel an obligation to them. I feel an obligation, indeed, to myself, because when I see what happened to Judge Brieant, I sometimes shudder to think what might happen to me were I to make freedom easy."

Judge Lord's phrase, "to make freedom easy," raised the issue of general deterrence, which B-J's attorney, Samuel Dawson, addressed eloquently. He said that B-J certainly deserved to be punished, for he had committed grave crimes and had confessed to them in "a final phase of a tragedy." He admitted that the idea of "rehabilitation" in B-J's case was irrelevant. But he argued that, in B-J's case, "the notion of general deterrence, I think, really is minor."

Dawson continued: "It is important for the public to know that if someone does something like this, there will be swift and sure prosecution and punishment. But to think that what we do in any one case will prevent crime is illusory at best, and we shouldn't take comfort in that at all. There are 250 million minds out there, and we can't say that what's done in any particular place will have everlasting effect on the rest of the public."

Dawson used the example of narcotics laws and convictions, observing that strict laws and long sentences haven't stopped drug sales. "People who are bent on certain courses of conduct don't plan on getting caught, let alone being sentenced," he said, noting that criminals still must be punished. His argument ultimately sought leniency in B-J's sentence. He described a choice between sentencing B-J, then sixty-two, to life in prison, or giving him the possibility of "a year or two" of freedom at the end of his life.

Needless to say, the assistant US attorney, James DeVita, strongly disagreed: "I believe that it is entirely possible that general deterrence is the most important consideration for Your Honor."

It wasn't the public at large that needed deterrence from trying to kill judges. Rather, it was "people of a criminal bent" who "do need a strong message that this society will not endure deliberate acts of terrorism against members of the judiciary who have to pass judgment on the criminal population, and that to say that no one would be deterred by significant, substantial sentence of incarceration in this case is simply erroneous."

In the end, Judge Lord admitted that after twenty-five and a half years on the bench, he still wasn't convinced one way or another about the effect of prison sentences on general deterrence. But, he said, "Certainly this man must be deterred as an individual.

"I see no mitigating factors whatsoever in this case," Judge Lord declared. "He has exhibited a complete disregard for the law. I see no reason to temper the sentence that was established by Congress."

Judge Lord imposed the maximum prison sentence: forty years in jail. B-J would become eligible for parole in ten years. THE NUTTY PROFESSOR GETS 40 YEARS, ran the *New York Post*'s uncharacteristically subdued headline. Its caption under B-J's photo certainly rang true: POISON PROF GETS THE BOOK.

8

Descent of a Man

WHATEVER MADE B-J COMMIT HIS MURDEROUS CRIMES AGAINST SO many real and imagined enemies came from a dark place in his personality, and he was going to the very heart of darkness in the American prison system: the United States Penitentiary at Marion in the rural, southern part of Illinois.

The abuses and brutality of the conditions at Alcatraz—the most repressive prison in the nation, much publicized in the media—had made its closure a political necessity. Marion, built to replace it, opened in 1963, the same year Alcatraz closed.

Before his incarceration at Eglin, B-J had written his friends and colleagues that "prison is just another place." But Marion was a distinctly different kind of place, the harshest prison in the country. Marion was constructed to hold about five hundred "difficult to control" adult male felons, according to George Pickett, superintendent of Marion in 1971. After two corrections officers were killed in separate incidents on the same day in 1983, the Marion penitentiary went into permanent lockdown, restricting most prisoners to solitary confinement for twenty-two and a half hours a day. The six-by-eight-foot cells had a concrete slab bed with thin padding, and inmates ate in their cells. Visitation was severely restricted, with no physical contact permitted. Guards arbitrarily and brutally enforced rules and regulations, and the regime became known as a "control unit," or, more broadly, "supermax" security.

B-J—held at the Otisville Federal Correctional Institution, a medium-security prison seventy miles northwest of New York City, before and after his sentencing—was moved to Marion on August 20, 1987. He was, by all accounts, a model prisoner. The change that came over him, evident in his many letters and prison files, was nothing less than remarkable. His letters reveal a calmness of mind largely unthinkable before his final incarceration. He assumed an almost obsequious tone in written requests to prison officials for a new battery for his hearing aid or for prescription sunglasses.

He still remained intellectually active, if not influential, in his field. He subscribed to scientific journals such as *Nature* and *Science,* and continued to follow developments in anthropology. His intellectual and cultural curiosity didn't abate. He subscribed to *Opera* and *Opera News* and read widely in the classics, from James Fenimore Cooper and Walt Whitman to Jane Austen and Marcel Proust. His letters to the Schlesingers especially teem with his thoughts on the many books that they sent him or that he recommended. But his letters could segue from literary chat to passages full of racial and ethnic slurs, especially disturbing for a man known as a progressive.

Of course, he also complained about the execrable food and the tedium of prison life. What was life like for a world-renowned scientist in jail? He answers that question in a letter to Klopfer: "One word seems to sum most of it up: boring as hell."

Klopfer, a Quaker, recalled his correspondence with B-J in his own book, *Politics and People in Ethology:* B-J's "many letters from prison provide a chilling picture of how our penitentiaries, originally conceived by their Quaker founders as places for meditation and penitence, have degenerated into medieval dungeons."

Marion wasted no effort on rehabilitation.

In December, however, B-J received some good news. Judge Lord had reduced his sentence by half, ruling that his two twenty-year sentences would run concurrently, making an earlier parole for B-J more likely.

In October 1989, B-J transferred to the high-security federal penitentiary at Terre Haute, Indiana, where conditions were less restrictive. Inmates received more freedom of movement outside their cells, they could eat together, and they had work details. B-J was first assigned to work in the electrical shop, but soon he became a clerk in the Correctional Medical Services office.

His enemies and friends have different narratives as to how B-J wound up in federal prison in the Midwest. Some of his supporters, to this day, refuse to believe that he was guilty of making illegal drugs in his NYU laboratory. There was no motive, for he was financially well off. He wouldn't possibly risk his career for such small advantage. He had no obvious, previous predilection toward either drugs or crime. Instead, he had a history as a law-abiding citizen, except for his incarceration during World War II for draft evasion, ostensibly a crime of conscience. His NYU lab work was transparent: He ordered chemicals openly and publicly through regular university channels. If he was engaging in criminal activity, wouldn't he have been more surreptitious about it?

Surely, then, their line of reasoning goes, some other explanation must exist. He was conducting legitimate scientific research on lemur behavior. Envious or vengeful colleagues conspired to frame him, with the help of students, perhaps planting drugs in his lab. His students, taking advantage of his sorrow over the death of Vina, changed a legitimate research project into a sordid, money-making drug operation. Concerned about his students' welfare, B-J took the rap for them.

But from the distance of several decades, the evidence of B-J's guilt is overwhelming. Two trials dealt with essentially the same evidence about drug manufacturing at Rufus D. Smith Hall at NYU from 1977 to 1979. B-J and one of his coconspirators, Bruce Greenfield, were separately found guilty by juries, and the judge at Greenfield's trial declared B-J mostly responsible. The government witnesses told essentially the same stories in trials five years apart, even those who originally had testified after cutting deals but who had little to lose by changing their testimony the second time around. Illegal drugs were manufactured with intent for sale. The lemur research story was a fiction. There were no lemurs. There was no serious experimental program. There were only inexperienced or inept persons attempting to make LSD or methaqualone under the careful watchfulness and control of B-J, who was no chemist himself.

B-J continued to promise his supporters to tell them the "real" story one day, but he never did. He always maintained his innocence of illegal drug-making, but he discussed only procedural issues—the constitutionality of the search of the lab, and whether certain drugs or documents should have been allowed into evidence. He never offered an explanation for his handwritten drug recipes or his frank statements about making drugs.

No one denied B-J's attempted-murder plot. He himself admitted his own guilt. But in the scenarios spun by some of his supporters, his unjust conviction for drug-making, perhaps caused by the distraction of his grief over Vina's death, drove him mad. Their argument—that B-J was unhinged by injustice—shouldn't be dismissed as self-delusion. Those of B-J's friends and advocates who felt this way simply knew another B-J: the person he wanted them or permitted them to see. Many didn't witness his curious lack of sadness over Vina's death. Instead, they saw feigned grief from someone who knew that this was the appropriate emotion to show, or who selfishly sought compassion and sympathy himself.

The B-J who directed students to make drugs in his lab and attempted to kill a federal judge, his wife, and others was the same brilliant, witty, and charming B-J capable of acts of extraordinary kindness and generosity.

The one key ingredient missing was empathy. Examples abound. He bullied many of his graduate students and, when he became chair at NYU, many of his colleagues in the anthropology department as well. He showed only perfunctory emotion at Vina's death. He exploited students and young staff by putting them to work in a drug-making scheme while he held power over their careers and paychecks. He never expressed remorse for the chaos he caused at NYU or, later, for his attempted murders.

At Marion and Terre Haute, he even prevaricated about his guilt in the attempted murders. He wrote Richard in 1989: "Three packages got sent to the wrong people because of . . . an error in transmitting data." In 1990, he wrote Klopfer, again saying he would tell the full story one day:

"Many of the things I was accused of doing are quite untrue. . . . The amount of material that was faked up by the so-called victim [the judge] turns out to have been quite great, and so perhaps there is ground for a RICO suit. . . . I did indeed send the judge doctored candy, but it was not poisoned, and it was not lethal. The only reason his wife got sick is that she probably ate all of the small number of doctored candies in the package. Or she was abnormally sensitive to the adrenergic chemical in it."

In other words, he meant it more as a prank than a crime, and the United States Postal System lay at fault for sending the packages to the wrong people. He still refused to take full responsibility for his actions.

Perhaps one of the most revelatory passages in his letters appears in passing in another 1989 letter to Richard. It masquerades in the language of emotion, yet it reveals a complete absence of empathy: "I feel badly about Ian [Tattersall]—what I did in no way involved him, and was not meant to, but it was, I am sure, felt as a sort of betrayal by Ian and Andrea. I think that is the one thing I regret most."

B-J turned Tattersall's home into a crime scene and nearly killed one of his close friends, but it "in no way involved him"? Empathy entails being able to see things from another person's perspective, which B-J was simply not capable of doing.

Frans de Waal—a Dutch-born primatologist who teaches at Emory University and serves as director of the Living Links Center at the Yerkes National Primate Research Center in Atlanta, Georgia—has devoted his life to the study of primate social behavior. He began by researching aggression and dominance behavior, but in recent years he has focused more on prosocial behavior, such as conflict resolution and empathy. He defines empathy as "the capacity to (a) be affected by and share the emotional state of another, (b) assess the reasons for the other's state, and (c) identify with the other, adopting his or her perspective."

In his book *The Age of Empathy: Nature's Lessons for a Kinder Society*, de Waal sees empathy as an evolutionary adaptation that has produced the glue that holds societies together. "It's now believed that empathy goes back far in evolutionary time, much further than our species. It probably started with the birth of parental care. During 200 million years of mammalian evolution, females sensitive to their offspring outreproduced those who were cold and distant."With such deep roots in evolutionary history, it is not surprising that neuroscientists have discovered that empathy lies hardwired in the brain's emotion-creating limbic system, particularly in the amygdala. Environmental factors of course shape our ability to experience empathy as well.

In his insightful book *The Science of Evil*, Cambridge psychologist Simon Baron-Cohen offers considerable insight into pathologies related to lack of empathy.

Baron-Cohen views evil as "empathy erosion," using terms for mental disorders from contemporary psychiatry—borderline, narcissistic, or psychopathic—and presenting them as a constellation of diagnoses that reflect low levels of empathy. Everyone lies somewhere on his bell-curve spectrum of empathy, but "zero degrees of empathy" makes for a lonely place, and can result in cruel behavior.

Baron-Cohen writes: "What is zero degrees of empathy like? What does it mean to have no empathy? And does this translate into what some people call evil? Zero degrees of empathy means that you have no awareness of how you come across to others, how to interact with others, or how to anticipate their feelings or reactions."

In an appendix, Baron-Cohen cites the criteria in the *Diagnostic and Statistical Manual of Mental Disorders* (fourth edition), the handbook published by the American Psychiatric Association, for various low-empathy personality disorders. Among the signs for narcissists are "a grandiose sense of self-importance," "a sense of entitlement," "a style of exploiting others," and "a complete lack of empathy." Signs of someone with antisocial personality disorder—akin to psychopathy, but diagnosed somewhat differently—include: "Failure to conform to norms of lawfulness," "deceitfulness," "impulsivity or failure to plan ahead," "irritability or aggression," and "lack of remorse." These aren't complete lists, but B-J, deeply lacking in empathy, easily could fit into either category, or both.

Because his friends and acquaintances never completely knew B-J's life story—his flirtation with Nazism as a youth; his bullying and exploitation of students and colleagues; his lies, large and small, that resulted in his conviction at NYU—many willingly forgave or forgot what flaws they did see.

After all these many years, diagnosing B-J is impossible, but viewing his actions through the lens of psychiatry helps to explain his destructive and self-destructive behavior, especially at NYU. Denied the NSF funding he was convinced that he deserved, he conjured a research project that seemed (to him) scientifically credible and potentially lucrative, legally or illegally. He became convinced that his professional reputation made him invulnerable to doubt or suspicion, so he operated the research project / drug laboratory openly. At the height of his self-delusion, the two enterprises were inextricably entwined, and both, in his mind, were legitimate. Cumulatively, he crossed the line from eccentricity to pathology. The perceived injustices of being denied tenure, his conviction for drug-making, and the insult of public criticism in the press led him to justify attempted murder. As Lady Caroline Lamb famously said of her lover, Lord Byron, B-J was "mad, bad, and dangerous to know."

Soon after entering Marion in 1987, B-J learned that he was HIV-positive, although he hadn't yet begun showing symptoms of AIDS. He parceled out the news gradually to his correspondents, including Sussman, Richard, and the Schlesingers. As always, he had an unexpected explanation, if a rather unlikely one: He had contracted it in a lab accident, possibly infected while packing blood samples at NYU, just before leaving for Eglin.

B-J contacted several students who had worked in his labs at Duke and NYU, among them Lon Alterman and Thomas Olivier, to warn them of the potential risk.

"I recall B-J writing my wife and me that he was HIV-positive, and that we should get tested," Alterman said. "She was pregnant at the time, and his letter was less than welcome." Neither was HIV-positive.

As for B-J's story about a lab accident, Alterman was skeptical. "BS," he scoffed. "He didn't deal with the blood samples. I did. The samples, which were frozen plasma [kept] in glass tubes, were put on dry ice and driven to the Duke Primate Center by *me*. Indeed, some tubes were broken in the process. My risk, not his."

B-J had one last bridge to burn. Around Christmas 1990, B-J sent a typed letter to Thomas Olivier, whom he often described as his "favorite student" at Duke. "This is not a Christmas greeting," it began portentously. B-J then informed Olivier that several people who worked at the Duke lab had tested HIV-positive, and suggested that he get tested. He didn't identify the people who had tested positive, nor did he mention that he himself had HIV, which Olivier learned later.

Olivier was, he said, "disgusted" with B-J. "It was a deliberate move to ruin my holiday." Olivier never contacted him again. However, when he heard from Richard that B-J didn't have long to live, he called the hospital only to learn that B-J had died. "I felt bad that I didn't have anything to do with him after that," he admitted, adding that even as a close friend, B-J was often extremely difficult. No one is known to have become HIV-positive from working in any of B-J's labs.

B-J's medical records show that he received good care. Shortly after the virus was discovered in his system, he began receiving AZT, a drug used to delay the onset of AIDS in people with HIV. But by the spring of 1992, things had taken a turn for the worse. In April, he wrote to Klopfer and his wife, Martha, about the DUPC's newborn aye-aye, a rare, endangered lemur so hideous that it's strangely endearing. B-J noted how cute it was and asked Klopfer for a photo. Then he mentioned that his HIV infection was seriously advanced. "I am now in the stage known as the 'wasting disease.' Since September I dropped from 220 pounds to 145, and am fighting to regain about 20 of them. I shall keep you posted."

During that same period, the parole commission denied B-J an early release, affirming a projected release date of January 1999, and setting his next statutory parole hearing for April 1994.

B-J's condition worsened. On May 28, he was transferred to the US Medical Center for Federal Prisoners in Springfield, Missouri, with pneumonia. He was treated with Pentamidine and underwent two blood transfusions. Hospital officials began notifying his friends and relations in June that the end was near. Only his sister, Theodora Letts, and her husband, David, managed to see him in time. David Letts said that when they saw B-J in the hospital he was still conscious, and seemed "at peace."

B-J died on July 2, 1992, at age sixty-seven, from "pneumonia complicating advanced HIV infection," according to the physician, Thomas Jones, who wrote his death summary. His body was shipped to Wisconsin, where he was cremated. His ashes were spread over Cranberry Lake.

Klopfer said recently that he believed B-J would be remembered for his scientific achievements rather than his crimes, but the *New York Times*, which headlined its obit JOHN BUETTNER-JANUSCH, 67, DIES; N.Y.U. PROFESSOR POISONED CANDY, led with his drug and attempted murder convictions. The *Times*, however, did devote a substantial amount of space to his career achievements. The British *Guardian*, under its headline BRILLIANT BUT FLAWED, focused mostly on his criminal convictions.

B-J as a young man on Cranberry Lake in Wisconsin, where his ashes were scattered after his death. COURTESY OF TERESA TRAUSCH

The *Times* reported that he died of pneumonia, without mentioning either HIV or AIDS. It also cited B-J's attorney, William Wachtel, as saying that B-J had been on a hunger strike protesting the parole commission's decision, and that he was being force-fed. B-J was being fed intravenously, true, and he did sometimes try to tear out his feeding tubes—but he was ill, and the hospital was doing what any hospital at the time would do: trying to keep a patient alive. No doubt profoundly depressed at the thought of dying in prison, B-J simply may have wanted to die. Whether that constitutes "a hunger strike" remains unclear.

Richard, Sussman, and Rogers, coauthors of B-J's obituary for the *American Journal of Physical Anthropology*, detailed his scientific accomplishments and only addressed his convictions for drug-making and attempted murder at the very end. The obituary offers some insight into

B-J the man: "Dynamic and colorful, John made a strong impression—sometimes good and sometimes bad—on everyone he met. He was a complicated person, and while we all knew parts of him, none of us knew him completely. Some of his actions in the last years of his life were, and will remain, unfathomable to us. . . . The world is a sadder and duller place without him."

As Richard said many years after the death of this most enigmatic man, "You never can really *know* anyone completely, can you?"

Epilogue

B-J's INTEREST IN AND PASSION FOR LEMURS CONTINUED TO INFLUENCE others, like ripples in a pond, for many years. His collecting of prosimians in the late 1950s and early 1960s while at Yale, his subsequent establishment of the primate facility that became the Duke Lemur Center, and his encouragement of others to study lemurs remain his most lasting legacies. The students and colleagues he inspired in turn spurred others to do research on lemurs.

Alison Jolly, now a visiting senior research fellow at the University of Sussex, returns to Madagascar every year for field research, and a species of mouse lemur, *Microcebus jollyae,* was named in her honor. She has become, after all these years, the Jane Goodall of lemurs.

Alison Richard studied under Jolly at Cambridge in the late 1960s and was persuaded by her to study lemurs in the wild. For more than three decades, she has been engaged in research on the ecology and behavior of the Verreaux's sifaka. Richard, along with Robert Sussman of Washington University and Guy Ramanantsoa of the University of Madagascar, helped establish the Beza Mahafaly Special Reserve in southwestern Madagascar, officially inaugurated in 1985. A native Briton, she had joined the anthropology faculty of Yale in 1972, rising to chair of the department from 1986 to 1990 and becoming provost in 1994. Until recently, she served as the first full-time female vice-chancellor of Cambridge University.

Ian Tattersall, curator emeritus of anthropology at the American Museum of Natural History in New York, has authored many scientific and popular books on human evolution, but he has never lost his love of lemurs. He has written numerous papers on prosimians and has contributed to the World Wildlife Fund's several editions of *Lemurs of Madagascar*. In 1974 he was the first Western scientist to discover and describe a striking lemur, the golden-crowned sifaka, in northern Madagascar. He thought at the time that it was a subspecies, but in 1988 Elwyn Simons identified it as an entirely new species and named it after him, *Propithecus tattersalli*—Tattersall's sifaka.

Peter Klopfer, Duke emeritus professor in biology, has mentored generations of students in the study of prosimians, both at the Duke Lemur Center and in Madagascar. His current research focuses on the sleep and hibernation behavior of the fat-tailed dwarf lemur.

The research of Robert Sussman, professor of physical anthropology at Washington University, ranges widely in the field of primatology, but he continues to conduct a long-term study of the ecology and social organization of ring-tailed lemurs at the Beza Mahafaly Special Reserve in Madagascar.

Elwyn Simons, Duke emeritus professor of evolutionary anthropology, served as director of the Duke University Primate Center from 1977 to 1991 and then as its scientific director until 2001.

As the first official director of the facility, now called the Duke Lemur Center, Simons took advantage of the expanse of the surrounding Duke Forest and created greatly enlarged natural habitat enclosures, ranging in size from one to twenty acres. The first group of brown lemurs was released in August 1981, and a second group of eight ring-tailed lemurs was "set free" in October that year.

Simons devoted himself to conservation in Madagascar as well. Among other projects, he helped lemur scientist and conservationist Patricia Wright to negotiate with the Malagasy government to establish the 100,000-acre Ranomafana National Park in the southeastern part of the island.

Simons was succeeded as director by Ken Glander (1991–2001) who also emphasized conservation, and William Hylander (2001–2005), who reinvigorated the research mission of the center. Anne Yoder, the current director, assumed her post in early 2006.

In 1997, under Glander's guidance, the center for the first time attempted to return several lemurs raised in captivity to the wild in Madagascar, to increase the native population's genetic diversity. Reintroducing captive-bred animals into the wild poses many difficulties, and many such attempts fail. Soon nicknamed "the Carolina Five," the highly endangered black-and-white ruffed lemurs (*Varecia variegata*) were released in the rain forest of the Betampona Reserve in the northeastern part of the island.

In the Wild: Lemurs with John Cleese, a PBS-BBC television documentary, examined their progress several months after their release. The Duke husband-and-wife team of Charles Welch and Andrea Katz tracked the lemurs via radio collars. Cleese learned that one had already died, but happily the other four were thriving.

Two more groups of lemurs were released in 1998 and 2001, some from other institutions, but all went through "boot camp training" in the Duke Forest enclosures. In 2007, ten years after the initial release, three of thirteen lemurs had survived, and at least six known offspring were produced. Increasing the gene pool of endangered lemurs through the reintroduction of captive-bred animals makes for a noble endeavor, but such projects can prove extremely expensive. Conservation currently takes place primarily through captive breeding in the United States and by protecting native habitats in Madagascar.

Current DLC director Yoder said recently that the facility's mission now has three prongs: research, conservation, and education. Fulfilling the last of these, the facility is open to very popular public tours. The DLC now contains the largest collection of prosimians outside Madagascar, with some 250 lemurs, galagos, and lorises, and about 100 individuals on loan to zoos and sanctuaries for exhibition and breeding.

Yoder also supervised the recently completed construction of entirely new facilities. Duke underwrote the building project's $10.4 million price tag, and included new offices and cages that permit the prosimians to move freely indoors and out. In good weather, many of the animals at the center roam in the natural habitat enclosures. At feeding time or in cold weather, staffers stroll down the forest paths banging on a tambourine, calling the lemurs like Pied Pipers. In winter, all of the animals stay in warm and comfortable indoor cages.

The center's grounds have grown from forty acres to eighty-five, the large outdoor runs surrounded by electric fences to keep the lemurs in and predators out. A few animals, such as the ugly yet wonderful aye-aye, always stay indoors, too rare to risk letting them roam freely.

What of the lemurs in Madagascar today? Sadly, political turmoil continues to prevail. The island nation has stagnated in a political crisis since March 2009, when Andry Rajoelina, a former DJ and mayor of the capital, ousted President Marc Ravalomanana with military backing. In September 2011, Madagascar's main political parties signed an agreement that called for elections within a year to end the nation's political crisis. Currently, the election is scheduled for 2013.

In the wake of the coup, most biological research in Madagascar stopped. But the failed state has regained some stability, and scientists have begun returning. Still, amid the chaos, Madagascar's national parks have fallen siege to illegal logging of endangered hardwoods, such as rosewood and ebony, and deforestation has further denuded lemur habitats. No one can say how many lemurs have been killed or died.

Indefatigable scientists continue their research in Madagascar despite the turmoil.

Much of this work surely wouldn't be taking place today if not for John Buettner-Janusch, the mad professor who put Madagascar and its prosimian creatures on the world's scientific and conservationist radar.

Acknowledgments

I FIRST CAME TO THE STRANGE SAGA OF JOHN BUETTNER-JANUSCH through my interest in environmental issues. Several years ago I visited the Duke Lemur Center in Durham, North Carolina, a remarkable institution for the study and conservation of those fascinating prosimians. A while later, I learned about Buettner-Janusch's role in establishing the facility—and, later still, his subsequent rise to chairman of the New York University Anthropology Department and, of course, his precipitous fall. His life story inextricably intertwined his love of lemurs and his exploitation of them as a cover for his drug-making "research." I needed to discover how this happened.

I must begin by thanking my agent, Martha Kaplan, for her support of a book idea steeped in cognitive dissonance: adorable mammals, illegal drugs, and attempted murder. She encouraged me to find a way to tell this story.

Several people helpfully shed light on this most enigmatic man. Teresa Trausch, B-J's niece, provided me with B-J's family history and many early photographs. Fortunately for a biographer, B-J was a prolific correspondent. Several of B-J's friends shared his letters with me, including Sondra Schlesinger, Alison Richard, and Peter Klopfer. Klopfer as well as Esteban Sarmiento and Richard Macris answered my endless queries about events that took place decades earlier.

Many thanks to the staffs of the Yale University Archives, the Duke University Archives, the New York University Archives, the National Archives and Records Administration in New York, and the National

Anthropological Archives, Smithsonian Institution. In particular, I thank NAA archivist Leanda Gahegan, who provided much appreciated assistance in sorting through B-J's correspondence and documents.

I am grateful for the help of many people at Globe Pequot Press, first and foremost my editor, James Jayo. His erudition helped greatly to improve this manuscript and to catch many errors, but he also kept me from straying too far off into the garden of forking paths that was B-J's life. I must also thank Ellen Urban, Meredith Dias, Melissa Hayes, Justin Marciano, Jennifer Renk, and Bret Kerr at Lyons Press.

Finally, my deepest gratitude goes to Ruta Duncia for her grace, patience, and understanding.

Of course, all errors in this book are my own responsibility.

NOTES

Introduction

ix. "I should say this": *United States of America v. John Buettner-Janusch,* sentencing, July 14, 1987.

x. "Madagascar has been isolated": E-mail from Alison Richard, May 15, 2011.

x. Buettner-Janusch was "peremptory": E-mail from Peter Klopfer, April 22, 2012.

1 Origins

1. John was born: Buettner-Janusch birth certificate.

1. Frederick Wilhelm Janusch and Gertrude Clare Buettner: Interview with Teresa Trausch, Buettner-Janusch's niece, April 27, 2011.

1. In the wake of the stock market crash: Ibid.

3. "Go to the Chicago Board of Trade": "Chicago: City of the Century," *American Experience,* PBS, 2004.

4. "Chicago was a town": Mailer, Norman. *Miami and the Siege of Chicago* (New York Review of Books Classics, 2008), p. 79.

4. "In Chicago, they did it straight": Ibid., p. 90.

5. John's father, heavily invested: Buettner-Janusch in pretrial interview with assistant DA Denise Cote, May 22, 1979.

5. The family moved in 1931: E-mail from Teresa Trausch, July 22, 2011.

6. Small-town life has its charms: Interview with Teresa Trausch, April 27, 2011.

6. "a brilliant student": FBI files obtained through the Freedom of Information Act in its 1952 loyalty investigation of B-J. The ensuing quotations about his Nazi leanings are all from FBI interviews at the time.

8. Public school in Eagle River: Eagle River school report cards and high school yearbooks.

8. His early sexual development: FBI, 1952.

10. With World War II raging: University of Chicago transcript.

12. He failed, however, to report: *United States of America v. Johannes Buettner-Janusch,* 1944, court docket.

13. After being released: Buettner-Janusch's movements and activities while on probation are documented by the FBI, 1952.

14. When his probation finally ended: University of Chicago transcript.

15. Washburn, scion of a Boston Brahmin family: Howell, F. Clark, "Sherwood Larned Washburn," *Biographical Memoirs,* Vol. 84, The National Academy Press, 2004, pp. 349–372.

15. The hypothesis has been: See, for example, Cartmill, Matt. *A View to a Death in the Morning: Hunting and Nature Through History* (Harvard University Press, 1996), and Hart, Donna, and Robert W. Sussman, *Man the Hunted* (Westview Press, 2008).

16. Also in the Anthropology Department: Interview with Constance Sutton, October 19, 2011.

16. Vina Mallowitz, yet another PhB candidate: University of Chicago transcript.

18. As he neared completion: FBI, 1952.

19. During the Korean War: Odell, Brig. Gen. J. C. "The New Quartermaster Research & Development Command," *The Quartermaster Review,* July/August 1954.

20. Beginning in September 1953: Correspondence and employment records, University of Utah Archives.

22. He finished his dissertation: University of Michigan transcript.

22. and even took time to teach: Wayne University employment records.

22. Frederick Thieme, who had studied: Kelso, A. J., "Frederick Patton Thieme (1914–1989)," *American Anthropologist,* September 1990, pp. 740–741.

22. On B-J's dissertation committee: Schull, William J. "In Memoriam: James Norman Spuhler (1917–1992)," *American Journal of Physical Anthropology*, 92:113–116 (1993).

23. At the University of Michigan: Interview with Milton and Sondra Schlesinger, January 31, 2011.

2 *Island Ecology*

24. Called the founding father: "Irving Rouse (1913–2006)," *American Anthropologist*, March 2007, pp. 235–237.

24. Murdock spearheaded a team: "George Murdock," *New World Encyclopedia*.

25. Murdock also collected information: Price, David H. *Threatening Anthropology: McCarthyism and the FBI's Surveillance of Activist Anthropologists* (Duke University Press Books, 2004), pp. 70–89.

25. Osgood, a scholar of Arctic and East Asian cultures: "Dr. Cornelius Osgood Dies; Ex-Curator of Yale Museum," *The New York Times*, January 7, 1985.

25. "Yale is very Yale": Buettner-Janusch letter to Andersons, September 16, 1958, John Buettner-Janusch Papers, National Anthropological Archives (NAA), Smithsonian Institution.

26. "The argument about New Haven": "Who Really Ruled in Dahl's New Haven?," G. William Domhoff, WhoRulesAmerica.net, http://sociology.ucsc.edu/whorulesamerica/local/new_haven.html. Accessed October 18, 2012.

27. "If you squinted": Interview with Richard Andrew, June 3, 2011.

27. "It has a genuine working fireplace": Buettner-Janusch letter to Andersons, September 16, 1958, NAA.

27. He appealed to Rouse: "S. Dillon Ripley II; Transformed Smithsonian, Started Magazine," *Los Angeles Times*, March 15, 2001.

27. Ripley wrote to Rouse: Letter from S. Dillon Ripley to Irving Rouse, June 17, 1959, Yale University Archives.

28. On another trip: Transcribed unpublished tape recording, January 13, 1962, NAA.

28. The photographs of chimpanzees: Peterson, Dale. *Jane Goodall: The Woman Who Redefined Man* (Houghton Mifflin Harcourt, 2006), p. 286.

28. Goodall's observations of tool use: Goodall, Jane. "Tool-Using and Aimed Throwing in a Community of Free-Living Chimpanzees," *Nature*, March 28, 1964.

29. "This is supposed to be": Transcribed unpublished tape recording, January 13, 1962, NAA.

29. "I made use of": Leakey, Richard E. *One Life: An Autobiography* (Salem House, 1983), p. 55.

29. A 1957 issue of *Life*: "The Gentle Lemurs," photographed by Loomis Dean, *Life*, August 12, 1957, pp. 51–59.

30. "We made it back safely": Buettner-Janusch letter to Washburn, December 3, 1959, NAA.

30. "Our galagos are doing beautifully": Buettner-Janusch letter to Washburn, December 3, 1959, NAA.

30. "the Island at the End": Jolly, Alison. *Lords and Lemurs: Mad Scientists, Kings with Spears, and Diversity in Madagascar* (Houghton Mifflin, 2004), p. 1.

30. Separated from mainland: Mittermeier, Russell A., et al., *Lemurs of Madagascar* (Conservation International, 2010), p. 19.

30. The island is rich: "Species Report: New Madagascar Species Discovered Weekly; Many Already Endangered," World Wildlife Fund website: www.wwf.mg/ourwork/cssp/species_report. Accessed October 18, 2012.

32. Lemurs were once: Jolly, *Lords and Lemurs*, p. 27.

32. Though it seems: Joyce, Christopher. "Did Madagascar's Menagerie Float From Africa?" NPR website: www.npr.org/templates/story/story.php?storyId=122813054. Accessed October 18, 2012.

32. They range in size: Mittermeier, *Lemurs of Madagascar*, pp. 124, 588.

32. Humans arrived: Godfrey, Laurie. "Isolation and Biodiversity," PBS website, www.pbs.org/edens/madagascar/eden.htm. Accessed October 18, 2012.

32. but in that relatively short time: Mittermeier, *Lemurs of Madagascar,* pp. 1–3.

32. According to Duke: Interview with Anne Yoder, January 6, 2011.

32. "May I announce": Gould, Lisa, and Michelle L. Sauther, eds. *Lemurs: Ecology and Adaptation,* "Notes on the History of Ecological Studies of Malagasy Lemurs," Alison Jolly and R. W. Sussman (Springer, 1996), p. 25.

33. Alfred Grandidier: Obituary, *Nature,* October 27, 1921, p. 286.

33. In more recent times: Gould, *Lemurs: Ecology and Adaptation,* p. 26.

33. announcing that B-J had brought: "Yale Plans Study of 25 Lemurs," *The New York Times,* November 23, 1960.

33. In 1961, British nature documentarian: "David Attenborough's Madagascar," BBC website, www.bbc.co.uk/nature/collections/p00db3n8. Accessed October 18, 2012.

34. He is credited: Sussman, Robert W., Alison F. Richard, and Jeffrey Rogers. "Obituary: John Buettner-Janusch (1924–1992)," *American Journal of Physical Anthropology,* 91: 529–530.

34. "What I am doing": Duffy, Robert. "The World of a Physical Anthropologist," *St. Louis Post-Dispatch,* April 22, 1976.

35. "keen to get into primates": Interview with Richard Andrew, June 3, 2011.

35. "They're early chapters": Interview with Elwyn Simons, January 8, 2011.

35. Also in 1960: Interview with Michael Coe, April 5, 2011.

36. "ebullient and charming": Interview with Richard Andrew, June 3, 2011.

36. Richard Andrew acted: E-mail from Alison Jolly, April 25, 2010.

36. "Basically I took": Interview with Alison Jolly, April 26, 2011.

36. There she kept several: E-mail from Alison Jolly, April 25, 2010.

37. One night, while Bishop: Ibid.

38. a couple of picky eaters: "Yale Zoologist Faces Dietary Problem: Tropical Snacks Lacking for Lemurs," *The New Haven Register*, February 14, 1962.

38. Her doctoral thesis: Interview with Alison Jolly, April 26, 2011.

38. That year, B-J was: Buettner-Janusch CV at Yale.

38. In the spring of 1963: Buettner-Janusch, John. "Trip to Fort Dauphin and Amboasary-Sud," unpublished, undated manuscript from Sondra Schlesinger.

40. the aristocratic de Heaulme family: Jolly, *Lords and Lemurs*, p. 8.

41. "In the end": Ibid.

41. "It was a funny little house": Interview with Alison Jolly, April 26, 2011.

41. "The house had no electric lights": Buettner-Janusch, "Trip to Fort Dauphin and Amboasary-Sud."

41. They were "aristocrats": Jolly, *Lords and Lemurs*, p. 8.

41. He also noted: Buettner-Janusch, "Trip to Fort Dauphin and Amboasary-Sud."

42. The three of them: E-mail from Alison Jolly, April 25, 2010.

42. "We went to stay": Buettner-Janusch, "Trip to Fort Dauphin and Amboasary-Sud."

42. Boggess had come to Madagascar: Interview with Preston Boggess, December 1, 2011.

43. Boggess's own private passion: Ibid.

43. "B-J could be very delightful": Ibid.

43. B-J, who had never been: Interview with Preston Boggess, February 2, 2012.

43. When they all arrived: Interview with Alison Jolly, April 26, 2011.

44. "John and Vina seemed to share": Ibid.

44. "Do not write to me": Undated letter from Buettner-Janusch to Bob Anderson, NAA.

45. "I decided, after much": Buettner-Janusch letter to Washburn, March 21, 1958, NAA.

45. "Being turned down": Showalter, Elaine. *Faculty Towers: The Academic Novel and Its Discontents* (University of Pennsylvania Press, 2005), p. 9.

46. According to B-J, Mintz: Undated letter from Buettner-Janusch to Bob Anderson, NAA.

47. only about a third: Donoghue, Frank. *The Last Professors: The Corporate University and the Fate of the Humanities* (Fordham University Press, 2008), p. 56.

47. "John was very outspoken": Interview with Elwyn Simons, January 8, 2011.

47. "he didn't respect": Interview with Michael Coe, April 5, 2011.

48. "Unfortunately, old Washburn": Undated letter from Buettner-Janusch to Bob Anderson, NAA.

48. The department chair: Undated letter from Buettner-Janusch to Bob Anderson, NAA.

48. "B-J loved animals": Interview with Michael Coe, April 5, 2011.

48. B-J put together: Unpublished proposal, Yale University Archives, G. Evelyn Hutchinson Papers.

49. Hutchinson wrote to experts: Letters dated December 1963 and January 1964, Yale University Archives.

50. A highlight of the: Pamphlet advertising Leakey's lectures, Yale University Archives.

50. A great deal: Seaver, Don. "Primates Are Studied at Duke," *The Rocky Mount* (NC) *Telegram*, October 17, 1965.

50. "I sure am going": Undated letter from Buettner-Janusch to Bob Anderson, NAA.

3 Going South

51. B-J, learning of: E-mail from Peter Klopfer, December 30, 2010.

52. "Our flight that August": Klopfer, Peter H. *Politics and People in Ethology* (Bucknell University Press, 1999), p. 65.

52. "Durham's airport": Ibid.

52. Klopfer recovered: Ibid., p. 69.

52. The battle against: Davidson, Osha Gray. *The Best of Enemies: Race and Redemption in the New South* (University of North Carolina Press, 2007), pp. 98–99.

52. Exactly one week: Ibid., p. 101.

53. A few days later: Ibid., pp. 103–105.

53. Klopfer's conscience: Klopfer, *Politics and People,* pp. 66–67.

53. While other protestors: Ibid., pp. 67–68.

53. Klopfer first met: Interview with Peter Klopfer, October 29, 2009.

53. "When he first asked": Ibid.

54. Klopfer had already: Klopfer, *Politics and People,* pp. 71–72.

54. he and Klopfer: Ibid., p. 78.

54. Moving the roughly: Buettner-Janusch, John. "Origin of the Prosimian Colony, Now the DUPC." The tale of moving the animals from Yale to Duke is in an unpublished memorandum in Peter Klopfer private collection.

54. The cofounders: Klopfer, *Politics and People,* pp. 78–79.

54. National Science Foundation: Seaver, Don. "Man's Cousins Get New Duke Home," *Durham Morning Herald,* June 24, 1968.

55. "In the months": Klopfer, *Politics and People,* pp. 78–79.

55. Workers finally: Seaver, "Man's Cousins Get New Duke Home."

55. During the 1966–67: *Duke Alumni News Register,* December 1970, Duke University Archives.

55. "one of the best books": Interview with Ian Tattersall, March 25, 2010.

56. Tattersall was a grad student: Ibid.

56. "I had the experience": Interview with Ian Tattersall, March 22, 2011.

56. "These creatures probably": Ibid.

56. "The lemurs are": Buettner-Janusch, John. *Origins of Man: Physical Anthropology* (John Wiley & Sons, 1966), p. 223.

57. "Lemurs move with": Ibid., p. 229.

57. "Some anthropologists have written": Ibid., p. 181.

58. "I must agree": Buettner-Janusch, John. Letter to the Editor, *Durham Morning Herald,* July 29, 1967.

59. "I usually tell": Buettner-Janusch, John. *Physical Anthropology: A Perspective* (John Wiley & Sons, 1973), p. 103.

59. "I have been asked": *Chapel Hill Weekly,* October 6, 1965.

59. He did get along: Interview with Alison Richard, January 21, 2011.

59. has fond memories: Interview with Robert Sussman, January 21, 2011.

59. latter's frequent rants: Interview with Alison Richard, January 21, 2011.

59. "The publication of nonbooks": Buettner-Janusch, John. Review of *Primate Ethology,* Desmond Morris, ed., *BioScience,* September 1968, p. 907.

60. serving as associate editor: Sussman, Robert W., Alison F. Richard, and Jeffrey Rogers. "Obituary: John Buettner-Janusch (1924–1992)," *American Journal of Physical Anthropology,* 91:529–530 (1993).

60. "Whenever she burst": Ibid.

60. B-J and Klopfer: Interview with Peter Klopfer, October 29, 2009.

60. went fishing with B-J: E-mail from William Hylander, January 10, 2011.

61. "As for our situation": Buettner-Janusch letter to Aaron Lerner, January 20, 1967, National Anthropological Archives (NAA), Smithsonian Institution.

61. "I shall get out": Buettner-Janusch letter to Michael Coe, December 11, 1968, NAA.

61. "Life in dismal": Buettner-Janusch letter to Harry Berger, October 31, 1968, NAA.

61. Male ring-tails engage: E-mail from Peter Klopfer, February 3, 2011.

62. University of Illinois: Buettner-Janusch letter to Michael Coe, May 21, 1968, NAA.

62. Hunter College: Ibid.

62. City College: Buettner-Janusch letter to Frederick Thieme, April 25, 1969, NAA.

62. "dictatorial powers": Buettner-Janusch letter to Michael Coe, May 21, 1968, NAA.

62. B-J and Vina visited: Buettner-Janusch letter to Jim Anderson, November 7, 1968, NAA.

62. "It is a pleasure": Buettner-Janusch letter to John Middleton, February 19, 1969, NAA.

63. "first-rate person": Buettner-Janusch letter of recommendation to the Department of Health, Education and Welfare, September 23, 1968, NAA.

63. The Aptes and the Buettner-Janusches: E-mail from Judit Katona-Apte, December 15, 2010.

63. Katona-Apte became: Ibid.

63. Once, while her husband: E-mail from Judit Katona-Apte, January 13, 2011.

64. "Both of them": E-mail from Sunita Apte, May 7, 2010.

64. people joked: E-mail from Judit Katona-Apte, December 12, 2010.

64. "an interesting upper-crust": Interview with Matt Cartmill, November 24, 2010.

64. "They shadowed": Interview with Peter Klopfer, November 19, 2010.

64. When they were neighbors: E-mail from Judit Katona-Apte, December 12, 2010.

65. "get on her broomstick": Interview with Elwyn Simons, January 8, 2011.

65. "I hereby submit": Vina Buettner-Janusch letter to John, November 30, 1971, NAA.

65. "B-J would invite": Interview with Peter Klopfer, November 19, 2010.

66. recalled a typical party: Interview with Elwyn Simons, January 8, 2011.

66. Returning from one of his trips: Interview with Peter Klopfer, October 29, 2009.

66. "We fought as often": Ibid.

66. But while in Tel Aviv: E-mail from Peter Klopfer, April 21, 2012.

67. He had a theory: *Chemistry*, October 1968, p. 9.

67. "Buettner-Janusch reasons thus": Ibid.

68. "Despite the fashionable": Buettner-Janusch, John. *Physical Anthropology: A Perspective* (John Wiley & Sons, 1973), p. 511.

68. "The bane of academic": *The* [Duke] *Chronicle*, April 6, 1973.

69. An apocryphal story: Interview with Peter Klopfer, October 29, 2009.

69. "I am leaving Duke": Buettner-Janusch letter to Peter Klopfer, March 19, 1973, NAA.

69. "No one who could": Buettner-Janusch letter to David Arneke, March 14, 1973, NAA.

69. Indeed, he seemed to feel: Buettner-Janusch retold these anecdotes often. See, for instance, Buettner-Janusch letter to Stanley Garn, September 27, 1967, NAA, and letter to "Jim," November 7, 1968, NAA. The recipient of the latter is possibly James Spuhler.

70. but Klopfer visited the site: E-mail from Peter Klopfer, February 11, 2011.

70. "peace negotiations": Interview with Matt Cartmill, November 24, 2010.

70. Wiggins grew up poor: E-mail from Charles Wiggins, February 19, 2011.

4 *Alpha Male*

72. Along with a salary: Raab, Selwyn. "Colleagues Offer View on N.Y.U. Professor in Drug Case," *The New York Times*, November 23, 1979.

72. B-J's apartment: Personal visit to current home of Thomas Nagel and Anne Hollander, May 11, 2011.

72. Inside it featured: Interviews with Teresa Trausch, April 27, 2011; Milton and Sondra Schlesinger, January 31, 2011; and Thomas Beidelman, October 5, 2011.

73. They held lavish parties: Wolfe, Linda. "The Strange Case of Dr. Buettner-Janusch," *New York*, September 15, 1980, p. 20.

73. "Dirty, dangerous, and destitute": For a fascinating photographic portrait of the period, see Allan Tannenbaum, *New York in the '70s* (Overlook TP, 2011).

73. Crime ran rampant: Hamill, Pete. "Our Times: From the 'Me' Decade to the Greed Decade," *New York*, April 4, 1988.

73. the city teetered: Roberts, Sam. "Infamous 'Drop Dead' Was Never Said by Ford," *The New York Times*, December 28, 2006.

73. still the poorest: Kamer, Foster. "The Poorest Congressional District in America? Right Here, in New York City," *Village Voice*, September 30, 2010. http://blogs.villagevoice.com/runninscared/2010/09/the_poorest_con.php. Accessed April 1, 2012.

73. in the postapocalyptic landscape: Flood, Joe. "Why the Bronx Burned," *New York Post*, May 16, 2010.

73. During Game Two: Ibid.

76. "In the early 1970s": Folpe, Emily Kies. *It Happened on Washington Square* (Johns Hopkins University Press, 2002), p. 312.

76. "In 1973, Oscar Newman": Ibid.

76. an eight-month siege: Kerr, Peter. "Crushing the Drug Dealers of Washington Square," *The New York Times*, November 9, 1987.

77. William Hylander interviewed: E-mail from William Hylander, February 9, 2012.

77. In the end: Interview with Lon Alterman, April 19, 2011.

77. found B-J intimidating: Interview with Owen Lynch, October 26, 2011.

78. Then-chairman: E-mail from Clifford Jolly, March 12, 2012.

78. deep misgivings: Interview with Constance Sutton, October 19, 2011.

79. "a truly cultured person": "Charles Miller Leslie, 1923–2009." Madan, T. N. *Contributions to Indian Sociology*, 2010: 44: 395.

79. "He actually hounded": Wolfe, "The Strange Case of Dr. Buettner-Janusch." p. 20.

80. B-J denigrated Leslie: Interview with Owen Lynch, October 26, 2011.

80. One day, he simply strode: Jernow, Allison L. "Drugs and Chocolate," *The Harvard Crimson*, April 23, 1987. Jernow was at the time an undergraduate reporter for the *Crimson*. She earned a law degree at NYU and became a legal adviser to the International Commission of Jurists in Geneva. But her feature story on B-J, after his arrest for the attempted murder of a federal judge, was deeply reported.

80. "I hated him": Ibid.

80. "Pay no attention": Buettner-Janusch letter to friends, January 1, 1980, Alison Richard private collection.

80. B-J went to the dean: Interview with Constance Sutton, October 19, 2011.

80. "I hope that all of you": Buettner-Janusch letter to friends, May 24, 1981, NAA.

80. despite B-J's denials: Buettner-Janusch letter to friends, January 1, 1980, Alison Richard private collection.

81. "But he did it": Interview with Peter Klopfer, October 29, 2009.

81. "Academic chairmen": Wilson, Robin. "Beggar, Psychologist, Mediator, Maid: The Thankless Job," *The Chronicle of Higher Education*, March 2, 2001.

82. heard numerous grievances: Raab, "Colleagues Offer Views on N.Y.U. Professor in Drug Case."

82. "I personally interviewed": Jernow, "Drugs and Chocolate."

82. "Civilization is a process": Cantwell, Anne-Marie, et al., eds., *Aboriginal Ritual and Economy in the Eastern Woodlands: Essays in Memory of Howard Dalton Winters*, "Howard Dalton Winters (1923–1994)," Anne-Marie Cantwell (Illinois State Museum Scientific Papers, 1994), p. 6.

82. Using this definition: Ibid.

83. The author of many campus novels: Edemariam, Aida. "Who's Afraid of the Campus Novel?", *The Guardian*, October 1, 2004.

83. Asked if they were friends: Interview with Thomas Beidelman, October 5, 2011.

84. "very truthful and honest": David Sabatini testimony in *United States of America v. John Buettner-Janusch*, 1980.

84. One of B-J's staunch friends: Interview with Alison Richard, January 21, 2011.

85. "early Beatle": Wolfe, "The Strange Case of Dr. Buettner-Janusch," p. 22.

85. deeply original paper: Jolly, Clifford J. "The Seed-Eaters: A New Model of Hominid Differentiation Based on a Baboon Analogy," *Man*. New Series, Vol. 5, No. 1 (March 1970), pp. 5–26.

85. "a milestone": Leakey, Richard. *The Making of Mankind* (E. P. Dutton, 1991), p. 51.

86. "paradigm shift": Lewin, Roger. *Bones of Contention: Controversies in the Search for Human Origins* (Simon & Schuster: New York), 1987, pp. 98–99.

86. Darwin's theory: Lewin, Roger. *In the Age of Mankind* (Smithsonian Books, 1988), p. 62.

86. Jolly's hypothesis: Lewin, *Bones of Contention*, pp. 98–99.

86. often praising: Interview with Jeffrey Rogers, March 14, 2012.

87. "We got along": E-mail from Clifford Jolly, March 12, 2012.

88. "I was just glad": Interview with Glenn Conroy, February 29, 2012.

88. hailed from a California: Interview with Robert Bettinger, March 12, 2012.

89. but in 1976, the unthinkable: Smith, R. Jeffrey. "Drug-Making Topples Eminent Anthropologist," *Science,* October 17, 1980, p. 299.

89. the NSF had conspired: Wolfe, "The Strange Case of Dr. Buettner-Janusch," p. 21.

90. called B-J's suspicions: Ibid.

90. "It was because": Interview with Lon Alterman, April 19, 2011.

90. "I was stunned": James, Laura. "The Very Nutty Professor," Clews blog. Comment by John Paulius, http://laurajames.typepad.com/clews/2005/08/the_very_nutty_.html. Accessed November 1, 2012.

91. An interesting portrait: Blunt, Sandra. "An Odd, Brilliant Professor, Long Forgotten, Is Remembered," *The New York Times,* August 23, 1987.

92. B-J often boasted: Smith, "Drug-Making Topples Eminent Anthropologist," p. 299.

92. *Sunrise Semester:* NYU website, "175 Facts about NYU," www.nyu.edu/library/bobst/research/arch/175/pages/sunrise.htm. Accessed November 1, 2012.

92. 1863 collection of essays: Huxley, Thomas H. *Man's Place in Nature* (Modern Library, 2001).

92. The course provided: Video from private collection of Robert Sussman.

92. Greatly annoyed: Interview with Owen Lynch, October 26, 2011.

93. B-J, incensed: Interview with Thomas Beidelman, October 5, 2011.

93. a diagnosis: Cartmill, Matt. "Deaths," *Anthropology Newsletter,* September 1992, p. 4.

93. B-J called William Hylander: E-mail from William Hylander, September 27, 2011.

93. at the CBS studio: Interview with Glenn Conroy, February 29, 2012.

93. She died on October 6: Vina Buettner-Janusch death certificate.

93. Her remains were cremated: E-mail from Teresa Trausch, August 10, 2011.

93. A brief obituary: "Mrs. Buettner-Janusch," *Durham Morning Herald,* October 12, 1977.

93. "in the dumps": Interview with William Hylander, November 23, 2010.

94. noted how matter-of-factly: Interview with Richard Macris, March 16, 2011.

94. also found it surprising: Interview with Owen Lynch, October 26, 2011.

94. The risk factors: "What You Need to Know about Liver Cancer," National Cancer Institute website, www.cancer.gov/cancertopics/wyntk/liver/page4. Accessed November 1, 2012.

94. During Christmas break: Buettner-Janusch deposition given to assistant DA Denise Cote, May 22, 1979.

5 The Tangled Web

95. "a steadying influence": Jernow, Allison L. "Drugs and Chocolate," The Harvard Crimson, April 23, 1987.

96. "flamboyant and tasteless": E-mail from Esteban Sarmiento, May 9, 2011.

96. a faculty photo: Duke University Archives.

96. leather jacket and boots: Interview with Thomas Beidelman, October 5, 2011.

96. Greek fishing cap: Interview with Lon Alterman, April 19, 2011.

96. fashion faux pas: Interview with Michael Coe, April 5, 2011.

97. "it did seem to make sense": Interview with Ian Tattersall, March 22, 2011.

97. "I think he was": Interview with Thomas Beidelman, October 5, 2011.

97. "He came out": Interview with Lon Alterman, April 19, 2011.

97. after the professor's indictment: Interview with Esteban Sarmiento, May 5, 2011.

97. boxes of amyl nitrite: Interview with Richard Macris, March 16, 2011.

97. "Colonel B-J's Poppers": Interview with Lon Alterman, April 19, 2011.

97. B-J considered: *United States of America v. John Buettner-Janusch,* 1980. Tape recording of a telephone conversation between Danny Cornyetz and John Buettner-Janusch, June 27, 1979, entered as evidence.

97. index cards: Interview with Lon Alterman, April 19, 2011.

98. "a secret legion": Clendinen, Dudley, and Adam Nagourney. *Out for Good* (Simon & Schuster, 1999), p. 12.

98. "the lives of millions": Ibid.

99. "Just about anyone": Buettner-Janusch deposition given to assistant DA Denise Cote, May 22, 1979.

99. an anthro grad student: Interview with Danny Cornyetz, March 20, 2010.

99. He occasionally napped: Testimony of Danny Cornyetz, *United States of America v. John Buettner-Janusch,* 1980.

99. middle-class family: E-mail from Richard Macris, March 23, 2012.

100. He began working: Testimony of Richard Macris, *United States of America v. John Buettner-Janusch,* 1980.

100. father was a stockbroker: E-mail from Richard Macris, March 23, 2012.

100. submitted a requisition: *United States of America v. John Buettner-Janusch,* Grand Jury Indictment filed on October 3, 1979, in the US District Court, Southern District of New York.

101. A book checked out: Testimony of Patricia Karatsis Berman, *United States of America v. John Buettner-Janusch,* 1980.

101. B-J ordered: *United States of America v. John Buettner-Janusch,* Grand Jury Indictment filed on October 3, 1979, in the US District Court, Southern District of New York.

101. Jolly said that: Testimony of Clifford Jolly, *United States of America v. John Buettner-Janusch,* 1980.

101. "it was possible": Testimony of Lisa Forman, *United States of America v. John Buettner-Janusch,* 1980.

101. "money was money": Testimony of Richard Dorfman, *United States of America v. John Buettner-Janusch,* 1980.

101. "You are as amoral": Testimony of Danny Cornyetz, *United States of America v. John Buettner-Janusch,* 1980.

102. LSD, first synthesized in 1938: Hofmann, Albert. *LSD: My Problem Child* (MAPS, 2009), p. 44.

102. "were weakly or not": Ibid., p. 60.

102. therapeutic use of LSD: Ibid., pp. 63–78.

102. which Sandoz offered: "LSD: The Drug," US Department of Justice, DEA, website: http://web.petabox.bibalex.org/web/20011116091659/ www.usdoj.gov/dea/pubs/lsd/lsd-4.htm. Accessed November 10, 2012.

103. "This joy": Hofmann, *LSD,* p. 79.

103. Schedule I drug: "Code of Federal Regulations: Schedule I," US Department of Justice website, Drug Enforcement Agency: www.dea diversion.usdoj.gov/21cfr/cfr/1308/1308_11.htm. Accessed November 10, 2012.

103. "Substances in this schedule": "Controlled Substance Schedules," Drug Enforcement Agency, Office of Diversion Control website, www.dea diversion.usdoj.gov/schedules/index.html. Accessed November 12, 2012.

103. In recent years, clinical studies: See Stix, Gary. "Return of a Problem Child," *Scientific American,* October 2009.

103. "one of its purposes": *United States of America v John Buettner-Janusch,* Grand Jury Indictment filed on October 3, 1979, in the United States District Court, Southern District.

103. "corporation is to be formed": Grand jury deposition by Martin Marion in *United States of America v. John Buettner-Janusch,* 1979.

104. which opened in 1936: "Staten Island Zoo," NYC-Arts: The Complete Guide website, www.nyc-arts.org/organizations/1841/staten-island-zoo. Accessed April 4, 2012.

104. "to launder money": prosecuting attorney Roanne Mann's opening statement in *United States of America v. John Buettner-Janusch,* 1979.

104. starting a nonprofit: Testimony of Martin Marion, *United States of America v. Bruce P. Greenfield and Mark Schwartz*, 1984.

104. an extremely endangered: "*Macaca silenus*," IUCN Red List website, www.iucnredlist.org/apps/redlist/details/12559/0. Accessed November 10, 2012.

104. They first approached: Testimony of Martin Marion, *United States of America v. Bruce P. Greenfield and Mark Schwartz*, 1984.

105. nonprofit never succeeded: Ibid.

105. had been arrested: Ibid.

105. "irresolvable personality differences": Ibid.

105. growing coldness: Ibid.

105. was completing a prospectus: Testimony of Patricia Pronger, *United States of America v. John Buettner-Janusch*, 1979.

105. "rich old ladies": John Buettner-Janusch deposition given to assistant DA Denise Cote, May 22, 1979.

105. didn't do a particularly good job: E-mail from Clifford Jolly, April 7, 2012.

105. Greenfield, like Cornyetz: E-mail from Lisa Forman, May 4, 2012.

106. Greenfield sometimes worked: Interview with Richard Macris, January 29, 2011.

106. "Claims that LSD": Hofmann, *LSD*, p. 93.

106. "The laboratory was": E-mail from Richard Macris, April 14, 2012.

106. "In order to isolate": Hofmann, *LSD*, p. 93.

107. "an extremely potent": Fox, Margolit. "Owsley Stanley, Artisan of Acid, Is Dead at 76," *The New York Times*, March 14, 2011.

107. "He also explained": Testimony of Richard Dorfman, *United States of America v. John Buettner-Janusch*, 1980.

107. Marion denied: Grand jury deposition by Martin Marion in *United States of America v. John Buettner-Janusch*, 1979.

107. but the three of them: Testimony of Richard Dorfman, *United States of America v. John Buettner-Janusch*, 1980.

107. Jolly didn't recall: E-mail from Clifford Jolly, April 7, 2012.

108. She committed an act: Testimony of Patricia Karatsis Berman, *United States of America v. John Buettner-Janusch*, 1980.

108. "took about eighteen months": Buettner-Janusch deposition given to assistant DA Denise Cote, May 22, 1979.

108. B-J came up three or four: Testimony of Lisa Forman, *United States of America v. John Buettner-Janusch*, 1980.

108. worked in the lab at night: Testimony of Richard Macris, *United States of America v. John Buettner-Janusch*, 1980.

108. Forman observed chemicals: Testimony of Lisa Forman, *United States of America v. John Buettner-Janusch*, 1980.

109. A few days after: Testimony of Richard Macris, *United States of America v. John Buettner-Janusch*, 1980.

109. "I liked the guy": Interview with Richard Macris, January 29, 2011.

109. Macris visited Jolly: Testimony of Richard Macris, *United States of America v. John Buettner-Janusch*, 1980.

109. "He was convinced": Interview with Richard Macris, January 29, 2011.

109. they shared a love: E-mail from Richard Macris, April 14, 2012.

109. The two of them: Interview with Lisa Forman, June 9, 2011

110. Cornyetz, playing: Testimony of Richard Macris, *United States of America v. John Buettner-Janusch*, 1980.

110. Curiously, B-J only: Testimony of Richard Macris, *United States of America v. John Buettner-Janusch*, 1980.

110. "too straight": Testimony of Danny Cornyetz, *United States of America v. John Buettner-Janusch*, 1980.

110. Macris continued working: Interview with Richard Macris, January 29, 2011.

110. "I was indignant": Ibid.

111. "What about your lemurs?": Testimony of Richard Macris, *United States of America v. John Buettner-Janusch*, 1980.

111. By the early 1970s: "Luding Out," *The Journal of the American Medical Association*, Darryl S. Inaba, George R. Gay, John A. Newmeyer, Craig Whitehead, June 11, 1973, pp. 1505–1509.

111. "luding out": "The Quaalude Lesson," *Frontline*, PBS.org, www.pbs .org/wgbh/pages/frontline/meth/faqs/quaaludes.html. Accessed November 12, 2012.

111. methaqualone abuse: "1980–1985," US Drug Enforcement Agency website, www.justice.gov/dea/pubs/history/deahistory_03.htm. Accessed November 12, 2012.

111. second most popular: "The Quaalude Lesson," *Frontline*.

112. Jolly began his own: Smith, R. Jeffrey. "Drug-Making Topples Eminent Anthropologist," *Science*, October 17, 1980, p. 298.

112. "I wouldn't call what I did": Raab, Selwyn. "Professor Sparked N.Y.U. Drug Charges," *The New York Times*, April 16, 1980.

112. Macris told his brother: Testimony of Richard Macris, pretrial hearings, *United States of America v. John Buettner-Janusch*, 1979.

112. He officially stopped: *United States of America v. John Buettner-Janusch*, 1980. Transcript of taped conversation between Richard Macris and John Buettner-Janusch, May 23, 1979.

112. Boyle got hold: Testimony of Edward Boyle, pretrial hearings, *United States of America v. John Buettner-Janusch*, 1979.

113. " 'I have good news' ": Ibid.

113. The university's 1974–75 budget: Fiske, Edward B. "Miracle of Washington Square," *The New York Times*, April 30, 1978.

113. asked in a headline: Brown, Stanley H. "Anybody Here Want to Be President of NYU?" *New York*, April 14, 1975.

113. Sawhill had expertly balanced: Fiske, "Miracle of Washington Square."

113. young, somewhat ascetic: Ibid.

113. Macris's brother Robert: Interview with Richard Macris, January 29, 2011.

113. Macris and Jolly were ushered: Ibid.

114. Later that afternoon: Ibid.

114. Schaffer thought: *United States of America v. John Buettner-Janusch*, US Court of Appeals, 2nd Circuit, summary of evidence, April 6, 1981.

114. Macris took the subway: Interview with Richard Macris, January 29, 2011.

114. Jolly went first: Testimony of Clifford Jolly, *United States of America v. John Buettner-Janusch*, 1980.

114. Jolly and Macris directed the agents: *United States of America v. John Buettner-Janusch*, US Court of Appeals, 2nd Circuit, summary of evidence, April 6, 1981.

114. The only actual LSD: Testimony of Jeffrey Weber, *United States of America v. John Buettner-Janusch*, 1980.

115. Only Jolly and the lab assistants: Interview with Richard Macris, January 29, 2011.

115. DEA Special Agent Toal arrived: Testimony of Jack Toal, *United States of America v. Bruce P. Greenfield and Mark Schwartz*, 1984.

115. "Could you just refrain": Transcript of deposition given by Buettner-Janusch to assistant DA Denise Cote, May 22, 1979.

115. "Witness flipped papers": Ibid.

116. "In the last three": Ibid.

117. "discussed this in generalities": Transcript of deposition given by Buettner-Janusch to assistant DA Denise Cote, May 22, 1979.

117. recalled no such conversations: Interview with Elwyn Simons, January 8, 2011.

117. he told Amorosa: Deposition given by Buettner-Janusch to assistant DA Dominic Amorosa, June 14, 1979.

118. "false, fictitious": *United States of America v. John Buettner-Janusch*, Grand Jury Indictment filed on October 3, 1979, in the US District Court, Southern District.

118. "As far as I know": E-mail from Cliff Jolly, April 7, 2012.

119. "I never heard B-J": Ibid.

119. "very unusual to set up": Ibid.

119. Amorosa pummeled B-J: Deposition given by Buettner-Janusch to assistant DA Dominic Amorosa, June 14, 1979.

120. "Everyone in the field": E-mail from Peter Klopfer, April 22, 2012.

120. he had never intended: Deposition given by Buettner-Janusch to assistant DA Dominic Amorosa, June 14, 1979.

120. ranging in purity: *United States of America v. John Buettner-Janusch,* Grand Jury Indictment filed on October 3, 1979, in the US District Court, Southern District.

120. Sarmiento hailed from: E-mail from Esteban Sarmiento, April 24, 2012.

121. There he had studied: Interview with Jeffrey Rogers, March 14, 2012.

122. "People have different": E-mail from Esteban Sarmiento, April 30, 2012.

122. B-J would talk for a while: E-mail from Esteban Sarmiento, May 9, 2012.

122. When Rogers first arrived: Interview with Jeffrey Rogers, March 14, 2012.

124. Richard made some: Smith, R. Jeffrey. "Drug-Making Topples Eminent Anthropologist," *Science,* October 17, 1980, pp. 298–299.

124. But Jolly knew Richard: E-mail from Clifford Jolly, April 11, 2012.

124. Rogers was subpoenaed: Interview with Jeffrey Rogers, March 14, 2012.

124. Soon, others got into the act: *United States of America v. John Buettner-Janusch,* 1980. Transcripts of taped conversations entered into evidence.

125. On May 22, Macris called: *United States of America v. John Buettner-Janusch,* 1980. Transcript of taped conversation between Richard Macris and Danny Cornyetz, May 22, 1979.

126. Over the course: *United States of America v. John Buettner-Janusch,* 1980. Transcript of taped conversation between Buettner-Janusch and Richard Macris, May 23, 1979.

127. Macris and B-J met again: *United States of America v. John Buettner-Janusch*, 1980. Transcript of taped conversation between Buettner-Janusch and Richard Macris, June 1, 1979.

127. Nat Laurendi: Nat Laurendi CV.

127. Cornyetz fetch him: Testimony of Danny Cornyetz, *United States of America v. John Buettner-Janusch*, 1980.

128. Macris, pretending concern: *United States of America v. John Buettner-Janusch*, 1980. Transcript of taped conversation between Buettner-Janusch and Richard Macris, June 1, 1979.

129. imagined the whole affair: Testimony of Lisa Forman, *United States of America v. John Buettner-Janusch*, 1980.

129. "beat any charges": *United States of America v. John Buettner-Janusch*, 1980. Transcript of taped conversation between Buettner-Janusch and Richard Macris, June 1, 1979.

129. substantial funding for research: *United States of America v. John Buettner-Janusch*, 1980. Transcript of taped conversation between Buettner-Janusch and Clifford Jolly, May 20, 1979.

129. "there's an enemy": *United States of America v. John Buettner-Janusch*, 1980. Transcript of taped conversation between Buettner-Janusch and Clifford Jolly, June 10, 1979.

129. It was a beautiful day: *United States of America v. John Buettner-Janusch*, 1980. Transcript of taped conversation among Richard Macris, Danny Cornyetz, and Lisa Forman, June 5, 1979.

130. Later at Rufus D. Smith Hall: *United States of America v. John Buettner-Janusch*, 1980. Transcript of taped conversation among Buettner-Janusch, Richard Macris, and Danny Cornyetz, June 5, 1979.

130. "I believe what he says": Ibid.

130. the day after graduation: *United States of America v. John Buettner-Janusch*, 1980. Transcript of taped conversation between Richard Macris and Danny Cornyetz, June 8, 1979.

131. quite skilled: *United States of America v. John Buettner-Janusch*, 1980. Transcript of taped conversation between Buettner-Janusch and Danny Cornyetz, July 2, 1979.

131. Greenfield was putting: Testimony of Richard Macris, *United States of America v. John Buettner-Janusch*, 1980.

132. to help him tape: Testimony of Danny Cornyetz, *United States of America v. John Buettner-Janusch*, 1980.

132. charged with lying: Ibid.

132. Indeed, the anxiety of: *United States of America v. John Buettner-Janusch*, 1980. Transcript of taped conversation between Richard Macris and Danny Cornyetz, June 8, 1979.

132. More than a rock venue: Blanks, Tim. "Mudd Quake," *The New York Times Magazine*, February 25, 2001.

133. Cornyetz wasn't a fan: Interview with Danny Cornyetz, March 20, 2010.

133. Without the prodding: Raab, Selwyn. "Professor Sparked N.Y.U. Drug Charges," *The New York Times*, April 16, 1980.

133. made him vulnerable: Smith, R. Jeffrey. "Drug-Making Topples Eminent Anthropologist," *Science*, October 17, 1980, p. 298.

133. "Something is going": Interview with Thomas Beidelman, October 5, 2011.

133. indicted on six counts: *United States of America v. John Buettner-Janusch*, Grand Jury Indictment filed on October 3, 1979, in the US District Court, Southern District.

135. At his arraignment: Lubasch, Arnold H. "Indictment Charges Professor Used N.Y.U. Laboratory to Make Drugs," *The New York Times*, October 5, 1979.

135. "an egregious abuse of trust": Ibid.

135. headline screamed: Smilon, Marvin. "Charge Famed Prof Ran NYU Drug Factory," *The New York Post*, October 5, 1979.

135. "his associates called": "NYU Professor Arrested on Drug-Making Charges," Associated Press, October 6, 1979.

135. "Something quite horrible": Buettner-Janusch photocopied letter to friends, December 1979, Alison Richard private collection.

136. "In his role": *United States of America v. John Buettner-Janusch,* Grand Jury Indictment filed on October 3, 1979, in the US District Court, Southern District.

136. university had cooperated: Lubasch, "Indictment Charges Professor Used N.Y.U. Laboratory to Make Drugs."

136. "he is an eminent": Bird, David. "N.Y.U. Is Reviewing Position of Professor Named in Drug Case," *The New York Times,* October 6, 1979.

137. continued to teach: Raab, Selwyn. "Colleagues Offer Views on N.Y.U. Professor in Drug Case," *The New York Times,* November 23, 1979.

137. ad hoc defense fund: Smith, "Drug-Making Topples Eminent Anthropologist," p. 296.

137. sources of donations: Buettner-Janusch letter to Michael Coe, November 28, 1979, Alison Richard private collection.

137. legal expenses: Interview with Milton and Sondra Schlesinger, January 31, 2011.

137. major issues: *United States of America v. John Buettner-Janusch,* Circuit Court of Appeals decision, April 6, 1981.

138. $5,000 a week: Buettner-Janusch photocopied letter to friends, May 24, 1980, Alison Richard private collection.

138. "a slut": Buettner-Janusch letter to Alison Richard and Robert Dewar, February 6, 1980, Alison Richard private collection.

138. "a fascist whore," "a Nazi whore": Buettner-Janusch photocopied letter to friends, May 24, 1980, Alison Richard private collection.

138. "the bitch" and a "foul insane fiend": Buettner-Janusch letter to Michael Coe, October 21, 1979, Alison Richard private collection.

138. "a fascist pig": Buettner-Janusch letter to Alison Richard and Robert Dewar, February 6, 1980, Alison Richard private collection.

138. "a lunatic": Buettner-Janusch letter to Alison Richard, undated, Alison Richard private collection.

138. "the worm and the jackal": Buettner-Janusch photocopied letter to friends, May 24, 1980, Alison Richard private collection.

138. letters were so crazy: Interview with Michael Coe, April 5, 2011.

138. "I shall certainly drive": Buettner-Janusch letter to Alison Richard and Robert Dewar, February 29, 1980, Alison Richard private collection.

138. "grand denouement": Buettner-Janusch letter to Alison Richard and Robert Dewar, April 11, 1980, Alison Richard private collection.

138. "seeing a shrink": Buettner-Janusch letter to Alison Richard and Robert Dewar, February 29, 1980, Alison Richard private collection.

6 Above Suspicion

140. ten a.m. on June 30: All of the testimony, quoted or paraphrased, comes from the transcript of *United States of America v. John Buettner-Janusch*, 1980. All evidence cited is from the trial as well.

140. "malaise" speech: Mattson, Kevin. *"What the Heck Are You Up To, Mr. President?": Jimmy Carter, America's "Malaise," and the Speech that Should Have Changed the Country* (Bloomsbury USA, 2010), p. xiii.

140. Iranian hostage crisis: Lewis, Paul. "Richard I. Queen, 51, Hostage Freed Early by Iranians in '80," *The New York Times,* August 21, 2002.

141. firefighter and police unions: Fox, Margalit. "Edward Silver, Who Led Police Review Panel, Dies at 83," *The New York Times,* October 3, 2004.

141. ran a four-page: Smith, R. Jeffrey. "Drug-Making Topples Eminent Anthropologist," *Science,* October 17, 1980, pp. 296–299.

141. "a stern presence": Hevesi, Dennis. "Charles L. Brieant Jr., Longtime Federal Judge, Is Dead at 85," *The New York Times,* July 27, 2008.

142. At twenty-nine, just a few years: Wolfe, Linda. "The Strange Case of Dr. Buettner-Janusch," *New York,* September 15, 1980, p. 21.

142. pin-striped chief counsel: "Jules Ritholz, 68, Dies; New York Tax Lawyer," *The New York Times,* September 16, 1993.

143. He described the trial: Buettner-Janusch photocopied letter to friends, May 24, 1980, Alison Richard private collection.

143. "Sentence first": Carroll, Lewis. Martin Gardner, ed. *The Annotated Alice: The Definitive Edition* (W. W. Norton, 1999), p. 124.

143. "Someone must have been": Kafka, Franz. Mike Mitchell, trans. (Oxford University Press, 2009), p. 5.

144. "a mystery figure": Raab, Selwyn. "Drug Trial of Professor at N.Y.U. Nearing Conclusion," *The New York Times,* July 12, 1980.

144. *LSD: A Total Study,* edited by: Sankar, D. V. Siva, ed. *LSD: A Total Study* (PJD Publications, 1975).

145. described the process: US Patent 2,438, 259, Albert Hofmann and Arthur Stoll, March 23, 1948.

145. "The use of LSD": Sankar, D. V. Siva. *LSD: A Total Study* (PJD Publications, 1975), p. 12.

147. could have produced: Smith, "Drug-Making Topples Eminent Anthropologist," p. 299.

149. NYU soon fired him: Wolfe, "The Strange Case of Dr. Buettner-Janusch," p. 22.

151. his boss could be generous: Interview with Danny Cornyetz, March 20, 2010.

153. Macris was certain: Interview with Richard Macris, January 29, 2011.

154. "We both felt": E-mail from Richard Macris, March 22, 2011.

154. "I did ask what": Smith, "Drug-Making Topples Eminent Anthropologist," p. 298.

157. "John was innocent": Interview with Michael Coe, April 5, 2011.

158. US Air Force researchers: Whitney, G. D., and G. M. Deavours. "Effect of Methaqualone on Behavior of the Chimpanzee," Technical Report, Aeromedical Research Lab (6571st) Holloman AFB NM, July 1968.

158. Vick liked B-J: Interview with Laura Vick, May 18, 2012.

159. "You can take": Ibid.

159. Called to testify: Ibid.

160. Vick said later: Ibid.

161. testimony had "saved" B-J: Interview with Peter Klopfer, October 29, 2009.

161. B-J had called Klopfer: Ibid.

161. B-J himself appeared: Ibid.

163. B-J personally called him: Interview with Elwyn Simons, January 8, 2011.

163. Simons had had an accident: Ibid.

164. "drugs to lemurs": Ibid.

164. after four and a half hours: Smith, "Drug-Making Topples Eminent Anthropologist," p. 297.

164. maximum sentence: Lubasch, Arnold H. "N.Y.U. Professor Guilty of Illegal Drug-Making," *The New York Times*. July 17, 1980.

7 *Punishment and Crime*

165. The *Times* reported: Lubasch, Arnold H. "N.Y.U. Professor Guilty of Illegal Drug-Making," *The New York Times*, July 17, 1980.

165. its cover story: Wolfe, Linda. "The Strange Case of Dr. Buettner-Janusch," *New York*, September 15, 1980.

165. detailed feature: Smith, R. Jeffrey. "Drug-Making Topples Eminent Anthropologist," *Science*, October 17, 1980.

166. written just two days: Buettner-Janusch photocopied letter to friends, July 18, 1980, Alison Richard private collection.

166. poignant and eloquent: Defense attorney Jules Ritholz reading Matt Cartmill letter, *United States of America v. John Buettner-Janusch*, 1980, sentencing hearing, November 14, 1980.

167. Macris, who had: Interview with Richard Macris, January 29, 2011.

167. Cornyetz got probation: Interview with Danny Cornyetz, March 20, 2010.

167. Dorfman received: Testimony of Richard Dorfman, *United States of America v. Bruce P. Greenfield and Mark Schwartz,* 1984.

167. Greenfield was tried: *United States of America v. Bruce P. Greenfield and Mark Schwartz,* 1984.

167. Forman, however: Interview with Lisa Forman, June 9, 2011.

167. "B-J has some chance": Smith, "Drug-Making Topples Eminent Anthropologist," pp. 298–299.

168. "All I know": Jernow, Allison L. "Drugs and Chocolate," *The Harvard Crimson,* April 23, 1987.

168. the risk involved: E-mail from Clifford Jolly, March 13, 2012.

169. "Ladies and gentlemen": Roanne Mann summation, *United States of America v. John Buettner-Janusch,* 1980.

169. At B-J's sentencing: Jules Ritholz, sentencing hearing, November 13, 1980, *United States of America v. John Buettner-Janusch,* 1980.

170. very detailed proposal: Notice of Motion from defense, January 26, 1981, *United States of America v. John Buettner-Janusch,* 1980.

170. In Judge Brieant's verdict: Judge Charles Brieant, sentencing hearing, November 13, 1980, *United States of America v. John Buettner-Janusch,* 1980.

171. Judge Brieant sentenced: "Professor Gets 5 Years in Drug Case," *The New York Times,* November 14, 1980.

171. working on an appeal: *United States of America v. John Buettner-Janusch,* 1980, US Court of Appeals, 2nd Circuit, argued March 5, 1981.

171. drips with sadness: Buettner-Janusch photocopied letter to friends, March 1981, Alison Richard private collection.

172. B-J's appeal was rejected: *United States of America v. John Buettner-Janusch,* 1980, US Court of Appeals, 2nd Circuit, decided, April 6, 1981.

173. The government had: US District Court, Southern District of New York, order, May 18, 1981.

173. emergency request: "Marshall Refuses to Block Case," Associated Press, May 21, 1981.

173. B-J's housekeeper: Interview with Thomas Olivier, October 17, 2011.

173. "I think I might not": Buettner-Janusch letter to Alison Richard, July 8, 1981, Alison Richard private collection.

173. during Olivier's visit: Interview with Thomas Olivier, October 17, 2011.

174. "That was the first": Interview with Lon Alterman, April 19, 2011.

174. Nearly everything: Interview with Milton and Sondra Schlesinger, January 31, 2011.

174. "It was like": Interview with Thomas Nagel and Anne Hollander, May 11, 2011.

175. incredibly biodiverse: "Eglin's Animal Hosts," *Airman* website, August 2004, http://web.archive.org/web/20050501193741/www.af.mil/news/airman/0804/eglinsb1.shtml. Accessed November 12, 2012.

175. "There are many": Buettner-Janusch letter to Alison Richard, July 8, 1981, Alison Richard private collection.

175. Other Eglin alums: Salter, Chuck. "From the Penthouse to the Big House," *Fast Company* website, www.fastcompany.com/45262/penthouse-big-house. Accessed November 10, 2012.

176. slave labor camp: Buettner-Janusch letter to Alison Richard, July 8, 1981, Alison Richard private collection.

176. As a newbie: Buettner-Janusch letter to Bob and Alma Anderson, June 21, 1981, John Buettner-Janusch Papers, National Anthropological Archives (NAA), Smithsonian Institution.

176. He moved to an: Ibid.

176. B-J began working: Buettner-Janusch letter to Alison Richard and Robert Dewar, September 20, 1981, Alison Richard private collection.

177. "Many of the men": Buettner-Janusch letter to Alison Richard and Robert Dewar, January 17, 1983, Alison Richard private collection.

177. "I got a call": Buettner-Janusch letter to Alison Richard, July 8, 1981, Alison Richard private collection.

178. "The head case manager": Buettner-Janusch letter to Alison Richard and Robert Dewar, January 17, 1983, Alison Richard private collection.

178. Supreme Court declined: "Anthropologist's Conviction Left Intact," Associated Press, October 5, 1981.

178. presumptive release date: *United States of America v. John Buettner-Janusch*, 1980, Memorandum and Order, Judge Charles Brieant, March 19, 1982.

178. The defense had learned: *United States of America v. John Buettner-Janusch*, 1980, Notice of Motion, defense attorney William Wachtel, January 26, 1982.

179. B-J read every page: Interview with Alison Richard, January 21, 2011.

179. "The next manuscript": Buettner-Janusch letter to Alison Richard and Robert Dewar, December 20, 1982, Alison Richard private collection.

179. one of the strangest: Interview with Thomas Olivier, October 17, 2011.

180. He complained to Richard: Buettner-Janusch letter to Alison Richard and Robert Dewar, June 28, 1983, Alison Richard private collection.

180. Once he brought him: Interview with Thomas Olivier, October 17, 2011.

180. "He had a lot of trouble": Interview with Robert Dewar, January 21, 2011.

180. "If I survive": Buettner-Janusch letter to Alison Richard, July 8, 1981, Alison Richard private collection.

181. "change the tradition": Buettner-Janusch letter to Alison Richard and Robert Dewar, August 30, 1983, Alison Richard private collection.

181. He had gained: Ibid.

181. a quarter-million: Buettner-Janusch letter to Alison Richard and Robert Dewar, December 20, 1982, Alison Richard private collection.

181. gave him $40: Buettner-Janusch letter to Alison Richard and Robert Dewar, June 28, 1983, Alison Richard private collection.

181. halfway house: Buettner-Janusch letter to Alison Richard and Robert Dewar, August 30, 1983, Alison Richard private collection.

181. Lon Alterman picked him up: Interview with Lon Alterman, April 19, 2011.

182. B-J praised: Buettner-Janusch photocopied letter to friends, August 18, 1984, John Buettner-Janusch Papers, NAA.

182. legendary Chelsea Hotel: Buettner-Janusch letter to Alison Richard and Robert Dewar, November 29, 1983, Alison Richard private collection.

182. frequent dinner guest: Interview with Ian Tattersall, March 22, 2011.

183. "We tried to take care": Ibid.

183. honorary research associate: Ibid.

183. "We would never": Interview with Ian Tattersall, May 17, 2011.

183. Two men were charged: "U.S. Says 2 Made Drugs at N.Y.U.," *The New York Times* (AP), May 25, 1984.

184. They were indicted: *United States of America v. Bruce P. Greenfield and Mark Schwartz,* 1984, Grand Jury indictment, May 15, 1984.

184. released the pair: "U.S. Says 2 Made Drugs at N.Y.U."

184. grand jury charged: *United States of America v. Bruce P. Greenfield and Mark Schwartz,* 1984, Grand Jury indictment, May 15, 1984.

184. offered the reasons: *United States of America v. Bruce P. Greenfield and Mark Schwartz,* 1984, Roanne Mann affidavit, July 23, 1984.

185. November 5, 1984: *United States of America v. Bruce P. Greenfield and Mark Schwartz,* 1984.

186. He had received immunity: Testimony of Stephen Lichtman, *United States of America v. Bruce P. Greenfield and Mark Schwartz,* 1984.

186. Lichtman's sad tale: Ibid.

187. Lichtman was high: attorney Michael Washor at bench speaking to Judge Whitman Knapp, *United States of America v. Bruce P. Greenfield and Mark Schwartz,* 1984.

187. "He's not the most": Judge Whitman Knapp, *United States of America v. Bruce P. Greenfield and Mark Schwartz,* 1984.

187. produced a document: Document entered into evidence by attorney Daniel Markewich, *United States of America v. Bruce P. Greenfield and Mark Schwartz,* 1984.

188. "No one intelligent": Daniel Markewich, defense summation, *United States of America v. Bruce P. Greenfield and Mark Schwartz,* 1984.

188. Judge Knapp summed up: Judge Whitman Knapp, sentencing hearing, January 14, 1985, *United States of America v. Bruce P. Greenfield and Mark Schwartz,* 1984.

189. Judge Knapp sentenced Greenfield: Judgment and Probation / Commitment Order, January 14, 1985, *United States of America v. Bruce P. Greenfield and Mark Schwartz,* 1984.

189. "Though this was": Selma Greenfield, sentencing hearing, January 14, 1985, *United States of America v. Bruce P. Greenfield and Mark Schwartz,* 1984.

189. going out to lunch: Interview with Esteban Sarmiento, May 5, 2011.

189. several long road trips: E-mail from Esteban Sarmiento, May 6, 2011.

190. "The modern conference": Lodge, David, *Small World* (Warner Books, 1989), prologue.

190. "And so it is": Hyatt, Susan Brinn. "A Badge of Honour," *Times Higher Education,* March 19, 2004.

190. Alison Jolly visited the States: E-mail from Alison Jolly, May 16, 2011.

191. "at peace with himself": Jernow, Allison. "Drugs and Chocolate," *The Harvard Crimson,* April 23, 1987.

191. Perhaps realizing: Buettner-Janusch letter to Alison Richard and Robert Dewar, January 6, 1984, Alison Richard private collection.

191. B-J frequently visited: Interview with Alison Richard, January 21, 2011.

191. B-J managed to collect: E-mail from Robert Sussman, January 25, 2011.

192. He vented to Sarmiento: E-mail from Esteban Sarmiento, May 9, 2011.

192. In a letter to Klopfer: Buettner-Janusch letter to Peter Klopfer, September 14, 1986, Peter Klopfer private collection.

193. planted hundreds: Buettner-Janusch letter to Alison Richard and Robert Dewar, November 15, 1986, Alison Richard private collection.

193. a lyrical letter: Buettner-Janusch letter to Alison Richard and Robert Dewar, December 14, 1986, Alison Richard private collection.

193. "English psychopath": Buettner-Janusch letter to Alison Richard and Robert Dewar, October 4, 1985, Alison Richard private collection.

193. "prosecutrix": Buettner-Janusch letter to Alison Richard and Robert Dewar, December 14, 1986, Alison Richard private collection.

193. "by the judge": Ibid.

193. "twit Charles Leslie": Ibid.

193. dog-sitting: Buettner-Janusch letter to Alison Richard and Robert Dewar, October 14, 1986, Alison Richard private collection.

193. had to get permission: McFadden, Robert D. "Judge Is Sent Tainted Candy; Man He Sentenced Is Charged," *The New York Times*, February 21, 1987.

194. Tattersall's assignment: Interview with Ian Tattersall, March 22, 2011.

194. On Valentine's Day: Interview with Alison Richard, January 21, 2011.

194. He had sent: McFadden, "Judge Is Sent Tainted Candy."

194. Found unconscious: Aig, Marlene. "Man Accused of Sending Poisoned Candy to Judge Who Sent Him to Jail," AP, February 20, 1987.

195. she was rushed: McFadden, "Judge Is Sent Tainted Candy."

195. ingested two substances: Ibid.

195. An FBI laboratory: Ibid.

195. squeeze drops of juice: Emsley, John. *Molecules of Murder: Criminal Molecules and Classic Cases* (Royal Society of Chemistry, 2008), pp. 47–48.

195. "hot as a hare": Stewart, Amy. *Wicked Plants: The Weed that Killed Lincoln's Mother and Other Botanical Atrocities* (Algonquin Books, 2009), p. 32.

195. hints at the suffering: "Atropine," Hazardous Substances Data Bank, US National Library of Medicine, http://toxnet.nlm.nih.gov/cgi-bin/sis/search/f?./temp/~sODXbq:1. Accessed November 12, 2012.

195. "curare-like paralysis": Reichl, Franz-Xaver and Leonard Ritter. *Illustrated Handbook of Toxicology* (Thieme, 2011).

196. Symptoms of overdose: "Pilocarpine," Hazardous Substances Data Bank, US National Library of Medicine, http://toxnet.nlm.nih.gov/cgi-bin/sis/search/f?./temp/~52r1v3:1. Accessed November 12, 2012.

196. 19,000 murders: Emsley, *Molecules of Murder*, preface.

196. became a suspect: McFadden, "Judge Is Sent Tainted Candy."

196. as a "sociopath": FBI files on the 1987 investigation of the attempted murder of Judge Brieant obtained through the Freedom of Information Act.

196. Patchin Post Office: Ibid.

196. his parole officer: Ibid.

196. identified a print: Ibid.

196. arrested at 11:45 p.m.: Ibid.

196. on his way home: McFadden, "Judge Is Sent Tainted Candy."

196. "Weary-looking": Ibid.

197. "danger to the community": Aig, "Man Accused of Sending Poisoned Candy to Judge."

197. without bail: McFadden, "Judge Is Sent Tainted Candy."

197. A public defender: *United States of America v. John Buettner-Janusch*, 1987.

197. permitted B-J: McFadden, "Judge Is Sent Tainted Candy."

197. "was sufficient to kill": Ibid.

197. "In less than a week": Blum, Andrew. UPI, February 20, 1987.

197. three other poisoned packages: FBI files on the 1987 investigation of the attempted murder of Judge Brieant obtained through FOIA request. Except for Judge Brieant, the names of the recipients are redacted. J. Bolling Sullivan was named in the court case against Buettner-Janusch. It is clear from the context (location and colleges) that the other recipients were Sidney Mintz and Charles Leslie. Mintz confirmed in an e-mail that he had received packages from Buettner-Janusch.

197. former graduate student at Duke: Interview with J. Bolling Sullivan, October 29, 2011.

198. The FBI soon learned: FBI, 1987.

199. In the mid- to late 1960s: E-mail from J. Bolling Sullivan, June 2, 2012.

199. near New Guinea: Interview with Ian Tattersall, March 22, 2011.

199. When the agents: FBI, 1987.

199. "a hideous mess": Interview with Ian Tattersall, March 22, 2011.

200. four charges: *United States of America v. John Buettner-Janusch*, 1987, arraignment hearing.

200. B-J by then had hired: Ibid.

200. cut a deal: Doyle, John M. "Ex-Professor's Guilty Plea Reveals Wider Poisoned Candy Plot," AP, June 10, 1987.

200. In exchange for a: Lubasch, Arnold H. "Professor Pleads Guilty in Poisoned Candy Case," *The New York Times*, June 10, 1987.

200. wider murder plot: Ibid.

201. B-J stood up: Ibid.

201. Shortly before: Moss, Debra Cassens. "Danger in the Courts," *ABA Journal*, July 1, 1987, pp. 18–19.

201. loomed large at B-J's sentencing: *United States of America v. John Buettner-Janusch*, 1987, sentencing hearing.

203. Judge Lord imposed: Lubasch, Arnold H. "Poison Candy Brings 40-Year Prison Term," *The New York Times*, July 15, 1987.

203. uncharacteristically subdued: "The Nutty Professor Gets 40 Years," *The New York Post,* July 15, 1987.

8 Descent of a Man

204. Marion, built to replace: "From Alcatraz to Marion to Florence—Control Unit Prisons in the United States," Committee to End the Marion Lockdown, 1992, http://people.umass.edu/~kastor/ceml_articles/cu_in_us.html. Accessed November 30, 2012.

205. moved to Marion: Buettner-Janusch's US Bureau of Prisons files on his incarceration for attempted murder were received through a Freedom of Information Act request. The files, which cover the years 1987–1992, deal primarily with his medical treatment for HIV/AIDS.

205. teem with his thoughts: Buettner-Janusch correspondence with Milton and Sondra Schlesinger, in the late 1980s and early '90s, Schlesinger private collection.

205. What was life like: Buettner-Janusch letter to Peter Klopfer, September 19, 1990, Peter Klopfer private collection.

205. "many letters from prison": Klopfer, Peter H. *Politics and People in Ethology: Personal Reflections on the Study of Animal Behavior* (Bucknell University Press, 1999), p. 80.

205. some good news: *United States of America v. John Buettner-Janusch,* 1987, Order by Judge Joseph Lord, December 16, 1987.

206. B-J transferred: US Bureau of Prisons records.

208. "Three packages got sent": Buettner-Janusch letter to Alison Richard and Robert Dewar, January 28, 1989, Alison Richard private collection.

208. "Many of the things": Buettner-Janusch letter to Peter Klopfer, May 15, 1990, Peter Klopfer private collection.

208. "what I did in no way": Buettner-Janusch letter to Alison Richard and Robert Dewar, January 28, 1989, Alison Richard private collection.

209. "the capacity to": de Waal, Frans B. M. "Putting the Altruism Back into Altruism: The Evolution of Empathy." *Annual Review of Pychology*, 59: 281.

209. "It's now believed": de Waal, Frans. *The Age of Empathy: Nature's Lessons for a Kinder Society* (Three Rivers Press, 2010), p. 67.

209. "lies hardwired": Baron-Cohen, Simon. *The Science of Evil: On Empathy and the Origins of Evil* (Basic Books, 2011), pp. 27–41.

209. "empathy erosion": Ibid., p. 6.XX. "What is zero degrees": Ibid., p. 43.

210. Baron-Cohen cites: Ibid., pp. 197–200.

211. Soon after entering: US Bureau of Prisons records, Death Summary, Dr. Thomas Jones, July 8, 1992.

211. unexpected explanation: Buettner-Janusch letter to Alison Richard and Robert Dewar, September 10, 1989, Alison Richard private collection.

211. "I recall B-J writing": E-mail from Lon Alterman, July 19, 2012.

211. "He didn't deal": E-mail from Lon Alterman, July 26, 2012.

211. "Christmas greeting": Interview with Thomas Olivier, July 8, 2011.

211. "disgusted" with B-J: Ibid.

212. B-J's medical records show: US Bureau of Prisons files.

212. "I am now in the stage": Buettner-Janusch letter to Peter and Martha Klopfer, April 29, 1992, Peter Klopfer private collection.

212. the parole commission denied: US Bureau of Prisons records, Notice of Action on Appeal, US Parole Commission, National Appeals Board, July 24, 1992.

212. David Letts said: Interview with David Letts, January 26, 2011.

212. death summary: US Bureau of Prisons records, Death Summary, Dr. Thomas Jones, July 8, 1992.

212. His ashes were spread: E-mail from Teresa Trausch, August 10, 2011.

212. scientific achievements: Interview with Peter Klopfer, October 26, 2009.

212. led with his drug: Lambert, Bruce. "John Buettner-Janusch, 67, Dies; N.Y.U. Professor Poisoned Candy," *The New York Times*, July 4, 1992.

212. focused mostly: "Brilliant but Flawed," *The Guardian*, July 7, 1992.

213. died of pneumonia: Lambert, "John Buettner-Janusch, 67, Dies."

213. try to tear out: US Bureau of Prisons records. In his final weeks at the US Medical Center for Federal Prisoners, Springfield, Missouri, nurses noted several attempts by Buettner-Janusch to remove his feeding tubes.

214. "Dynamic and colorful": Sussman, Robert W., Richard, Alison F., and Rogers, Jeffrey, "Obituary: John Buettner-Janusch (1924–1992)," *American Journal of Physical Anthropology*, 91:529–530 (1993).

214. "You never can": Interview with Alison Richard, April 6, 2011.

Epilogue

215. a species of mouse lemur: "Microcebus jollyae," IUCN Red List of Threatened Species, www.iucnredlist.org/details/136458/0. Accessed February 2, 2013.

215. studied under Jolly: E-mail from Alison Richard, May 9, 2011.

215. helped establish the Beza Mahafaly: Weber, William, ed., et al., *African Rain Forest Ecology and Conservation*, "Politics, Negotiation, and Conservation: A View from Madagascar," Richard, Alison F. and Robert E. Dewar, pp. 535-544. (Yale University Press, 2001).

216. the first Western scientist: "Propithecus tattersalli," IUCN Red List of Threatened Species, www.iucnredlist.org/details/18352/0. Accessed February 2, 2013.

216. sleep and hibernation: Jabr, Ferris. "The Mysterious Brain of the Fat-Tailed Dwarf Lemur, the World's Only Hibernating Primate," *Scientific American* blog "Brainwaves," http://blogs.scientificamerican.com/brain-waves/2012/06/18/the-mysterious-brain-of-the-fat-tailed-dwarf-lemur-the-worlds-only-hibernating-primate. Accessed February 2, 2013.

216. continues to conduct: Sauter, M. L., et al., "The Socioecology of the Ringtailed Lemur: Thirty-five Years of Research," *Evolutionary Anthropology*, 8: 120–132.

216. Simons took advantage: Fleagle, J. G., and C. C. Gilbert, eds. *Elwyn Simons: A Search for Origins*, "Decades of Lemur Research and Conservation: The Elwyn Simons Influence," Patricia C. Wright (Springer, 2008), p. 290.

216. he helped: Ibid., p. 300.

217. under Glander's guidance: Bates, Karl. "Into the Wild," www.duke news.duke.edu/2007/11/lemurs.html. Accessed November 22, 2012.

217. examined their progress: *In the Wild: Lemurs with John Cleese*, directed by Justine Kershaw (PBS Home Video, 1998).

217. Two more groups: Bates, "Into the Wild."

217. facility's mission: Interview with Anne Yoder, January 6, 2011.

218. completed construction: "World Renowned Duke Lemur Center Gets Updated, Expanded Facilities," Lord Aeck Sargent Architecture, www .lordaecksargent.com/profile/news_and_awards/news_releases/2010/ world_renowned_duke_lemur_center_gets_updated_expanded_facilities. Accessed November 30, 2012.

218. The center's grounds: Duke Lemur Center website, http://lemur. duke.edu/about-the-duke-lemur-center. Accessed November 30, 2012.

218. The island nation has: Bearak, Barry. "Coup Attempt by Military Is Reported in Madagascar," *The New York Times*, November 17, 2010.

218. signed an agreement: Iloniaina, Alain. "Madagascar to Hold Presidential Election Next May," Reuters, August 2, 2012.

218. have fallen siege: Draper, Robert. "The Pierced Heart of Madagascar," *National Geographic*, September 2010, pp. 80–109.

Further Reading

Baron-Cohen, Simon. *The Science of Evil: On Empathy and the Origins of Evil* (Basic Books, 2011).

Buettner-Janusch, John. *Origins of Man: Physical Anthropology* (John Wiley & Sons, 1966).

———. *Physical Anthropology: A Perspective* (John Wiley & Sons, 1973).

Clendinen, Dudley, and Adam Nagourney, *Out for Good* (Simon & Schuster, 1999).

Davidson, Osha Gray. *The Best of Enemies: Race and Redemption in the New South* (University of North Carolina Press, 2007).

de Waal, Frans. *The Age of Empathy: Nature's Lessons for a Kinder Society* (Three Rivers Press, 2010).

Donoghue, Frank. *The Last Professors: The Corporate University and the Fate of the Humanities* (Fordham University Press, 2008).

Emsley, John. *Molecules of Murder: Criminal Molecules and Classic Cases* (Royal Society of Chemistry, 2008).

Fleagle, J. G., and C. C. Gilbert, eds. *Elwyn Simons: A Search for Origins*, "Decades of Lemur Research and Conservation: The Elwyn Simons Influence," Patricia C. Wright (Springer, 2008).

Folpe, Emily Kies. *It Happened on Washington Square* (Johns Hopkins University Press, 2002).

Godfrey, Linda S., *Strange Wisconsin: More Badger State Weirdness* (Trails Books, 2007).

Gould, Lisa, and Michelle L. Sauther, eds. *Lemurs: Ecology and Adaptation*, "Notes on the History of Ecological Studies of Malagasy Lemurs," Alison Jolly and R. W. Sussman (Springer, 1996).

Hofmann, Albert. *LSD: My Problem Child* (MAPS, 2009).

Howell, F. Clark, "Sherwood Larned Washburn," *Biographical Memoirs*, vol. 84 (The National Academy Press, 2004).

Huxley, Thomas H. *Man's Place in Nature* (Modern Library, 2001).

Jolly, Alison. *Lords and Lemurs: Mad Scientists, Kings with Spears, and Diversity in Madagascar* (Houghton Mifflin, 2004).

Klopfer, Peter H. *Politics and People in Ethology: Personal Reflections on the Study of Animal Behavior* (Bucknell University Press, 1999).

Leakey, Richard E. *The Making of Mankind* (E. P. Dutton, 1991).

———. *One Life: An Autobiography* (Salem House, 1983).

Lewin, Roger. In the Age of Mankind (Smithsonian Books, 1988).

———. *Bones of Contention: Controversies in the Search for Human Origins* (Simon & Schuster, 1987).

Mittermeier, Russell, ed., et al. *Lemurs of Madagascar* (Conservation International, 2010).

Peterson, Dale. *Jane Goodall: The Woman Who Redefined Man* (Houghton Mifflin Harcourt, 2006).

Price, David H. *Threatening Anthropology: McCarthyism and the FBI's Surveillance of Activist Anthropologists* (Duke University Press Books, 2004).

Reichl, Franz-Xaver, and Leonard Ritter. *Illustrated Handbook of Toxicology* (Thieme, 2011).

Sankar, D. V. Siva, ed. *LSD: A Total Study* (PJD Publications, 1975).

Showalter, Elaine. *Faculty Towers: The Academic Novel and Its Discontents* (University of Pennsylvania Press, 2005).

Stewart, Amy. *Wicked Plants: The Weed that Killed Lincoln's Mother and Other Botanical Atrocities* (Algonquin Books, 2009).

(Italicized page numbers indicate photographs.)

activism, 51, 52–53, 58
Age of Empathy, The (Waal), 209
Alterman, Lon, 77, 90, 97, 174, 181, 211
American Anthropological Association conferences, 190
American Anthropologist, 47
American Association of Physical Anthropology (AAPA) conventions, 189
American Graves Registration Service, 18–19
American Journal of Physical Anthropology, 47, 60, 116, 179–80, 213
American Museum of Natural History, 183
Amorosa, Dominic, 114, 115, 117–20
Amoroso, Frank, *166*
amyl nitrite, 97
Analamazaotra Special Reserve, 43
Andasibe, Madagascar, 43
Anderson, Alma, 21
Anderson, Robert, 21, 44
Andrew, Richard, 27, 35, 36, 49
Annals of the New York Academy of Sciences, 47
appeals, 171–73, 178
Apte, Mahadev, 63
Apte, Sharad, 63
Apte, Sunita, 64
archaeological digs, 19, *20*
arraignments, 135, 200–201
arrests, 90, 115–19, 196–97
atropine poisoning, 195
Attenborough, David, 33
aye-ayes, 29

baboons, 27–28, 29
Baron-Cohen, Simon, 209–10

"Beggar, Psychologist, Mediator, Maid: the Thankless Job of a Chairman" (Wilson), 81
Beidelman, Thomas, 83–84, 97, 133
belladonna, 195
Berenty Private Reserve, 40–41
Berger, Harry, 61
Berkowitz, David, 74, 88
Berman, Patricia Karatsis, 100, 108, 143–44, 145–46, 167
Bettinger, Robert, 88–89
Bishop, Allison. *See* Jolly, Allison (Bishop)
Blow-Up (film), 98–99
Boggess, Preston, 40–41, 43
Bond, Edna, 8
book reviews, 59
Booth, Wayne C., 98
Boyle, Edward, 112–13
Brieant, Charles L., Jr.
    murder attempt on, 194–97, 198, 200, 201
    as trial judge, 137, 141, 147, 150, 153, 170–71
Brieant, Virginia, 194–95, 197, 200
Buettner, Gertrude Clare, 1, *2*, 5–6, *11*
Buettner-Janusch, John (Johannes) "B-J." *See also related topics*
    as associate editor, 60
    birth and early childhood, 1–6, *2*
    at Cranberry Lake, *213*
    death of, 212–14
    description, *26*, 51, 64, 90, 95–96, *96*, 121, 181
    education, 6–7, 8–11, *9*, *11*, 14–16, 21–22
    employment, academic, 19–20, 23–27, 44–50, 53, 55, 68, 77–89
        (*see also specific universities*)
    employment, early, 13–14, 16, 18, 19, *20*

health, 9, 13, 138–39, 211–12
interpersonal relationship issues,
     15–16, 43, 48, 59, 70, 77–89
in Madagascar, *31, 39*
marriage, 16, *17,* 64–65
in NYC during first trial, *134*
in NYU office, *75*
penmanship, 8
personality, 47, 68–69, 87, 90, 91, 98,
     168–69, 189–91, 207–10
residences, post-prison, 181–82,
     192–93
sexual orientation, 9, 96–98
teaching style, 90–91, 92–93, 121–22
with Wachtel and Amoroso, *116*
wartime views and conscientious
     objection, 7–8, 12–13
wife's death response, 93–94, 207
Buettner-Janusch, Vina (Mallowitz)
on archaeological dig in Illinois, *20*
associates of, 22, 63
background, 16
death of, 93–94, 207
description, 64, *64*
early employment, 21
as husband's editorial consultant, 60
inheritance, 92
Kenya trips, 38
as laboratory assistant, 65, 174
in Madagascar with husband, 38–44, *39*
marriage and relationship, 16, *17,*
     64–65, 85, 95
bullying, 79–81
bush babies (galagos), 29, 30, 36, 49, 66
Byrnes, John, 197

Cantor, Norman, 82
Cantwell, Anne Marie, 82
capitalism, 3–4
Carter, Frank, 8
Carter, Jimmy, 140
Cartmill, Matt, 64, 70, 166–67

CBGB, 132
chairmen, academic, 81
Chemistry (magazine), 67
Chicago, Illinois, 3–4
Chicago Board of Trade, 3
chimpanzees, 28–29
civil rights movement, 8, 51, 52–52, 58
Clendinen, Dudley, 98
cocaine, synthetic, 147, 149, 151, 164, 186
cockroaches, 40
Coe, Michael, 35–36, 47–48, 61, 96,
     137, 157
Columbia University, 74
Commerson, Philibert de, 32
conferences, 189–90
Conroy, Glenn, 87–88, 93
conscientious objection, 12–13
Controlled Substances Act, 103
Cornyetz, Danny
     background, 99
     description, 99
     drug production admission, 109–10
     drug production purpose, 101–2
     Greenfield lab testing and, 132
     as lab director, 99
     lifestyle, 132–33
     Macris relationship with, 109
     post-trial education, 167
     as prosecution witness, 143, 150–52, 163
     recipe search assignments, 108
     tape-recorded conversations, 124–26,
          129, 130
Cote, Denise, 115–17
Cranberry Lake, 5–6, 212, *213*
Crick, Francis, 117
crosses, burning, 69–70
Cylert, 149, 150

Dahl, Robert, 26
Dawson, Samuel, 201–2
Delysid, 102
DeVita, James, 197, 202

Dewar, Robert, 124, 180, 191
Doin' Times, The, 176–77
Domhoff, G. William, 26
Donoghue, Frank, 47
Doran, William, 196
Dorfman, Richard
  as administrative assistant, 100
  aftermath, 167
  on drug production purpose, 101
  drug sales, 147
  as prosecution witness, 107, 143,
    147–50, 163
drug case. *See also* LSD; methaqualone
  arraignment, 135
  arrests and interrogation, 115–19
  B-J's version of events, 135–36, 207, 208
  cover story and defense, 116–19, 123,
    128, 139, 155–56, 158
  defense funds and costs, 128, 137
  indictments, 133–34
  investigation, 124–33
  laboratory procedures as evidence, 106
  laboratory searches, 114–15, 125–26,
    127, 133, 137–38
  media coverage, 135
  plea bargain deals and government
    witnesses, 147, 151
  pretrial hearings, 137–38
  sentencing, 166, 169–72
  supporters' defense arguments,
    166–69, 206
  tape-recorded conversations as
    evidence, 102, 124–26, 128
  trial (see *United States of America v.
    John Buettner-Janusch*)
Drug Enforcement Agency, 114
Duke Forest, 54
Duke Lemur Center (*formerly* Duke
  University Primate Center), 50,
  54–55, 71, 216–18
Duke University
  academic writings at, 55–59

anatomy department appointments,
  50, 53, 55
civil rights movement, 52–53
faculty photo at, 96, *96*
lecture series at, 50
primate center at, 50, 53–55, 71,
  216–18
resignation, 69
views on, 60–61
wife as lab assistant and resignation, 65
Dunaif, Andrea, 193
Durham, G. Homer, 20
Durham, North Carolina, 51–53, 60–61
Durham Morning Herald letters to
  editor, 58

Eagle River, Wisconsin, 5–6
"Effect of Methaqualone on Behavior of
  the Chimpanzee" (US Air Force
  study), 158
Eglin Air Force Base prison, 173,
  175–81
electrophoresis, gel, 34–35
empathy, 207–10
Emsley, John, 196
*Evolutionary and Genetic Biology of
  Primates* (Buettner-Janusch, J.), 47

Faculty Towers (Showalter), 45–46
fires, 69–70
Folpe, Emily Kies, 76
Ford, Gerald, 73
Forman, Lisa
  aftermath, 167
  on B-J's laboratory time, 108
  drug production explanation given
    to, 101
  as graduate lab assistant, 100
  on Macris-Cornyetz relationship, 109
  perception of B-J, 106
  perception of drug case, 129
  tape-recorded conversations, 124

Fossey, Dian, 28
Franks, Bobby, 5
Fried, Bernard, 112–13

galagos (bush babies), 29, 30, 36, 49, 66
Galdikas, Biruté, 28
gay liberation movement, 98
Giuliani, Rudolph, 197
Glander, Ken, 217
Gonzalez, Nancy, 90
Goodall, Jane, 28–29
Grandidier, Alfred, 33
Greek mythology metaphors, 169
Greenfield, Bruce
    aftermath, 167
    arrest, 115
    B-J's arrest, 115
    coconspirator charges and trial,
        184–89
    description, 105–6
    as graduate lab assistant, 100
    late-night lab testing and toxic
        materials, 131–32
    nonprofit organizations cofounded
        by, 104, 107
    as scapegoat, 131
    tape-recorded conversations, 124
    in trial testimony, 144
    Vick dissertation critique, 159–60
Greenwich Village, 97–98
Griesa, Thomas P., 184

halfway houses, 181–82
Harvey, Florence, 13
Herzog, Arthur, 137
Histoire physique, naturelle et politique de
    Madagascar (Grandidier), 33
HIV, 211–12
Hoebel, E. Adamson, 20
Hofmann, Albert, 102, 106, 145
Hollander, Anne, 174
Homo sapiens, 57–58

homosexuality, 9, 96–98
Homo urbanus, 1
Hoover, J. Edgar, 18, 25
hunting hypothesis, 15
Hutchinson, G. Evelyn, 36, 49, 137
Huxley, Aldous, 145
Huxley, Thomas H., 92
Hyatt, Susan Brin, 190
Hylander, William, 60, 77, 84, 93–94, 217

incarceration, 173, 174–81, 204–6
indictments, 133–35
inheritance, 92
Insull, Samuel, 5
interpersonal relationship issues, 15–16,
    43, 48, 59, 70, 77–89
In the Wild: Lemurs with John Cleese
    (television documentary), 217
Iranian hostage crisis, 140

Jacobs, Stephen, 136
Janusch, Frederick Wilhelm, 1, 2, 3, 5–6
Jennings, Jesse, 20–21
Jolly, Allison (Bishop)
    doctoral studies at Yale, 36–37
    lemur studies, 215
    in Madagascar, 38–44
    post-prison visits with, 190
    students influenced by, 85
    at trial, 159
    trial testimony, 160
Jolly, Clifford
    aftermath, 167–68
    background, 85–86
    character reference requests, 129
    chemical requisition explanations to, 101
    description as mentor, 121
    on drug production cover story,
        118–19
    drug production investigations with
        Macris, 109, 112
    drug production reporting, 113–14

as Greenfield's adviser, 187
investigation collaborations, 124, 133
lab assistants of, 100, 105
lab facilities of, 99
nonprofit organization knowledge, 107
personality, 86
as prosecution witness, 143, 154, 164
recommendation letters for, 62
relationship with B-J, 86–87
revenge fantasies and grudges
    against, 192, 193
Jolly, Richard, 43
Jungle, The (Sinclair), 4

Kacker, Indra Kishore, 111
Kalban, Philip, 127
Katona-Apte, Judit, 63
Katz, Andrea, 217
Kaufman, Irving, 172
Kenya, 27, 28, 38
King, Martin Luther, Jr., 53
Klopfer, Martha, 52, 65
Klopfer, Peter
    background, 52–53
    on burning cross incident, 70
    on controlled substance permits, 120
    as defense witness, 160–61
    friendship with, 51–52, 53, 60, 65
    on interpersonal relationships of B-J, 81
    lemur studies, 53–54, 216
    mongoose pets, 66
    on parties of B-J, 65–66
    primate facility development, 54–55
    prison letters to, 205, 212
    on temperament of B-J, 66–67
Knapp, Whitman, 185–89
kokolampo, 43
Korean War, 18

Larkin, Joyce, 7–8
Last Professors, The (Donoghue), 47
Laurendi, Nat, 127

Leakey, Louis, 28–29, 48, 50
Leakey, Richard, 29, 85
lemur behavior research project
    as drug production cover story, 116–
        19, 123, 128, 139
    questioning legitimacy of, 164
    trial defense witnesses and legitimacy
        of, 155–61
lemurs
    academic research studies on, 33,
        34–35, 38, 53–54
    behavior of, 61–62
    Cold War theories on, 67
    collecting, 24, 28, 29, 30–31
    dissertations on, 36
    extinction of, 30, 32
    legacy of study, 215–18
    in Madagascar natural habitat, 41,
        43, 56, 218–19
    newspaper articles on, 38
    overview, 30, 32
    as pets, 66
    television shows featuring, 33
    writings about, 56–57
Lemurs of Madagascar (field manual), 43
Leopold, Nathan, 4–5
Lerner, Aaron, 61
Leslie, Charles, 15–16, 79–80, 198, 200
letters
    accusation, 80
    to the editor, 58
    to persecutors, 138
    from prison, 175, 177–78, 180
    of recommendation, 62–63
    to supporters, 166–67, 171–72
Letts, David, 212
Letts, Theodora Buettner-Janusch, 1, 212
Levine, James, 72
Lewin, Roger, 86
Lichtman, Stephen, 186–87
lidocaine, 147, 148, 151, 164, 186
Liebling, Louis, 147, 148, 149

Life magazine, 29
Lodge, David, 190
Loeb, Richard, 4–5
Lord, Joseph, 200, 201–2, 205
Lords and Lemurs (Bishop), 36, 41
LSD (lysergic acid derivatives), 102–3,
    106–7. *See also* LSD production
LSD: A Total Study (Sankar, ed.), 101,
    144–45, 148, 151
LSD: My Problem Child (Hofmann),
    103, 106
LSD production
    assistants and coconspirators, 105–6,
        109–10
    books with recipes, 101, 144
    laboratory time, 108
    lab research explanations for, 101
    nonprofit organization for
        concealment of, 103–5, 107
    pretrial testimony and cover story for,
        116–19
    process and challenge of, 106–7
    purpose of, 101–2
    supply requisitions, 100–101, 107
    trial testimony on, 148, 153
Lunch of the Loving Couples, 44
Lynch, Owen, 77–78, 80, 84, 92–93, 94

macaques, 66, 104
Macris, Richard
    background, 99–100
    Cornyetz conversations with, 129, 130
    Cornyetz relationship with, 109
    description, 100
    drug production investigations, 109,
        110, 111, 112
    drug production recruitment, 108–11
    drug production reporting, 113–14
    investigation collaborations, 124–26,
        128–29
    as lab assistant, 94
    post-trial education, 167

as prosecution witness, 143, 152–53,
    154, 163–64
    resignation, 112
    revenge fantasies and grudges
        against, 192
Macris, Robert, 112, 113
Madagascar
    current conditions, 218–19
    early exploration of, 32–33
    geographical descriptions, 30, 32
    reserves on, 40, 43
    specimen collecting in, *31*, 38–44, *39*
    specimen collections from, 24, 28–29,
        30, 32, 33–34
    trips to, 29–30, 33
Mailer, Norman, 4
Mallowitz, Vina. *See* Buettner-Janusch,
    Vina (Mallowitz)
Manhattan Project, 10
Mann, Roanne
    background, 141–42
    Greenfield prosecution, 185
    letters to and about, 138
    media quotes, 135
    motives, 142–43
    prosecution witness questioning,
        143–49, 151, 156
    sentencing assessment questionnaires,
        178–79
    summations, 161–63
"Man's Place in Nature" (course), 92
Mantadia National Park, 43
Marion, Martin, 104–5, 107, 185–86
Marion United States Penitentiary,
    204–3
Markewich, Daniel, 184
Marshall, Thurgood, 173
"Me Decade, The," 74
mental illness, 13, 138–39
methaqualone (Quaalude)
    behavior studies using, 158
    drug category, 111

history of, 111
pretrial testimony and cover story for
    production of, 116–19
production of, 101, 102, 106–11
production statistics, 120
production street value, 147
supply requisitions, 107
trial testimonies on production of,
    148, 186
Metropolitan Opera, 60, 72
Miami and the Siege of Chicago (Mailer), 4
Mintz, Sidney, 44–45, 46, 48–49, 50,
    198, 200
Molecules of Murder (Emsley), 196
mongooses, 66
monkeys, 28
Morgan, John, 158
Morris, Desmond, 59–60
Mudd Club, 132–33, 151–52
murder plots, attempted
    arrest and plea bargain, 196, 200–201
    empathy issues and, 208
    sentencing, 201–3
    victims, 194–98
Murdock, George, 24–25

Nagourney, Adam, 98
National Science Foundation, 50, 54,
    89–90
Nazism, 7–8, 18
New Haven, Connecticut, 26–27
Newman, Oscar, 76
New York City, 60, 72–75
New York magazine, 140, 165
New York Post, 135, 140, 203
New York Times, 91, 135, 140, 165,
    212–13
New York University
    academic writings, 89
    anthropology department
        appointments, 68, 75
    benefits, 72

history, 74, 76
interpersonal relationships at, 15–16,
    77–89
research laboratories at (*see* Rufus D.
    Smith Hall laboratory)
response to indictment, 136–37
response to verdict, 165
teaching style as professor at, 90–91,
    92–93, 121–22
trial verdict and criticism of, 170–71
Nute, Peter, 54, 199

Olin, Philip, 13
Olivier, Thomas, 77, 173–75, 179, 180, 211
Origins of Man: Physical Anthropology
    (Buettner-Janusch, J.), 44, 47,
    55–58, 60, 191
Osgood, Cornelius, 24, 25
Out for Good (Clendinen and
    Nagourney), 98
Owsley Stanley, Augustus, III, 106–7

paranoia, 90, 127
parole, 181, 193
parties, 65–66, 73
Paulius, John, 90
Périnet, Madagascar, 43
pets, 66
Petter, Jean-Jacques, 33
Petter-Rousseaux, Arlette, 33
Phillips-Conroy, Jane, 88
Physical Anthropology (Buettner-Janusch,
    J.), 55, 58–59, 68
Pilbeam, David, 137
pilocarpine hydrochloride, 195
plagarism, 71
poisonings, 194–200
Politics and People in Ethology (Klopfer,
    P.), 52
polygraph tests, 127–28, 149, 151
pottos, 29, 36, 37–38, 49
prescription drugs, 102, 147, 148, 149, 150

presidential elections, 141
Primate Ethology (Morris), 59–60
Primates in Nature (Richard), 179
prison time, 173, 174–81, 204–6
Pronger, Patricia, 105, 155–57
Proteus (Greek mythological figure), 169

Quaalude. *See* methaqualone
Quartermaster Corps (US Army), 16, 18

Ramanantsoa, Guy, 215
requisitions, 100–101, 107
revenge fantasies, 138, 180–81, 192
Rhetoric of Fiction, The (Booth), 98
Richard, Allison
    on B-J's revenge fantasies, 138
    on B-J's treatment of students, 59
    defense fund begun by, 137
    on description of B-J, 84–85
    on Jolly, Clifford, post-trial, 167
    lemur studies legacy, 215
    obituary authorship, 213–14
    papers and books edited for, 177, 180
    post-prison visits with, 191, 194
    prison letters to, 175, 180, 208
    students of, 124
Ripley, S. Dillon, 27, 36, 42
Ritholz, Jules
    background, 142
    defense and witness questioning, 142,
        149–50, 151–52, 154, 155–56, 159
    summations, 161, 163–64
Robertson, J. David, 137, 157
Rogers, Jeffrey, 120–24, 167, 213–14
Rorer, William H., 111
Rothschild, Nan, 135
Rouse, Benjamin, 24, 27, 46
Rufus D. Smith Hall laboratory (NYU)
    access to, 99
    chemical supply requisitions to,
        100–101, 107
    employees and assistants in, 99–100

law enforcement search of, 114–15,
    125–26, 127, 133, 137
time spent in, 108, 122–23
Ruona, Martin, 9

Sabatini, David, 84
sabotage, 108, 145
Salvation Army, 181–82
Salwen, Bert, 137
Sankar, D. V. Siva, 144–45
Sarmiento, Esteban
    background, 120–21
    on description of B-J, 95–96
    personality, 121
    post-prison relationship with, 189
    post-prison revenge rants to, 192
    on sexual orientation of B-J, 97
    on teaching style of B-J, 122
Sawhill, John, 113–14
Schaffer, Andrew, 114
Schlesinger, Milton, 22, 84, 137, 205
Schlesinger, Sondra, 22, 84, 127, 174, 205
Schwartz, Mark, 115, 184–87
Science magazine, 165
Science of Evil, The (Baron-Cohen), 209
"Seed-Eaters, The" (Jolly, C.), 85
Selective Training and Service Act, 7,
    12–13
sentencing hearings, 166, 169–72,
    201–3
Showalter, Elaine, 45–46
sifakas, 29
Silliman Memorial Lectures, 50
Simian Expansions, 103–5, 107, 155
Simons, Elwyn
    on Buettner-Janusch marriage,
        64–65, 66
    on interpersonal issues of B-J, 47
    lemur project defense and, 117,
        156–57, 164
    lemur studies, 35, 216–17

primate research colony proposal
collaboration, 49
trial absence, 162–63
as Yale faculty member, 35
Simonton, Joe, 6
Sinclair, Upton, 4
sisal plant, 40
slow lorises, 36, 37
Small World (Lodge), 190
Smith, Geoff, 42, 43
sodium barbital, 147, 148, 151
sparteine poisoning, 195
Spuhler, James, 22, 168
Staten Island Zoo, 104–5
Stonewall Riots, 98
strikes, 141
Sullivan, J. Bolling, 197–98, 198–99, 200
Sunrise Semester (television course), 90,
92, 93
supporters, 166–69, 171–72, 206–7
Sussman, Robert
on B-J as mentor, 59
as defense witness, 160
friendship with, 84
lemur studies, 215, 216
obituary authorship, 213–14
as party bartender, 66
Sutton, Constance, 15, 78–79, 80
swine-pink skin, 58

Talese, Gay, 76
tape-recorded conversations, 102, 124–
26, 128–30
Tattersall, Ian
apartment as crime scene, 199–200, 208
background, 56
gifts to, 200
lemur studies legacy, 215–16
museum lecture touring, 194
on *Origins of Man,* 55–56
post-prison relationship with, 182,
183, 191, 193

on sexual orientation of B-J, 97
Tenney, Charles, 135
tenure, 45–47
Terre Haute federal penitentiary, 206
therapy, 138–39
Thieme, Frederick, 22
Toal, Jack, 114, 115, 186
toluene, 108
trials. See *United States of America v.*
Bruce P. Greenfield and Mark
Schwartz; United States of America
v. John Buettner-Janusch
Triangle Shirtwaist Factory, 74–75
Twichell, Joseph, 37
Tyler, Joel, 197

Union Stock Yards, 4
United States of America v. Bruce P.
Greenfield and Mark Schwartz
(drug trial), 185–89, 206–7
United States of America v. John Buettner-
Janusch (drug trial)
books with drug recipes as evidence,
144–45, 148, 151
character witnesses, 155, 157–58
charges, 140, 154–55
defense arguments, 142
defense attorneys for, *116,* 142
judges for, 141
jury instructions on government
witnesses, 147
media coverage, 140–41, 165
motive, 142–43
in New York during, *134*
plea bargain deals and government
witnesses, 147, 151
prosecuting attorney for, 141–42
sell, conspiracy and intent to, 147–
49, 150
summations, 161–63
verdict, 164
with Wachtel and Amoroso, *116*

witnesses for defense, 155–64
witnesses for prosecution, 143–55
University Hospital, 13–14
University of Chicago, 10, 14, 21
University of Illinois at Urbana, 62
University of Michigan, 16, 21–22
University of Utah, 19–21
urban culture and lifestyle, 60, 67–68, 95
US Army civilian employment, 16, 18
Use of the Hand in Lower Primates
    (Bishop), 36

Vick , Laura, 158–59
Vietnam War, 51

Waal, Frans de, 208–9
Wachtel, William, *116*, 157, 213
wanderoos, 104
Washburn, Sherwood "Sherry," 14–15,
    16, 18, 45, 48, 95, 127
Washington Square, 74, 76–77
Washor, Michael, 184, 187
Watson, James, 117
Wayne University, 22
Welch, Charles, 217
Who Governs? (Dahl), 26

Wiggins, Richard, 70–71
Wilson, Robin, 81
Winder, R. Bayly, 82
Winters, Howard, 19, *20*, 82, 89
Wolfe, Linda, 85
Wolfe, Tom, 74
World War II, 7–8, 11–13, 18

Yale University
    academic writings at, 47
    anthropology department
        appointments, 23–27
    anthropology faculty at, 35–36
    lemur studies at, 34–35, 50
    primate colony proposals, 49–50
    species collections at, 27–30, 36–38
    tenure denial and interpersonal
        conflicts, 44–48, 50
Yearbook of Physical Anthropology, 60
Yoder, Anne, 32, 217

Zaccaro, Ron, 136
Zaheer, Syed Hussain, 111
Zoo Quest to Madagascar (television
    series), 33